Is Britain Dying?

Is Britain Dying?

PERSPECTIVES ON THE CURRENT CRISIS

EDITED BY
Isaac Kramnick

Cornell University Press
ITHACA AND LONDON

First published 1979 by Cornell University Press
Published in the United Kingdom by Cornell University Press Ltd.,
2-4 Brook Street, London W1Y 1AA.

International Standard Book Number 0-8014-1234-X
Library of Congress Catalog Card Number 79-12895
Printed in the United States of America
Librarians: Library of Congress cataloging information appears on the last page of the book.

Contents

Preface

Mountains of garbage in Leicester Square; ambulance drivers on strike; attendants turning patients away from hospitals; terrorist bombings of gasoline storage tanks; schools closed; striking lorry drivers huddled around makeshift fires; civil servants refusing to work; trains idle; no *Times*; no *T.L.S.*; a bewildered prime minister juggling election days; a Trades Union Congress helpless before militant shop stewards; a peppery leader of the opposition shouting, "Resign!" This was the British winter of discontent—1978–79.

It was the winter when the world saw on television revolution in Iran and paralysis in Britain. The one was lightning fast and unexpected. The other seemed all too predictable and unfolded like a tragedy whose plot was dictated by the decade of the 1970s, if not the third of a century that had passed since World War II.

The British crisis did not spring on an unsuspecting world in the winter of '79. Much of the drama was familiar, all too familiar, though the players may have changed. Throughout the 1970s, pundits and public figures, watching the play unfold, have worried about and analyzed Britain. This volume is an example of that decade-long concern. It is an outgrowth of the conference "The British Crisis: Real or Imagined?" held at Cornell University, April 13–15, 1978. The conference, which Daniel Baugh of Cornell's history department and I conceived and organized, was sponsored by the Western Societies Program of the Center for International Studies. All the essays published here were originally presented at the conference.

Many people were responsible for the success of the conference. At the Center for International Studies, Milton J. Esman, the director, and Sean Killeen, the executive director, were involved in every detail of planning the event. Special thanks are due Sally Kramer, whose many months of work made it possible

7

for the conference to take place. Just before and during the conference she was admirably aided by Alan Cafruny. At the Society for the Humanities, Michael Kammen provided financial assistance and warmly opened up the Andrew Dickson White House for our proceedings. Pamela Armstrong cheerfully and helpfully welcomed us into the Society.

Others at Cornell deserve mention. President Frank H. T. Rhodes graciously took time from his busy schedule to welcome and introduce Edward Heath. Jennie Farley was responsible for many of the arrangements that made possible Barbara Castle's visit. Robert Smith was a delightful help at the news office. Thanks are also due Joseph Leeming and Bryant Robey on that score. Arline Blaker of the Cornell Department of Government lent her usual helpful and calming influence to the proceedings.

Various sources were generous with their support: the Western Societies Program of the Center for International Studies; the Oliphant Speakers' Fellowship of Sigma Phi fraternity; the Women's Studies Program; the Kappa Alpha Theta Lecture Program, administered by the University Lecture Committee; the University Unions Program Board; the Interfraternity Council Speakers' Forum; and the Center for the Humanities. The British Information Service in New York and the director of its policy and reference division, Stephen Wright, were of great assistance, too.

Miriam Brody Kramnick was invaluable to the entire enterprise. She did, to be sure, chauffeur the former prime minister, but more significant, she adapted Barbara Castle's question-and-answer session to the essay on women in Britain that appears below. In addition, she helped edit the entire volume for style and substance.

Acknowledgments are due the *British Journal of Sociology* for permission to use in revised form Ralph Miliband's "A State of Desubordination," which it published in December 1978. Acknowledgment is also due *The New Republic* for permission to reproduce passages from Robin Marris's "Is Britain an Awful Warning to America?" (17 September 1977) in his "Britain's Relative Economic Decline: A Reply to Stephen Blank." The introductory essays by Edward Heath and Barbara Castle were published earlier in *Cornell Review* 4, Fall 1978.

ISAAC KRAMNICK

Ithaca, New York

Is Britain Dying?

1 | *Introduction: The Making of a Crisis*

ISAAC KRAMNICK

Something seems very wrong with Britain. Once the very model of a modern major power—stable, rich, and smug—it appears beset now by political and economic instability and by civil unrest and disorder. One observer has even taken to calling it "the sick man of Europe."[1] Hardly a month passes without the appearance of a new book or learned article on the decline and imminent demise of once proud Britain, or on the annoying (sometimes called quaint) inefficiencies and relaxations of British daily life.[2] To be sure, the British themselves seem immune to this sense of despair. A recent worldwide Gallup survey has shown that they are among the happiest people in the world.[3] For some, this complacency is *prima facie* evidence that no crisis exists. For others, it is itself a most glaring symptom of that very crisis and decline.

Whether and how one perceives a crisis in modern Britain is, of course, very much a function of one's politics. The conventional left in Britain and elsewhere sees a crisis and assigns the blame to bankers, managers, and the class system.[4] The right in Britain and elsewhere, especially in America, sees a crisis and indicts unions, socialism, and intellectuals.[5] The radical left also sees a crisis, but one that undermines the entire social order of capitalist Britain. While still pointing to the conventional villains—profits, exploitation, and international bankers—it has more stridently added another in recent years: the Labour Party serves in its view as a "guarantor of the postwar capitalist order," diffusing pressures from below which threaten the system.[6]

11

The less partisan observer of Britain discerns there a general mood of malaise and stagnation on the one hand, and on the other the growth of unrest, discontent, and disorder. This sense of crisis and accelerating decline is rendered all the more dramatic in view of the great distance Britain has had to fall. The three salient features of its power and reputation in recent centuries have been slowly eroded. This first and most intensively industrialized nation, once the world's factory, now has a growth rate lower than that of virtually all other industrialized nations. This world power on whose empire the sun never set seems now bereft of even moral influence in the international arena. And finally, this nation of peaceful continuity, homogeneous and free of strife, seems racked by regional, racial, and social tensions that threaten to break up the nation if not the entire social fabric itself.

The Political and Economic Background

This decline has not happened overnight. Few could have known in July 1945 what was in store for a Britain whose industrial might had withstood Hitler, whose empire was intact, and whose tradition of peaceful continuity would see the socialists in the Labour Party easily take over the reins of His Majesty's Government from Sir Winston Churchill. The Labour Party, under Clement Attlee, captured a majority of parliamentary seats for the first time. Safe in its overwhelming mandate, the party set about translating into legislation the recommendations of the two great social documents that had emerged during the war—the 1942 Beveridge Report on Social Welfare and the 1944 Report on Full Employment in a Free Society. It committed itself to ensure adequate subsistence for all. The state would be responsible for maintaining full employment and a minimum standard of living. To fulfill these goals the Labour Government nationalized the Bank of England, the railroads, and the mining, gas, electricity, road transport, and steel industries. By passing the National Insurance Act of 1946, covering unemployment, sickness, maternity, death, and retirement, it provided a basic scheme of social security for all. The National Health Act of 1946 provided a health service offering free medical care for all.

Not only were these years of great commitment to new

priorities of equality and justice; it would appear in retrospect that these years of the postwar Labour Government also saw truly impressive gains in the annual rate of growth and in the rate of productivity.[7] But to many British they were still gray years of austerity and rationing. Attlee won reelection by a slender majority in 1950, but in 1951 Labour was turned out and Winston Churchill, at the head of the Conservative Party, returned as prime minister. His party would govern for the next thirteen years. Elections would take place in 1955 and 1959, and each time the Tories would win by unprecedented increases in their parliamentary majorities. Three more men would live at 10 Downing Street in those years of Conservative hegemony as death or retirement removed its occupants. Churchill was replaced by Anthony Eden in 1955, Eden by Harold Macmillan in 1957, and Macmillan by Sir Alec Douglas-Home in 1963.

The 1950s saw what many called then the era of Tory prosperity. Such Tory leaders as R. A. Butler and Churchill reformed their party, and the Conservative Government left intact most of Labor's welfare state. Standards of living improved for a wide spectrum of the population and there was a dramatic explosion in mass consumption. Macmillan told the voters they had "never had it so good." Meanwhile, the Labour Party fiercely debated the extent of its commitment to socialism and nationalization. The party was split between those who, like Aueurin Bevan and his younger disciples Harold Wilson and Barbara Castle, sought to create a truly socialist commonwealth in Britain and the more pragmatic Labourites, such as Hugh Gaitskell, who saw nationalization as only an optional tool in the course of a more efficiently managed mixed economy. With Gaitskell's assumption of the party leadership, Labour moved right during those long years in opposition.

Equally notable, the 1950s saw the Tory government continue another postwar Labour reform, the liquidation of the Empire, which had begun in earnest with the independence of India. But the Conservatives under Churchill and Eden were by no means resigned to playing bit parts in world politics. In 1954 Eden pledged that Britain would keep a sizable defense force in Europe for an unlimited period. In 1956 there was, of course, Suez. But even here the Tories were following the lead of Labour, which after all had begun this renaissance of great-power talk with its massive rearmament in 1950 in the wake of the Korean war. Bevan and two other ministers had resigned in 1950, but American prodding of Attlee's government won the day and set the tone for at least the early years of Tory rule.

Thirteen years of Tory dominance came to an end with the critical election of 1964. Macmillan had resigned in 1963 and been replaced as prime minister by the elegant aristocrat Lord Home. Gaitskell had died that same year and the Labour Party chose as its leader Harold Wilson, somewhat shorn of the fiery radicalism that he had earlier directed at Gaitskell's leadership. The next year's election could hardly have provided a more disparate choice in party images. The landed Scottish laird at the head of the Conservative Party offered the electorate more prosperity, more consumer goods, more housing. If there were storm clouds on the economic horizon—indeed, if they had been there for some time—Home talked of the Common Market and of economic planning via the Tory innovation of 1961, the National Economic Development Council (or "Neddy"), as solutions. But to many, Home's ability and knowledge of modern economics seemed archaic. Wilson, on the other hand, cultivated an image not of the partisan Bevanite but of the pipe-smoking Oxford economics don. He offered the electorate a vision of industrial efficiency through technological advance. A Labour government would preside over a white-hot technological revolution. His rhetoric depicted the Labour Party as a group of modern, efficient scientific managers. They stood for technology, growth, and management. Short on talk of justice and equality, Wilson offered the socialists as better planners and technicians. He won and Britain seemed poised at the entrance to a new age, Harold Wilson's technocratic utopia.

All of the new prime minister's talk of planned expansion and growth presided over by white-coated scientists and a new breed of managers coordinated by Neddys big and small came to nothing. Despite the reaffirmation of its mandate by the election of 1966, the new technocracy and Wilson's government foundered in a sea of economic troubles. Wilson was obsessively committed to the strength of sterling and doggedly resisted any devaluation. When he finally did devaluate in 1967, it was too late. From 1965 until it lost power in 1970, Labour presided over a stop-go economy, with most of the emphasis on the stop cycles. Concern for the pound, for the balance of payments, and for inflation led to retrenchment and restrictive economic policies. Investment was held back, and efforts to expand output and raise productivity were limited.

The nadir of Wilson's government was reached in 1969, when the simmering dispute between the unions and the Labour Party came to a head. A new generation of union leaders and workers was unhappy at being asked to curb its demands, even if by a Labour government. Restraint in the face of higher unemployment, inflation, and lower real income became impossible. The workers fought back with their only weapon, the strike. From 1967 on, a wave of strikes and unofficial work stoppages swept Britain. Matters came to a head in 1969 with the publication by Barbara Castle, the secretary of state for employment, of the government white paper *In Place of Strife,* calling once again for the restraint and cooperation of union members. What was novel in the document, and an unprecedented break from party traditions, was the government's threat to impose legal restraints on union activities. Mandatory cooling-off periods and secret ballots of union members were some of the projected reforms. The left of the Labour Party and the entire union movement felt betrayed by Wilson's government. In the debate on *In Place of Strife* in the House of Commons, fifty-three Labour members voted against the government. If that were not enough for one year, August 1969 also saw Wilson's fateful decision to send troops to Northern Ireland. They were to be there temporarily; ten years later they would be there still.

No surprise, then, that in the election of 1970 Harold Wilson was rejected at the polls by the biggest swing of votes in the postwar era, and the Conservatives returned to power under Edward Heath. Heath immediately set about junking the consensus on the mixed economy that had persisted throughout the postwar period. He talked of reducing government's economic role, of whittling down the public sector, of encouraging competition and free enterprise. He promised a veritable renewal of British capitalism.

Two Heath initiatives were crucial in this grand design for revitalizing a "free economy." In the first he was successful. After centuries of denying its Europeanness, Britain was brought in 1973 into the European Economic Community (the Common Market). In his second initiative he failed—so miserably, indeed, that his government was undone. While taking Britain into Europe, Heath took on the unions. He brought in and passed the Industrial Relations Act of 1971, which carried out Wilson's threat to impose legal restraints on the unions, and then some. With its outlawing of the closed shop, its cooling-off periods, and its establishment of a National Industrial Relations Court with power to declare strikes illegal and assign fines and award damages, the act was the cornerstone in Heath's efforts to take wage fixing out of the hands of negotiators for labor and management. However paradoxical it may have been to subject labor relations to the judicial arena in light of his commitment to free the economy, Heath dug in, and so did the unions. Union violations of the law met with a good deal of public support.

Heath was no more successful in managing Britain's fragile economy, free or mixed. The balance of payments still was a nagging problem, and inflation, especially after the 1973 oil crisis, was getting out of hand. In the fall of 1972 the Conservative Government introduced the most stringent wage and price controls in Britain's peacetime history. Nor was Heath, even with his new industrial relations act, able to reduce the number of strikes. In fact, 1972 saw more lost workdays in Britain through strikes than any previous year since 1926.[8] And it was the militant unions and a strike that brought down Heath's government. The Middle East oil crisis led in late 1973 to a fuel shortage that was exacerbated by the miners' refusal to work overtime while negotiating a new contract. Heath moved Britain to a three-day workweek, and no amount of persuasion by either the government or the Trades Union Congress could keep the miners from calling a national strike.[9] Heath called an election. which fell in the midst of the strike. He lost. and Labour under Harold Wilson returned to power to settle the strike and once again seek to manage the ailing economy.

Wilson's return was less than triumphal. His party won only 37 percent of the vote and translated this small share into a parliamentary majority only by enlisting the support of the Liberals and members of splinter parties. Labour's record was equally unspectacular. Under Wilson and his successor, James Callaghan, the party was able to do little with this vulnerable majority. For five years Britain's economic woes persisted, lightened only occasionally by the sense of having a savior in North Sea oil. This third postwar Labour government presided over a period of uncertainty, confusion, and crisis. The rise of Scottish and Welsh nationalism, the growth of a fascist right, the enduring labyrinth of the Irish stalemate, and the return of crippling strikes filled the late 1970s with new imponderables and new uncertainties. The victory of Margaret Thatcher settled little. As the decade came to an end many asked: What's wrong with Britain?

What Crisis?

Anthony Howard, the editor of the prestigious left weekly *New Statesman,* has described Britain and its government as "without any bearings, let alone a sense of direction." He finds Britain's "economic policy in ruins" and its leaders "playing an increasingly ludicrous game of blindman's bluff."[10] Stephen Blank questions whether, with its government exhausted and social conflict intensifying, British democracy can survive.[11]

This sense of something wrong is not totally new. In the early 1960s a mood of introspective self-evaluation swept through British life. Arthur Koestler's *Suicide of a Nation* was joined by Michael Shanks's *Stagnant Society* and a whole series of Penguin books on *What's Wrong with . . .*(various British institutions). The media chimed in with *Private Eye,* "Beyond the Fringe," and "That Was the Week That Was."[12] This mood soon dissolved in the first flurry of enthusiasm over Wilson's vision of the new technocracy that Britain would become. But these self-doubts of the early 1960s pale beside the concern of the late 1970s, when crisis seemed to be on everyone's mind.

What exactly is the nature of this crisis? What diverse tendencies combine to give the overwhelming sense that something is wrong in Britain? An analysis of the aggravated conditions of Britain today can best be organized about the three salient features of its former grandeur. They cluster around its industrial economy, its position in the world, and its ability to resolve conflict peacefully with democratic continuity.

Most dramatic of Britain's problems seem to be the economic

ones. Its rate of growth is mired between 2 and 2.5 percent a year, far short of government goals of 4 percent. Inflation in Britain was for some twenty years no higher than 3 percent a year; in the early 1970s it averaged about 10 percent a year and later in the decade it rose much higher, nearing on occasion 20 percent. Successive governments have allowed unemployment to rise in an effort to reduce the economy's inflationary tendencies. From the years of postwar recovery until 1961, unemployment remained constant at the low figure of 1.5 percent. In the late 1960s it began to climb. From 1967 to 1970 it averaged 2.4 percent. In 1971 it had reached 3.6 percent. By the end of the decade unemployment approached 8 percent, considerably higher than at any other time since the Great Depression. Preoccupation with adverse balance of payments and the stability of the pound, combined with the evident failure of the planning efforts begun in the early 1960s, has produced an economy that has "failed to increase production, to maintain stable prices, to invest more, to get more satisfactory returns in productivity from investment, to export more."[13] Strikes, labor unrest, and failed enterprises seem endemic. The plight of such venerable institutions as Rolls-Royce and the London *Times* conjures up, especially among journalists, an overwhelming sense of crisis.

Many explanations have been offered for Britain's poor economic performance. For some it represents the paradoxical but inevitable fruits of Britain's early industrial preeminence. "Assets can turn into liabilities." A worn-out industrial pioneer, Britain confronts a world economy that has far surpassed it technologically. Meanwhile, it agonizes over "remodernization."[14] Others write of Britain as a classic example of the postindustrial society with its relaxed attitudes toward work, profit, and productivity.[15] For some the explanation lies in the sad state of British management. Peter Calvocoressi concludes: "The economic failures of our period were essentially industrial and however the blame might be apportioned among different groups or classes, the main share rested on those with prime responsibility—the owners and their nominees or agents."[16] Oligarchic, nepotistic, amateurish, uneducated management is the culprit. But unions fare no better in the view of those who emphasize the "new group politics" and "pluralistic stagnation" as the cause of Britain's economic problems. Samuel Beer and Gerald Dorfman, for example, single out the unions for their power to undermine national economic policy.[17]

Finally, political factors are blamed. The analyses of Andrew Shonfield, Susan Strange, and Stephen Blank emphasize the subordination of British domestic economic policy to the goals of foreign policy. Continuous concern with the balance of payments, for example, has led successive governments to restrain domestic investment. The related political efforts to defend sterling and maintain a strong international posture are the culprits, not any deficiencies inherent in British economic attitudes, according to this school.[18]

While international political concerns clearly loom large in any analysis of the sources of today's economic crisis, few would claim that Britain's role in the world, the second salient feature of its former grandeur, plays a crucial role in shaping the sense of its current crisis. It is central, to be sure, in creating the sense of decline. To the popular mind, there is no more vivid symbol of British decline than the demise of empire and Britain's floundering search for a new international role. Labour's decision in 1967 to end the British presence east of Suez finally put to rest the lingering memory of international strength. But the Commonwealth, the American alliance, nuclear power, moral stewardship, and the Common Market have not proved adequate substitutes. And it is here, of course, that international issues do link up with today's crisis, for this search for a new international role and the inability to accept a subordinate world position led to the emphasis on international financial stature and influence as a compensatory symbol of grandeur. Even more overt failures of foreign and military policy probably contribute to the sense of crisis today. Who, for example, can estimate how much Britain's inability to effect a settlement in Northern Ireland or even Cyprus or Rhodesia helps create the sense that something is wrong with the country?

Much more critical than international issues in shaping the sense of crisis in Britain today is the apparent rise of social and political tension, the acceleration of unrest and violence within the country. The centuries-old tradition of continuity and peaceful democratic resolution of conflict seems in jeopardy. Inflation, un-

employment, and poor economic conditions in general breed inevitable and justifiable class tensions. The country's poor economic performance of late has only exacerbated the already
smoldering economic inequities in British life. Despite the welfare
state, two million people live below the poverty line in Britain, and
it still has "about the most unequal distribution of incomes and of
wealth in the world."[19] Of the 15 million houses in England and
Wales, 6 million were built before World War I and at least a
million are over a hundred years old. One million are rated as
slums; the number without baths, lavatories, and running hot
water is reckoned in the millions.[20] Parallel to and no doubt partly
derived from the rise of class tensions during the recent years of
economic difficulty is the rise of racial tension, which has provided fodder for a fascist resurgence in the National Front. Race
riots and political confrontation are no longer uncommon in Britain. While the regional tensions created by the politicization of
Scottish and Welsh nationalism (itself clearly linked to Britain's
economic crisis) may produce less violence than class and racial
tension, they do portend utterly unpredictable possibilities in a
nation traditionally so stable and so linked to the past.

One cannot avoid a gnawing sense that something is wrong with
Britain when one reads that the left fears the emergence of an
authoritarian regime that will "be firm with greedy workers, picketing strikers, presumptuous trade unions, subversive teachers,
noisy students, tiresome blacks, welfare scroungers, sinister Marxists, misguided libertarians, and everybody else standing in the
way of national renewal by way of 'free enterprise' and the ownership of capital."[21] Some might dismiss this fear as a typical
paranoid fantasy of the radical left. But is all well in a Britain
where Sir Oswald Mosley, a chilling voice from the past, could in
1974 denounce "the prevailing pessimism and almost universal
defeatism" of his countrymen, and the *Times* could in all seriousness carry an editorial by Lord Chalfont bearing the headline
"Could Britain Be Heading for a Military Takeover?"[22]

Perspectives on the Current Crisis

Whether Americans care about what happens to Britain
or not, they seem unable to avoid thinking about it. At both popu-

lar and scholarly levels, the British example is dangled before American eyes to show the dire consequences of one line of policy or the obvious benefits of another. Particularly at the popular or journalistic level, the American sense of British social, political, and economic life is informed by people with axes to grind. Britain's woes are cited often by Milton Friedman and the authors of *The Future That Doesn't Work* as a warning to Americans of the follies of government spending and state socialism.

Americans have, of course, an alternative to these bleak inferences drawn from current British history. The case can be made that Britain is once again in the vanguard of progress, setting forth new and innovative patterns of life for a postindustrial age. Its humane and efficient provision of social and human services has much to teach America. Its arts and culture thrive, and here, too, it can be a model for emulation.

Anthony Lewis, one of America's most astute observers of Britain, has written that despite all that may be wrong with Britain, it is unfair to say "that in these sins Britain is worse than other countries."[23] A consideration of the United States, he declares, will turn up the same problems. Barbara Castle, pointing to American unemployment, inflation, and an adverse balance of payments, develops the same theme. Commentators thus do tend to dwell on America's similarity to Britain. To be sure, America's language and culture, its political and legal system, even its industrial society have been molded by its English connection. And now it seems to share the common malaise confronting the industrial West.

But America differs from Britain. While America shares with Britain, for example, the problem of reconciling bureaucracy and social welfare with an Anglo-Saxon concept of freedom, the British example has been misused and misunderstood. Britain's bureaucracy has a longer history than America's, has developed differently, and functions within a different network of political institutions. America and Britain are very different societies. Homicides and manslaughter cases number about 500 a year in Britain, while in the United States the figure is about 17,000. Britain's *public* expenditure for health care is slightly larger than its expenditure for defense.[24]

What is happening in Britain, however, does not owe its significance only, or even primarily, to its relevance to America. The fate of Britain is of intrinsic interest and historic moment. It is this conviction that informs this volume, which brings together various perspectives on the crisis, various explanations and interpretations of Britain's problems, and even some denials that anything is wrong.

Part I gives two politicians the first word. Edward Heath and Barbara Castle, both incredibly active and influential figures over three decades of British public life, make up in wide-ranging overview for what their comments lack in analytic depth. Their reflections, offered in April 1978, cover a variety of international and domestic themes. Reading Heath's remarks, one easily forgets that he was in opposition to the ruling government and that an election was but a few months away. He is full of bullish confidence. Far from facing a crisis, Britain thrives. To make a case for crisis, he contends, is not to single out Britain but to describe a condition facing the West in general. There is a singular lack of party polemics here as Heath takes the highroad. Totally missing are accusations that after 1974 (when Heath left office) the Labour Party brought disaster to Britain. The British socialists are not depicted as sinister culprits. Any problems that do exist, and few do, are the products of the world economy, brought about by the steep increase in the price of oil in 1973.

This is vintage late-1970s Heath. Gone is the outspoken champion of a rejuvenated capitalism, eager to take on the trade unions. Ever since February 1975, when Heath was replaced as head of the Conservative Party by Margaret Thatcher, he has bided his time, hoping that eventually his more moderate posture would win away the party faithful from the more strident conservatism of the new leader. In these remarks he reads like a statesman, hoping that Thatcher should lead their party to defeat in the upcoming election, the party would remember just such a tone and turn once again to him.

Castle's remarks stand in glaring opposition to Heath's. Yes, she contends, there is a British crisis, but in no sense is her governing Labour Party responsible. The culprits are the international banking community, misguided Conservative policy in the past, American mistakes, and, of course, Britain's decision to join the Common Market. She has a long enemies list, and with lively partisanship she ticks them off. The British crisis is their responsibility, and no wonder her own party faced all those problems in 1978.

In Part II, dealing with the British economy, Gerald Dorfman re-creates the bitter mood of confrontation that characterized Heath's last few months in office. His assessment of the power of British unions is more than the simple tale of how the miners brought down Heath's government. The study of those few months, Dorfman suggests, offers important clues to the enduring problems that will plague the relationship of the union movement to any Conservative government.

In contrast to Dorfman's intensive look at a particular traumatic episode in recent British politico-economic life, Stephen Blank provides a sweeping survey of the British economy over the past four decades. He finds much to be pleased with and has little truck with those who bad-mouth Britain as permanently disabled economically. Far from being a terminal patient among Europe's economies, Blank suggests, the British economy has never been allowed to realize its potential, as it is traditionally subordinated to political and international concerns. Blank links any problems that exist to the state of rather advanced crisis in which he finds the British parties and party system. Nor does the civil service escape its share of the blame in Blank's analysis. Robin Marris, on the other hand, is convinced that fundamental problems do exist in the British economy. In comparing Britain with other "rich" nations, he finds its performance inadequate in area after area. The culprit, he feels, is an outdated economic world view that assumes, for example, that a modern economy can be run by dilettantes.

An article in *The Economist* was the inspiration behind Jorgen Rasmussen's piece, which opens Part III, on the modern British state. *The Economist* chose Guy Fawkes Day in November 1977 to publish a root-and-branch attack on British political institutions that culminated in the suggestion (one hopes figurative) that the time had come for "blowing up a tyranny."[25] British parliamentary institutions had much to learn from American practices, *The Economist* argued, especially in terms of legislative power vis-à-vis the potential for executive tyranny. Rasmussen finds little of value in *The Economist*'s reading of American institutions and even less in its indictment of British practices. Perhaps the most significant part of Rasmussen's rebuttal is his detailed analysis of changes in the relationship between the Commons and the cabinet during the 1970s.

In recent years Britain, no less than the United States, and perhaps even more, has seen issues of sexual politics enter the mainstream of state concerns. Barbara Castle's remarks provide a vivid personal perspective on recent political developments in women's quest for equality in Britain. She describes the visible advances made in the numbers of women entering public life, but also details what still remains to be done. She concentrates on the intricacies of welfare and pension reform, not terribly dramatic and glamorous topics, but the legislative battlefields where many of the advances of women are being won in today's Britain.

Ira Katznelson draws attention to what he suggests are decisive changes within the working class and hence in the Labour Party as it expresses the aspirations and ideals of that class. The British Labour Party, no longer committed to an egalitarian socialist commonwealth, has succumbed to the reformist distributive politics conventionally identified with American labor. This change of course is closely linked to the disappearance of traditional working-class communities and subcultures in Britain, under the impact of the national media, urban redevelopment, and geographic mobility. The result, Katznelson argues, is that English workers and their party have increasingly embraced middle-class values.

While Katznelson characterizes diffuse, varied, and persistent challenges to authority by ad hoc movements and groups that cross class lines as an American pluralist style of political conflict, and as such by no means a step forward, Ralph Miliband is unable to dismiss them so easily. His survey of politics and class relations in the last four decades culminates in his perception of new pressures on the British social system—not a coherent socialist challenge yet not altogether outside of the context of class. He coins the term "desubordination" to describe efforts by people in subordinate positions to "mitigate, resist, and transform the conditions of their subordination." He has no sense of where these efforts will lead in the long run. Convinced, however, that the Labour Party is today an inappropriate vehicle for any such effort at desubordination, he has short-range misgivings about the British state that are bleak indeed.

For how long can we blithely continue to talk about this British state? Part IV looks at the very real possibility that out of today's crisis may indeed come the breakup of Britain. That Scottish football and rugby crowds have replaced "God Save the Queen" with "O Flower of Scotland" is but the symbolic tip of the iceberg, Jack Brand argues in his paper on Scottish nationalism. Brand traces the recent rise of national feeling in Scotland and its translation into a political movement. He is convinced that it has profound implications for the future of British politics in general. Milton Esman is also concerned with this contemporary Scottish renaissance. His discussion places it in a broader analytical framework of comparative ethnic and economic discontent. Indeed, he reads the resurgence of political nationalism in Scotland as symptomatic of a general state of development characteristic of late industrial societies.

Part V looks at the international dimension of the British crisis. Lawrence Freedman surveys Britain's agonizing search for a unique and exceptional role in its postimperial stage. While he is critical of those who simplistically link Britain's slide from great-power status with its dismal economic performance, he does emphasize Britain's international vulnerability and its considerable stake in the health of the international fiscal order. He concludes with a most sobering analysis of recent British travails in the world's money markets.

Richard Rosecrance continues this emphasis with a vivid summary of two centuries of British foreign policy. He assumes that Britain's power in the world was a direct result of its economic preeminence. The heart of his argument is his detailed discussion of the nature of that economic hegemony with its concentration of international energies on services and invisibles. As the world economic order has changed, so has Britain's economic strength, and thus its international power. In the course of his piece Rosecrance provides some fascinating commentary on Britain's military performance over the last 150 years. But central to his article is the theme that runs through so much of this volume, the inextricable linkage of Britain's political strength with financial and economic variables.

The volume closes with two very distinct kinds of analyses of the British crisis and speculations about the future. Tom Nairn provides a brilliant polemic against all that is pious and pompous in contemporary Britain. He offers as a prelude to his rather frightening vision of the future a dazzling tour of a crisis-ridden civilization. Peter Stansky, in the final piece, is by no means as convinced as Nairn that all is rotten in Britain. Much is wrong, Stansky admits, and he effectively uses George Orwell's writings and misgivings to highlight these shortcomings. But, the calendar notwithstanding, 1984 is not around the corner. The future Stansky sees for Britain is more hopeful: for British problems he foresees civil and humane British solutions.

This may well be the theme on which all the contributions to the volume converge. No doubt much is wrong with Britain. Some of the wrongness is unique to Britain and some of it is the inescapable result of the new social and economic order that has emerged in the last third of the twentieth century. All the contributors have been self-consciously reluctant to offer much mawkish praise of "muddling through," but it is a latent theme throughout the volume. Would that Britain's problems could be solved by British solutions! The possibility that they may not may itself be what is truly wrong with Britain.

Notes

1. Peter Calvocoressi, *The British Experience, 1945–1975* (New York: Pantheon Books, 1978), p. 65.
2. See, for example, R. Emmet Tyrell, Jr., ed., *The Future That Doesn't Work: Social Democracy's Failures in Britain* (New York: Doubleday, 1977); Daniel Bell, "The Future That Never Was," *Public Interest*, Spring 1978; Robin Marris, "Is Britain an Awful Warning to America?," *New Republic*, September 17, 1977; note also Milton Friedman's periodic warnings reported in the popular press and in his *Newsweek* columns. For an alternative reading, see Bernard D. Nossiter, *A Future That Works* (Boston: Houghton Mifflin, 1978), and Philip Green, "Social Democracy and Its Critics: The Case of England," *Dissent*, Summer 1978.
3. Cited in Ralf Dahrendorf, "Is Britain Really That Sick?," *Wall Street Journal*, August 18, 1977.
4. See, for example, Barbara Castle's paper below, Robin Marris's "Is Britain an Awful Warning to America?" and his piece below. See also Peter Calvocoressi, *The British Experience, 1945–1975.*
5. See Tyrell, ed., *The Future That Doesn't Work,* and Bell, "The Future That Never Was."
6. One of the best arguments from this perspective is found in the work of Leo Panitch. See, for example, his "Ideology and Integration:

The Case of the British Labour Party," *Political Studies* 19, no. 2 (1971); "Profits and Politics: Labour and the Crisis of British Capitalism," Conference on British Studies, Claremont, Calif., April 16, 1977; *Social Democracy and Industrial Militancy* (Cambridge: Cambridge University Press, 1975). See also the papers by Tom Nairn and Ralph Miliband below.

7. See Sir Henry Phelps Brown, "What Is the British Predicament?," *Three Banks Review,* no. 116 (December 1977); see also Stephen Blank's piece below and his "Britain: The Politics of Foreign Economic Policy," in *Between Power and Plenty,* ed. Peter J. Katzenstein (Madison: University of Wisconsin Press, 1978).

8. See Blank, "Britain," p. 126.

9. For details of these events, see Gerald Dorfman's piece below.

10. Anthony Howard, "Angry Wage Earners, Floundering Politicians," *New York Times Magazine,* December 26, 1976, p. 36.

11. Blank, "Britain," p. 92.

12. See D. E. Butler and Anthony King, *The British General Election of 1964* (London: Macmillan, 1965), chap. 2.

13. Blank, "Britain," p. 90.

14. Richard Rose, *Politics in England* (Boston: Little, Brown, 1974), p. 55.

15. See Bell, "The Future That Never Was"; Leslie Lenkowsky, "Welfare and the Welfare State," in *The Future That Doesn't Work,* ed. Tyrell; see also Nossiter, *The Future That Works.*

16. Calvocoressi, *British Experience,* p. 191.

17. See Samuel Beer, *British Politics in the Collectivist Age,* rev. ed. (New York: Random House, 1969), chap. 12; Gerald Dorfman, *Wage Politics in Britain, 1945-1975: Government vs. TUC* (Ames: Iowa State University Press, 1973), p. 75, and his piece below; Jack Hayward, "National Aptitudes for Planning in Britain, France, and Italy," *Government and Opposition* 9, no. 4 (Autumn 1974).

18. See Andrew Shonfield, *British Economic Policy since the War* (London: Penguin Books, 1958); Susan Strange, *Sterling and British Policy* (London: Oxford University Press, 1971); Blank, "Britain," and his piece below.

19. Calvocoressi, *British Experience,* p. 123.

20. Ibid., p. 140.

21. See Miliband's piece below.

22. See *Times* (London), August 5, 1974.

23. "QE 2 and Other Sore Points," *Sunday Times,* January 12, 1969.

24. See Rose, *Politics in Britain,* p. 397, and Calvocoressi, *British Experience,* p. 36.

25. *The Economist,* November 5, 1977, pp. 11-16.

PART I ::

The Politician's Perspective

2 | *A Tory View*

EDWARD HEATH

Since I first started taking an active part in politics as a student at Oxford just over forty years ago, there has been the most rapid transformation in world affairs that we have noted in any period of history. After the Second World War we established organizations to deal with the international, political, economic, social, and cultural aspects of our lives together. We believed that we had established stability such as the world had not known before. Certainly at my time as a student in the thirties we had the utmost degree of instability, massive unemployment, the growth of the dictatorships in Europe, which were leading inevitably, we believed, to a world war.

That was what my generation lived through. It was, therefore, to a certain extent our pride that after the war the institutions were established to deal with these problems: the United Nations for the international political problems; the International Monetary Fund to deal with the question of currencies; the World Bank to deal with the development of less fortunate countries; the committees of the United Nations to deal with social and cultural matters; the Atlantic Alliance to assure our security. And so for a decade, two decades, we were convinced that this was a state of affairs which would continue as far as we could see and of which we could take advantage.

I think now the world is realizing that the stability has been gravely eroded in almost every sphere. If we look at international affairs, then the UN is no longer expected to deal with individual problems. If we look at monetary affairs, then instead of having stable currencies and fixed parities we now have a world in which currencies are for the most part floating. From the point of view of the developing countries, the World Bank helped, but the disparity between the standard of living of the thousand or twelve hundred million people of the developing world and what we in the developed world have has become greater despite everything which has been done. Perhaps in the cultural sphere we have been somewhat more successful. But when it comes to the question of security, then we see the growth of Soviet power in recent years, which is obviously a threat in particular to the sea lanes of the world and, as now in Africa, to other continents and possibly to Europe itself. So the stability which we thought we had established has in fact been undermined in practically every aspect of our international and, therefore, our national life.

Very well then, how does Britain, how does the United States stand in all of this? Let me just submit one thing about the United States as the background to what I want to say about Britain and Europe. I think that what we are now seeing in the international sphere is a major change in America's attitude toward international affairs and its policy toward many parts of the world. Again, in the forty or more years since I started taking interest in politics—going back even to sixth-form days at school—I have watched a continuous process of movement of power from Congress into the White House. It started with Roosevelt because he was elected to deal with the economic crisis of 1931. To do so he indulged in what would now be called government intervention, though by comparison with modern times it was of the mildest sort—the Tennessee Valley Authority and so on. Then, after Pearl Harbor, the United States had to fight for its own survival, not just by sending troops to Europe to help friends and allies, and more power went into his hands. Truman's power grew because of Korea; Kennedy's, Johnson's, and Nixon's because of Vietnam. As an outside observer, what I see now is that after Vietnam and Watergate, Congress has said, in effect, we are not going to have the president going off on these ventures of his own again. But as a practical politician, all I know is that when a democratic assembly gets an idea like that into its head it does not drop it very easily. Since we have seen four decades in which the movement was in one direction, we must be prepared to see a period in which it goes in the other.

This, of course, will impose a grave restraint on what the president can do in foreign policy and international affairs. And it forces the rest of us to recognize the fact. The first to recognize this were, of course, the Russians, and the first instance was in Angola. They made a correct assessment of the change in American attitude. This did not happen under President Carter and Mr. Vance; it happened under President Ford and Mr. Kissinger when Congress would not allow Kissinger to send funds to Angola, let alone men or matériel. As a result, the Soviet Union has pursued its policy in Africa secure—it believes—from any interference. We have seen a lack of American action in Ethiopia or Somalia or any other aspect of the African continent. Of course, in the Pacific we have also seen indications of the withdrawal from South Korea. If there are to be full diplomatic relations between the United States and China, then the United States will have to withdraw from Taiwan and she will not get any understanding from Peking as to how the problem will be settled after withdrawal.

Then what matters in this situation? If this is a correct analysis, what matters is the relationship between the United States and Europe and the United States and Japan. Those are two prime issues. We in Europe will no longer be able to expect the United States to take action in any part of the world to put right something which we do not like, and then to blame the United States for the way in which she does it. That luxury in the future will be denied us. I think it is very important that we should see the developments in Britain and in Europe against this background.

It is vital that the Atlantic Alliance be maintained for the security of both Europe and the United States. Very well, in that case Europe must be prepared to make a greater contribution toward the security of the alliance as a whole. In this, Britain is certainly playing her part: a greater proportion of the gross domestic product toward security in Europe than any other single country. So as far as our security is concerned, there is no crisis. Many of us would like to see more done, but that depends upon economics, having the strength to deal with the provisions of what is required. I will touch on this when I come to economic matters.

In some quarters detente has become a dirty word. It is said to be the soft option. Detente is not something new; I remember hearing the speech in which it was proposed by Mr. Churchill in 1953 and nobody would term Winston Churchill a soft option. He made that speech after the death of Stalin, when I was a whip in my party and sat on the steps by the speaker's feet. On the whole it is sometimes more useful to be able to watch the faces of one's own party than the backs of their heads. Mr. Churchill apologized for Mr. Eden's illness and announced that he had taken over the Foreign Office himself—no mean undertaking for a prime minister of nearly eighty. Then he made a long, very boring speech about the Middle East and I wondered at the time why it was so bad. I realized on rereading it that of course it had been written by the Foreign Office and he had not had time to change it in any way. Then came this dramatic intervention in which he suddenly switched from the Middle East and said, now I have a message to give, Stalin is dead and now we can re-create the working arrangement which we and the Americans had with the Soviet Union for so much of the Second World War. Together we can work. And that was the beginning of detente.

All the time, the doctrine was to maintain superiority over the Soviet bloc. Of course, it was bound to lead to a race between two cars, or two alliances. It was only when President Nixon said that he was prepared to accept parity that you could enter upon SALT and discussions about disarmament. But what is essential is that in negotiating on parity you do not allow yourself to get into a position of inferiority. That is what the West must always guard against, that in negotiating for genuine disarmament we do not allow ourselves to be put into a position of disadvantage.

Europe is essential in this formula. If we are looking at the general world strategy in which both of us have to play a part, then China also has an increasingly important role. A country which by the end of the century will be a thousand million people, which has nuclear weapons, which has very large conventional forces, and which has immense resources of raw materials must be reckoned with. China wants a strong Europe on Russia's western flank, understandably. It is in the Alliance's interest and in the interest of Europe that there be a strong China on Russia's eastern flank. As we see, the world strategy begins to fit together. This, then, is what we should be working jointly for in international affairs and in the field of security.

Perhaps I could just touch on a phrase which has already been used about the relationship between the United States and Britain, sometimes termed the *special relationship*. I myself never use this term, I dislike it and I much prefer to call it a *natural* relationship. It is natural because of our common history, our common heritage, language—despite its misuse and abuse—the common law background to our work. I dislike the term *special arrangement* because the United States has very important relations with other European countries, the Federal Republic of Germany, for example, and with Japan. I see no reason why we in Britain should try to have something which cannot be established by other friends and allies. So I prefer to look at our arrangement always as a natural understanding which comes from all those things we have in common.

Very well then, what about British policy in particular? Of course, in this time which I have lived through we have changed our comparative positions. After all, when I was in Oxford we talked about the Powers. What did it mean? We meant Britain, Germany, France, Italy, and the Netherlands. In the late thirties one did not think of the United States as a power, one did not think of the Soviet Union as a power. But today, nobody regards Europe as a power in itself or the individual member countries. We had the greatest empire of all. We have seen a change into a commonwealth of free, independent nations. We try to pass on to them all the Westminster democratic system—like yours, the most difficult system in the world to work successfully. Apart from the old commonwealth, there is hardly a country which has been able to maintain the Westminster parliamentary system. But we were able to make the change without violence and it has been successful, with the one remaining exception of Rhodesia. There is now more hope than at any time in the past ten years, with the internal settlement in Rhodesia, to move to a more stable condition there.

I want to quote two figures which indicate the sort of problem which confronts us in the European Economic Community. The latest estimate available for economic production in the United States was 1514 billion dollars in 1976. The figure for the European Community was 1345 billion dollars—not a very great difference and a diminishing gap. The differences are much greater, of course, if you take the next: the Soviet Union at 850 or Japan at

450. But look what the United States succeeds in doing with a production of that size—a massive defense program, including all the nuclear weapons; a massive space program, rightly or wrongly; an immense computer industry which scoops the world pool; an immense civil aviation construction industry; and many other major industries, such as the automobile industry.

What does Europe do which can compare with that? On such a scale? At the moment, nothing. It cannot compete with defense and nuclear technology, with space, computers, construction of aircraft, or these other great industries. I think the lesson is that if we in the Community are not yet using our resources efficiently and rationally, as happens to a much larger degree in America, then we must remember that America has been for so much longer a single market and then urgently develop the proper use of our resources. The Community was fashioned and formed mainly on the political basis that from greater European unity we could have not only greater economic strength but political strength which could influence the rest of the world. We are already advancing along these lines through the Lomé Agreement for the developing countries; forty-seven countries united with us whom we are able to help. And so Britain's role now—in the political as well as the immediate defense sphere, in the economic interest and the interest of developing countries—is in the European Community. Looking at it from this point of view, there is no "British crisis" as far as our national affairs are concerned or our role in Europe. I regret that we have not been able to give greater leadership to the Community in the last three or four years. I regret that the Community has not made greater progress during these years. But I understand that the pressure on individual heads of government from the combination of inflation and unemployment has been so great that they have turned inward instead of recognizing the fundamental truth that the Community exists to find common solutions to common problems. I hope now that with the summit meeting in July we are moving out of this phase and into a new phase of international cooperation.

I have indicated that such problems of international relations and security as we have in Britain are shared by others. This is also true of most aspects of the economic sphere. We are still seeing today high inflation and massive unemployment in the Western world. In Britain we have the particular problem that we were the first industrial nation, that others were able to take advantage of our experience, our knowledge and mistakes. We still have not remedied the weaknesses which arose from this: lack of investment, low productivity, trade union restrictions (the consequence to a large extent of the great depression of the thirties), and outdated equipment.

But these are problems which can be overcome. We now have North Sea oil, and we must look at this from two points. First, regarding the effect on the balance of payments, it should enable us—with careful handling—to maintain a slight surplus. Second, oil revenues through the normal tax system can be used for the repayment of debt, the reduction of taxes, increased public expenditure, or to encourage investment in industry whether it is private or nationalized. Each government in its time will have to decide the balance which it wants to create among the different possibilities.

The fact that we ought to be able to maintain the balance of payments in moderate surplus means that constraints which Britain has had for the last thirty years on expanding its economy could be gradually removed. On each occasion in the past when we have expanded we have come up against the problem of deficit, inevitably because if you have no raw materials of your own—as we do not, except for coal—then you have to import before you can export. And this leads, inevitably, to a growing deficit before you can make it up with increased exports. Of course, the oil will not last forever and in the course of the next ten or fifteen years we must make sure that both the revenues and the balance-of-payments advantage should be used for basic industrial reconstruction in Britain.

Again, some of the problems which we suffer from here are common. Let us take the steel industry, a major industry in raw materials. From 1950 to 1974, the production of steel in the West increased from 150 million tons to 450 million. It increased 300 percent. In Britain, it increased 23 percent. You can say that this was a consequence of nationalization, denationalization, threatened renationalization, final renationalization, and that all of this had to lead to a lack of investment and paralysis in the industry.

But during the same time in the United States, the greatest free-enterprise country in the world, steel production increased by 29 percent. That is not a very great difference, and the United States became a great steel importing country. The Japanese increased their production in this period from 4.4 million tons to 120.2 million—an increase of 2030 percent. Those are staggering figures, and if you say that Britain has a crisis in the steel industry or a crisis with certain aspects of its industrial production, then let us look at the position as a whole.

What I find worrisome is that in the West we are seeing our industries more and more replaced by the products of countries around the Pacific. We have seen enormous progress in Japan and a very substantial surplus in her balance of payments. We now see the same developments in South Korea, the Philippines, beginning in Indonesia, already well developed in Hong Kong and Singapore. And in the Middle East we tend to assume that the money will be spent in the West. Today much of it is being spent in South Korea, the Philippines, and Indonesia. The Middle East is using the construction industries in those countries instead of the United States or Germany or Britain. If we take each of these industries in turn, then we see the sphere of the automobile industry diminishing and we will see—we have seen it already—competition in electronics. The answer to this problem can come only from an expanding world economy which is able to absorb more and more of the products of both the developed and developing countries.

Here I come to what is really the crux of the present situation. I do not think that the world is grasping the significance of what happened in the autumn of 1973, when OPEC suddenly increased the price of oil fourfold. That meant a massive transfer of financial resources across the exchanges to those member countries, estimated at $120 billion per year. If you withdraw $120 billion from the West it does two things: it reduces the standard of living of everyone there and removes the value of jobs. If the money is then respent, it creates jobs but it does not restore your standard of living. We have seen that some of the money has been respent, but there is still today a gap of at least $40 billion per year accumulating year after year—some would put it as high as $60 billion. It may be placed on deposit, but it is all short term, forty-

eight hours or a week or a month. It cannot be used for productive investment in any country in the West. And so the net result
of this is that underneath any cyclical trends we have heavy unemployment caused by the continuous transfer of a vast sum of
$40 to $60 billion per year into OPEC members which are not
organized—as they freely admit—to spend it. This is the underlying problem which faces the world economy today. It is why Britain has 1.5 million unemployed, a rate of 6 or 6.1 percent. It is
why the United States has a rate roughly the same. It is why there
is a total of 17 million unemployed in the West. Businessmen say
to me, "You know it's taking a long time to pull out of this trade
cycle." But this is not just a trade cycle.

The steel industry provides a single instance of the effects of
this turn. In 1974, Western steel production dropped by 18 million tons. That was a direct consequence of the state of affairs
after the autumn of 1973. Britain has its problems, of course; we
ought now to be able to maintain a reasonable balance of payments and we have high reserves. But we have to face the fact that
these reserves are not the result of successful trading. They are
the result of deposits in sterling by other countries that wish to
halt the slide in London.

I want to touch on the very large public sector in the British
economy. This, of course, is the direct policy of successive Labour
governments to which I have always been opposed. But I have to
recognize that in a country of our size, with such a closely integrated economy, if a private enterprise finds itself in difficulties
from which it cannot recover, then there is a responsibility for
the government to take action to maintain that firm. This was the
problem that faced us over Rolls-Royce. We as a government
could not possibly stand by and watch Rolls-Royce crash, leaving
over seventy air forces in the world without any maintenance for
their engines and many more civil airlines without any possibility
of spare parts or replacements. At the same time, President Nixon
could not afford to watch Lockheed go to the wall. Lockheed and
Rolls-Royce were, of course, bound together on the Tristar and
211 engine. Here is clear proof of not only the close network
within Britain itself, but the network across the Atlantic in a single
product. But as far as the public sector is concerned, my view is
that changing ownership solves nothing. It does produce im-

mense problems for the budgetary action which any government has to take. When you are looking at the British budget and the question of the borrowing requirement, then you have to recognize that the budget is responsible for investment in the steel industry, the coal industry, the electricity industry, the gas industry, and the nuclear power industry. It is responsible for civil aviation and air transport, for the whole of the railways, for road freight, and therefore the figures include investment for a public sector which must now be roughly 50 percent. It is very important to recognize that if one of these industries was in private hands or was to say our investment program for next year is 500 million, then you would pat it on the head and say, well done, thou good and faithful private enterprise. If a nationalized industry has 500 million out of the budget, then everybody says this is a disgrace and a public scandal.

Now this is not a tolerable intellectual approach to the problems of the public sector. I must also recognize that once an industry becomes part of the public sector it is only with the utmost difficulty that it can be returned to the private sector again—if only because the threat of renationalization will prevent investment. It is, after all, difficult to persuade private citizens to put their money into railways which are losing several hundred million pounds a year. We did have two successes in the government of 1970-74 in denationalizing publicly owned concerns. One was a brewery in Carlisle that was nationalized during the First World War, and as the beer was not what everybody expected, we were able to get away with it. The other was Thomas Cook's travel agency, and we were able to sell that to a bank. One cannot really visualize either of those as commanding the heights of the British economy.

British political institutions are among the oldest in the parliamentary democracies. You may say that we have been slow to adapt, and in some ways this is true: slow in the parliamentary system, though we did reform the local government system. There was much criticism of it; there will always be when one reforms local government. But now we have the problem of devolution for Scotland and Wales.

My view for the last ten years has been that for the sake of good government in Scotland and Wales there should be devolution. In

Scotland there is a strong feeling that they want their own parliament and administration. In Wales this feeling is less strong, but I know from my experience in the last twenty-five years that what Scotland has today Wales wants tomorrow. But Scotland does not want separatism, nor does Wales. I do not believe that a threat to the unity of the United Kingdom exists. Only a small percentage of Scots would like to have independence, even though they believe in that way they would gain the oil revenues. In fact, it is possible for any good navigator to draw a line off Barick Head which would show that very little oil is in Scottish territory. At the moment it is unnecessary to do that, though I am quite prepared to learn my navigating for the purpose if the issue ever arises.

Our problem is that we are trying to develop devolution not in a federal system but in one in which there is no written constitution. All the problems of trying to find answers to financial power and political power in a double system arise very simply from this single fact. On the other hand, the rest of the United Kingdom is not prepared at the moment to accept a federal system. So the debates in Parliament and in the country have been coming out of this one great problem: how do we maintain our present unwritten constitution, but at the same time introduce very clear, specific powers under devolution?

It is interesting to look at this aspect of our life and compare it to the Federal Republic of Germany. The United States and Britain together after the war arranged the system for the Federal Republic. First, we gave them central government in a federal system at Bonn. The Bundestag last year sat for 500 hours. The Westminster Parliament sat for 1505, a large number of them through the night. The Bonn system on the whole is not only more comfortable but sensible. We gave them devolution in the *Länder,* and there is no point in saying that there is a great difference between this and England and Scotland. Schleswig-Holstein and North Rhine Westphalia have their own parliaments, their own premiers, and they deal with matters which are not dealt with at Bonn—local matters of health, education, and so on. It works.

We also gave them a trade union movement limited to fourteen unions. We in England have 376 and this makes negotiation difficult in an industry where you have sixteen or eighteen to deal with. The trade union movement in Germany cannot be allied with a political party. In England, the unions are allied, of course, with the Labour Party.

These things have proved to be the strength of German development in the postwar period. They are things which we in Britain cannot give to ourselves. But the next aspect one has to mention is the social side, the most widely discussed part of which is the health service. I believe that the health service has been invaluable to the British people in removing anxiety and worry about how they are going to be cared for in times of sickness. Of course, it needs more resources. And if one takes education, then here again we have a very wide state system that needs resources, too. Our so-called public school system has a quarter of a million children, the state system has ten and a quarter million. So the responsibility of the government must always be very largely in looking after the educational system under the state. But neither the health service nor the educational system can be improved without further resources. This, again, is where we come back to the question of an expanding economy and dealing with world problems.

I want to say one word about the educational system in particular. What we have seen develop in these last two decades is the movement toward comprehensive education and away from a system in which selection was made either for academic, technical, or general education. I believe that this is a movement in the wrong direction, that it is connected with one of the basic facts of British political and administrative life. We pride ourselves in having a permanent civil service that has the highest standards of conduct. It is incorruptable and fair. It is, in fact, the best administered civil service in the world. It was founded at the end of the nineteenth century, very largely on the Oxford modes and grades and the similar Cambridge tradition. What I find we are lacking in is those capable of policy formulation. This was first brought to my attention acutely during the negotiations on Britain's entry into the EEC in 1960–63, for which I was responsible. When I sat around the negotiating table with the ministers from the other countries and their key men, I saw how capable they were in this regard—particularly the French.

I well remember the number three man in the French delegation, who has just been made minister of foreign trade, a brilliant young man who came to me one night and said, look, we can't go on trying to find a solution to commonwealth problems as we are doing. Whatever it may be, foodstuffs or tariffs, your chap sits there and puffs his pipe and says, yes, well, yes, I think we shall find a solution and if we don't, well, we'll get used to it just as we've got used to the commonwealth. Then the Frenchman told me that he had worked out a system, that I must study it and tell him where the shoe pinches. We may not be able to meet every problem, but at least we have a system on which we base the whole of the relationship between the commonwealth countries. I said that the shoe pinched on Hong Kong and on dry grapes from southern Australia, that we would have to make a special arrangement outside the system for that. But this became the system on which, finally, ten years later, we entered the EEC. This is what I mean by policy formulation. I do not believe you can get it with a system which becomes flatter and flatter, as comprehensive education does. You must have a pyramid, as the French do.

There is no crisis in any of the aspects I have mentioned. Problems, yes; deep-seated, yes; difficult to solve, yes; but not of a crisis nature.

I want finally to touch on cultural aspects. In culture, I think we can take pride in Britain for what we have. London is the music capital of the world today. No other city has five major symphony orchestras and two opera houses, both packed the whole time. No other city has eight weeks of promenade concerts with seven thousand young people packed there every night. If one looks to painting and sculpture, then Britain gives a lead in modern work. If one looks to drama, then London still has the best theater of any capital city in the world. And so I believe that in cultural matters, which may be as true a test of a civilized country as we know, not only do we not have a crisis but we can say that we are giving a lead not only to Europe but to the rest of the world. I think that at a time of mass unemployment, at a time when people are leaving school, leaving universities for jobs they cannot find—certainly not jobs that meet their qualifications—then society needs to give even more emphasis to the arts than in normal times. The arts embody our values, and what we have to show is that however difficult the economic problems may be, we can maintain the standards of our civilization, which are European, which we have given to America.

This has been a wide-sweeping review with a very broad brush. I look back, of course, to the thirties constantly because then we had so many similar problems. We were not able then to solve the problems because we were not working together. If the world conference on economic affairs in 1932 had reached agreement on a program for action, then the whole tale of the thirties would have been different. Today we cannot afford to lose the opportunity. The world cannot have a stable foundation unless the United States, the EEC, and Japan agree on the fundamentals. We can then begin to make progress toward an expanding economy to ensure the prosperity on which our security in the West can be based.

3 | *A Socialist View*

BARBARA CASTLE

I want to refer to some important indices which in America's obsession with Britain's troubles she may have overlooked. British crisis? America has recently run up a massive balance-of-payments deficit; the largest, I understand, in her history. Britain's is moving into surplus. The dollar's weakness has become an international embarrassment. It is sterling's new strength that is worrying us. America's unemployment is nearly as high as Britain's. Taking the Organization for Economic Cooperation and Development (OECD) adjusted figures, at the end of 1977 America's was nearly 7 percent and Britain's about 8. Or let us take the English sickness, strikes. The International Labor Organization (ILO) has shown in its published figures that between 1967 and 1976 America lost far more workdays per thousand population than strike-prone England did. Or let us take some social indices. Britain's crime rate is rising, but not as fast as America's. Britain has the problem of neglect and dereliction in her cities just as America has, but London has never gone bankrupt—New York has. Or taking one of the essentials of civilized living, Britain happens to believe that one cannot have national unity without equality of opportunity to defeat pain and death. In Britain our National Health Service is a strong, unifying force.

I wonder if you noticed something rather interesting in Mr. Heath's remarks. Did you hear him denounce socialized medicine? It is true that the Conservatives voted against the introduction of the National Health Service, but with 99 percent of the British population drawing their medical care from it, all he said was that it needs more resources—and so it does. But it does not need resources more severely than those Americans who after a long illness face the medical bills they cannot afford, even with all the heavy private insurance they have taken out.

Now I want to assure you that I am not just making a few debating points, not just engaging in patronizing persiflage. My central case is that the crisis, if there be one, is general. Is there a crisis? There is certainly tragedy—the tragedy of depression, of wasted resources as we prove ourselves in advanced societies incapable of putting our people to work, of poverty. But this is worldwide. Within the world depression it is true that Britain is struggling to deal with special difficulties which arise from her history. On these I would not basically disagree with Mr. Heath's analysis. He seems right that Britain was the leading industrial nation in the past century and that in recent years we have lost our way. And it is quite right that over the years newer industrial nations have overtaken us. I agree with him on the causes of this. We have been pushed by the need to make ourselves industrially competitive to keep in the swim. We have been cushioned not only by the possession of a geographical empire but by the development of a financial one. In Britain the invisibles—banking, insurance, interest on overseas investment—have become more important than our factories. But what Mr. Heath did not say is that this fact lies at the heart of the British political argument.

Historically, the Labour Party has been the mouthpiece of the industrial worker and of the trade unions. Indeed, it grew out of the trade unions, which grew out of the needs of the workers on the factory floor. Because labor was insecure and desperate, trade unions came into existence and then created the labor movement to fight the political battles which were necessary because sectional trade union interests could not do the trick. For their part, the Tories have instinctively been a mouthpiece of City and banking interests. I do not believe that there is a single prominent banking company that subscribes to the funds of the Labour Party. Certainly, the City regards the Labour Party as its most dangerous enemy. So we are the party that by history has put the industrialization of Britain first. This should be obvious, because the strength of British industry is as vital to the Labour Party's political support as to Britain's livelihood. Industry does not live on invisibles; it needs something very visible, indeed, in the form of jobs at home. It does not live on the strength of overseas investments—some people can, even when industry is flat on its back, but not the people who support the Labour Party. This is why there is a very steep conflict of national interest. The interest of trade unions in the labor movement is a national, if you like, a *patriotic* interest. Our future depends on what happens within our home boundaries. It is the Labour Party that has fought against the creeping disease in Britain of the past few years.

What is the center of the problem that faces us? The deindustrialization following that brief, glorious lead in the Industrial Revolution years. This is why Labour governments have historically been compelled to carry out tough policies, very often to the disappointment of their supporters' hopes in the short term. We say to our people, sorry, love, we know you voted for us for higher wages and fatter social services, but sky's the limit until this country has reversed the slow industrial decline by investing more in basic industry. During the postwar years, the political pattern has been that Labour fights for the industry that gave our people jobs, and then the Tories come along and say with solemn voices, oh, we know these sacrifices are not really necessary. If we came back you'd have more in your pockets—cut the taxation and private investment would take care of itself. Mr. Heath said that the oil revenues we now face—not as large as some people imagine, certainly not enough to give us a gold rush—must be used for basic industrial reconstruction. I agree with him. But the important thing to remember about Mr. Heath is that the Conservative Party has rejected him. On almost every policy issue he disagrees with the present Conservative leadership.

In the House of Commons a great debate is going on about what use Britain should make of the North Sea oil revenues. At the very top of the priorities set out by the Labour Government's white paper is new investment and additional capacity in our own industry. Mrs. Thatcher has risen in her indignation to denounce this policy. She has a very different and a very simple formula which will have powerful demagogic appeal in the next election. She is going to say vote Conservative and we'll use the North Sea oil to cut your income taxes, leaving you with more money in your own pockets. Some of you will save it and then it will get invested in private industry. But this assumption runs counter to our whole history.

It is crucial to grasp two major factors that are at the heart of the economic impasse in which Britain finds herself. First is the chronic propensity of Britain to invest overseas, far more than her competititors do. This has something to do with that old imperial history, the fact that we had an escape route as long as the empire was there and our overseas connections were so strong. Mr. Heath touched upon this. In the years between 1966 and 1976 British direct investment overseas increased by 579 percent while manufacturing investment at home increased by 17.6 percent. Do you think that any of Britain's major industrial competitors engage in this kind of insanity? According to OECD figures for 1976, British overseas direct investment was running at nearly three times that of France, half again as much as West Germany, and nearly twice that of Japan. It is hardly surprising that Britain is struggling with the problem of low productivity. Some people would say that it is all due to some innate British sluggishness or lack of will to be rich or those beastly trade unions, but faced with these figures how can anyone deny that the basic cause is lack of comparable motor power?

I have an example in my own constituency in the industrial North, Blackburn, near Manchester in Lancashire. Until recently one of the major sources of new employment as the textile industry died out was the firm of Mullard. I have been to that vast factory, looked down at the factory floor and seen a few hundred men, with large numbers of machines per person, where formerly there were 3000 women assembling the conventional radio and TV tubes manually. There are about three hundred of these workers left and they will go soon, another blight striking my constituency, which has been through the trauma of the decline of textiles as the developing countries came along. What will replace the conventional TV tube? The electronics component industry in Britain has been crying out for government help. We have not the money, they say, to build up the alternative sophisticated technologies without government help. This is why the Labour Government set up new institutions like the National Enterprise Board, in order to channel government funds into industry—which Mrs. Margaret Thatcher loses no opportunity to deride, of course.

The second factor from which we are suffering is a consequence of the first; that is, Britain's far greater propensity to
import from her competitors. Because of this endemic industrial
weakness, every time we want to expand our economy we suck in
imports. Import penetration of British markets has been increasing steadily and alarmingly. Manufacturing production in Britain
today is barely higher than it was seven years ago, but the value of
imports of manufactured goods has risen two and one-half times.
No wonder unemployment has risen from 600,000 to nearly 1.5
million during the same period. Britain has circled desperately in
this trap in the postwar years.

This weakness has been exacerbated by two traumatic developments within the past thirty years. The first was the war in
which we were mockingly called the victors, following which we
were left more impoverished than the vanquished as all the international agencies and the United States rushed to give help to
countries like Germany as a barrier against the onrush of com-
munism. Nothing comparable was done to build up our industrial
strength. On the contrary, when I was a young new entree in the
House of Commons in 1945, I was faced with the challenge of
whether I should vote against my own government over the issue
of the American loan. The need for that loan on impossible terms
had arisen because of the conventional analysis that was bedevil-
ing international developments. During the war, my constituency
had stopped most of its textile production under an agreement
struck between Britain and the United States. Oh, said the United
States, we'll give you lend-lease, we'll have international cooperation, we'll share each other's burdens. Lend-lease was apparently
a magic formula. We were told that we must become the Allies'
arsenal, so my women textile workers were sent into the munitions factories. Never mind about the exports, said America,
lend-lease will pay for them. Certainly as long as the war lasted
this was a viable partnership, but literally within hours of peace
having been declared, lend-lease was stopped. There were ships
on the high seas bringing us the wherewithal to live. We under-
lined *lease* because we were doing the munitions work. And half-
way across the Atlantic those goods became payable.

We had no export trade because America asked us to abandon
it. We had to start paying our way without an export trade under
the conventional financial orthodoxy. To help us, the Americans

offered silver, but on the conventional terms that within two years
sterling had to become convertible. I was one of sixteen in a
crowded House of Commons to vote against it. And I walked in
intense loneliness across the chamber floor while our chief whip
nearly had apoplexy. But I was right; within less than a year those
terms had to be revised. They were unworkable, but in the meantime British revival had been struck another blow. This legacy of
the war should not, in my view, be underestimated.

Mr. Heath referred to the second trauma that has knocked
Britain sideways, the dramatic increase in oil prices. Here again, I
agree with his analysis. What it has meant is that the OPEC members have acquired huge surpluses that they cannot spend. I have
tried to help them spend it; as secretary of state for the social
services I went to Saudi Arabia, Kuwait, and Iran, talking to
health ministers and trying to get them to use some of that surplus
to buy our health know-how. But they are slow to play and in the
last few years $40 to $60 billion has been taken out of international circulation. Mr. Heath's analysis was right, but again he has
failed to draw the political lesson that is obvious. It is clear that in
such a situation the only way to sustain world trade is to encourage deficit countries like Britain to maintain their own economic
activity by borrowing. This is not a national weakness, a national
sin. It is international virtue and common sense if world trade is
not to slump into a depression that would hit all of us. Of course,
one does not want to borrow to engage in a spending spree. We
have not had much of a spending spree in Britain for the last few
years.

Once again we had to face the harsh realities under a Labour
government. But it was economic folly to force us to deflate demand below our productive potential in order to maintain our
credit worthiness in conventional terms. Yet this folly was forced
upon us by the International Monetary Fund (IMF), with, of
course, the Conservatives trying to suggest it was due to socialist
profligacy that we were borrowing at all. Here we really come to
the heart of the political argument. Ever since the war, a battle
of ideas has been going on between two rival groups; on the one
hand, the free-market mystics and, on the other, those of us who
stubbornly persist in believing that unemployment can be
overcome without bringing problems of inflation down on our
shoulders.

Here in the discussion of Britain's crisis we usually hear a lot about the trade unions. We are told that it is their power which causes inflation by forcing wages up and that it is their restrictive practices which cause the problem of low productivity. There is, of course, an element of truth in this; after all, trade unions were brought into existence as defensive mechanisms. But one does not make people less defensive by beating them about the head. One cannot run industry without the cooperation of those who work in it. It is this cooperation that the Labour Party has sought by voicing and practicing one simple principle. People will accept sacrifices only if those sacrifices are not unilateral. Trade unionists will not drop restrictive practices until they believe there is a better way to safeguard jobs. They will not hold down wage demands to make profits for industry unless they have a say in how those profits are employed. And the British trade union movement is no longer prepared to make profits for industry so that those who pocket the profits can then proceed to invest them overseas.

One of the essential problems in a democracy, particularly a modern industrialized democracy like Britain's and America's, is this: how, in a free society where trade unions can exercise power, do you persuade workers not to eat the seed corn of tomorrow's harvest? How do you persuade them to take the longer view? Britain had a great inflationary outburst of wage demands in 1974, but by patient argument we convinced the trade unions that this was suicide. By 1975, we had the trade union movement of Britain voluntarily instructing their members to accept one of the toughest income policies in our history—voluntarily. In the years 1975 and 1976 we had something unprecedented, I think, in the democratic world. For two years trade unions accepted and encouraged their members to accept a reduction in their standard of living—not under a statutory income policy, which the Labor government rightly scrapped, but voluntarily.

The tragedy that haunts Britain at the present time is that this social contract has been jeopardized by the IMF's deflationary policies. Instead of workers finding that their sacrifices have been saving their jobs, they have seen unemployment go up relentlessly. Even in the wealthy European Community there are over six million unemployed, over sixteen million in OECD countries. As for the developing countries, the position is desperate.

I was at a socialist international convention on unemployment recently which covered a wide range of countries from all parts of the world. There were twenty-eight of them there, a number of the delegations led by important prime ministers like Helmut Schmidt, chancellor of West Germany. One of them was Michael Manley of Jamaica, who, after listening to us wring our hands at our 6 percent unemployment, got up and said, do you realize that in my country unemployment is 25 percent, among the women it is 50 percent? This is the curse of the modern world.

It is not enough to say, "Cure inflation and unemployment will disappear." In Britain we have seen the opposite. Unemployment is high because the world is suffering from a lack of demand. The deficit countries are afraid to expand because that sucks in imports, and the surplus countries insist on exporting their unemployment by maintaining their surpluses. Of course, the answer must be international, not autarkic. And it must include the developing countries. Manley reported that 70 to 80 percent of Jamaica's foreign exchange goes to service the debts it must incur just to pay interest. The terms of world trade have turned brutally against the weakest.

As for Britain, I agree with the Cambridge economic planning group that we must be loosened from the shackles of Common Market membership and IMF policies. We must have ceilings on imports to protect our main industries—not so that we can export our unemployment (we are helping to export unemployment now with deflationary policies that contribute to the flatness of world trade). We must give priority to investment in our industry and continue to make sacrifices in consumption. These ideas are on the march and I say no, Britain is not in a crisis, but the world is, and Britain can help to show the way out.

PART II : :

The British Economy

4 | *The Heath Years: Some Further Thoughts about Union Influence*

GERALD A. DORFMAN

This essay takes another look at union-government relations during the Heath years. It examines labor's efforts to press its own economic policy views on the Heath government, using the leverage that unions won in battle with the same government during its first two years in office.

The story of the unions' successful struggle against the industrial and economic policies of the Heath government is well known. They beat back Tory efforts to impose a framework of laws in British industrial relations and otherwise alter and reduce the power of unions in national economic decision making. These battles climaxed three decades of argument about the extent of union responsibility for behaving in the "national interest." Union victories against the Heath government did not settle the argument but did reconfirm the power of the trade union movement to veto policies to which it objects but which require a high degree of union cooperation for success.

These victories also raised new questions about whether the Trades Union Congress (TUC) could convert this awesome veto power into more positive influence on the terms of alternative economic policy. The changing nature of economic problems, especially the twin problems of high unemployment and high inflation, caused the TUC to take a more active role in proposing economic policies it wished the government to adopt. It was no longer sufficient—as it had been for decades—for the TUC simply to deliver its veto against government policies it disliked and then leave the government alone to find some new policies that would fill the remaining vacuum.

A Brief Look Back at the
Pattern of Union Power

The pattern of postwar union behavior has been dominated by TUC efforts to preserve the free collective bargaining system against periodic government demands that it help in restraining wage inflation. Unions suffered few costs for their intransigence against wage restraint because they knew that the government of the day, whether Labour or Conservative, would protect their members' general economic well-being—especially ensuring a high level of employment.

Unions enjoyed two reinforcing bases for their confidence. First, the Beveridge Report of 1944 had promoted an all-party commitment that guaranteed economic security, including such contradictory policies as full employment, low inflation, a healthy balance of payments, a high and rising standard of living, and steady expansion of the economy. Second, the subsequent political bidding process in Britain had acted for more than two decades constantly to renew these 1944 promises. For example, from 1945 until the middle sixties at least, no government would dare risk allowing unemployment to rise above 2 percent of the work force.

The unions, working through the TUC, were in an even stronger position when dealing with Conservative governments throughout these years. Whereas Labour politicians and union leaders came from the same "family"—that is, the labor movement—and therefore could exert inordinate influence on each other, the Conservatives suffered from distance, hostility, and sheer ignorance of the union movement. Tory leaders didn't know union leaders very well, and the experience of the General Strike of 1926 caused them to fear that their poor relationship was a real disadvantage in the collectivist era. Winston Churchill had used this argument when he instructed his minister of labour, Walter Monckton, to settle with the unions and preserve industrial peace at all costs. Successor Tory governments through the Home period took this advice very much to heart, and the unions had the advantage of an intimidating relationship. Tory governments would hesitate to ask the unions for cooperation on such sensitive issues as income policies. When they did ask, in 1956 and 1961, for example, the TUC could say no and withdraw from future dialogue without fear that the Tories would press the issue or take reprisals.

The union-Tory relationship remained in this condition until the middle sixties. It began to change in 1965, when Edward Heath, as the new Conservative leader, responded to the growing demand, particularly among the party faithful, that something be done about the unions. Heath established a study group within the party to examine future Tory policy on industrial relations. The report of that group, *Fair Deal at Work* (1968), set the stage for the union-Heath conflict by its recommendation that British industrial relations be brought under a framework of laws as established by an industrial relations act.

The union defeat of the Labour Government's *In Place of Strife* proposal in 1969 pumped new life into the Conservatives' alternative proposals to do something about the unions. The stage was thus well set for battle when the Heath government took office in June 1970. Within weeks the government's strategy became clear. *Fair Deal at Work* would translate into an attempt to change fundamentally the pattern of industrial relations in Britain. The government would seek to reduce indiscipline on the shop floor and otherwise reduce the influence of trade unionism at the national level by defusing the intimidating instrument of the unofficial (wildcat) strike. Moreover, the government at the same time intended to end traditional bargaining with the Trades Union Congress about wage policy by using the example of its resistance in the public sector to spread progressive wage restraint through the economy.

There was little argument within the General Council about how to react to this government strategy. The trade union movement very simply could not passively accept the loss of the basis and instrumentality for the influence it had exerted over the previous two and one-half decades. The first approach to the government would be made with gentleness and good manners; in private and public the government would be advised to readopt the traditional wisdom about keeping peace with the trade union movement. But if that tactic did not work, the members of the General Council unanimously agreed, the general secretary would lead an all-out struggle to *force* the government to readopt Churchill's prescriptive warning.

Gentleness and good humor quickly failed. Beginning in late 1971, the TUC waged a massive and eventually disruptive campaign against the industrial relations bill. Later there were serious arguments and confrontations in the public sector over the government's de facto wage restraint. By early 1972 the Prime Minister recognized the sorry consequences of his confrontation. As he said at the end of the miners' strike of that winter, which produced a very inflationary settlement, some other way needed to be found to settle the country's problems. Within a few weeks he proceeded to scrap confrontation and instead sought union participation in a new round of bargaining about solutions to Britain's mounting economic problems.

The union victories not only saved the TUC's place at the center of national economic decision making, they added strength to the force of TUC influence. For the second time in four years the unions had defeated a government challenge to its powerful role in public policy making. The Prime Minister had acknowledged his defeat, and during the late summer and early fall of 1972 he openly courted the union movement with promises of full and permanent influence on the decision-making process.

Opportunity and Failure

The Trades Union Congress thus stood at the zenith of its power and influence during the summer of 1972. Its victories, moreover, had come at an opportune moment because the General Council recognized that Britain's economic problems posed a serious threat to union interests. High inflation together with high unemployment was a dangerous combination, made more frightening by the government's waverings on its commitment to the terms of the 1944 all-party agreement on economic security. The Prime Minister's pleadings for collectivist negotiations thus offered a golden opportunity for the TUC to use its strength to press for remedial policies that would place special emphasis on restoring full employment and freezing price levels.

But this opportunity for influence and, as Heath offered, for having a share in the management of the economy injected a new element of tension into the General Council. It quickly became apparent that the possibility of cooperating with a Tory government, however potentially rewarding in policy terms, would produce conflict and fissures between factions of union leaders. This effect was almost precisely the reverse of the effect that conflicts with the Tories had produced during the first two years of the Heath government. The struggle against the Industrial Relations Act and the de facto wage policy in the public sector had created new unity while ending the long struggle between national union leaders and their shop stewards' movements. Now cooperation with the Tories threatened to destroy that unity.

The media largely failed to consider this intraunion political argument in their speculations about the possible success of the tripartite talks during the summer and fall of 1972. Instead, journalists reported on the jousts between the TUC, the Confederation of British Industries (CBI), and the government over the question of whether there would be talks. and once talks began, on the details of the counterproposals. They mistakenly took heart at the fact that negotiations continued, assuming that the chances for some sort of agreement rested primarily on compromising the differences over the terms of wage and price controls.

The General Council entered the negotiations from quite a different perspective. Militant and moderate leaders finally agreed to join the talks only after serious argument. The mediating efforts of the general secretary, Victor Feather, prevailed. Feather convinced the council that the TUC had everything to gain and nothing to lose by talking with the government. The TUC certainly had no need to reach agreement at the end unless the Prime Minister was prepared to accept TUC terms, which would give the union movement substantial policy gains. Feather argued persuasively that the TUC had won its chance to put those terms to the government and therefore had no need to continue to shout its views from a distance. While he recognized that the Tory Government had shown itself to be a dangerous adversary, the General Council should, as a matter of self-interest, test Heath's offer of influence on policy making, which the unions had so powerfully earned by their struggles.

The more militant members of the General Council reluctantly agreed to go along with the talks on this basis. But they made it clear that they were opposed to reaching agreement with Heath on any terms short of the government's unqualified acceptance of TUC proposals. Moreover, they wanted no part of the Prime Minister's offer to include the TUC in a permanent triumverate that would manage the economy. They were determined to protect the free bargaining process. They were also determined to protect the voluntary system of industrial relations which they believed they had earned by their struggles first against *In Place of Strife* and then against the Industrial Relations Act. They were completely unwilling, therefore, to submit to what they believed was a Tory strategy to win by stealth what could not be forced by confrontation.

From the beginning of the tripartite talks, therefore, TUC negotiators could do no more than play out their role with mock seriousness. Without near unanimity in the General Council there was virtually no chance that they could conclude any sort of agreement with this government. Once it became apparent that the government was totally unwilling to cave in in the way that the more militant union leaders had demanded, the talks bogged down in stalemate. The TUC negotiators in late October 1972 moved to force the bargaining to its climax by demanding that the government agree to every point in their package of proposals. These proposals included demands that Heath had already refused, including comprehensive statutory price controls and assurances about the nonoperation of the Industrial Relations Act.

The talks finally broke down in complete disagreement in early November, and the government moved to legislate a freeze on both prices and wages. In the end Heath rejected what he characterized as union "double standards." Heath objected especially to the union proposals that he operate a voluntary wage-restraint policy while enjoying the benefits of statutory price controls. Also, he vehemently refused to negotiate about changes in the Industrial Relations Act, the Housing Finance Act, or British policy in the EEC. These policies, he said, were the business of government and not subject to negotiations.

Quite relieved, the TUC negotiators withdrew, charging that the Prime Minister had insincerely invited the TUC to join in the management of the economy. But in withdrawing the TUC also harbored considerable frustration because it had chosen to sabotage the talks, in part in order to preserve its own unity at the expense of genuine policy goals that it believed would have been helpful for the interests of its member unions.

A second opportunity for TUC cooperation on much the same basis developed during the following year but produced similar results. Rapid inflation in food and housing costs during the winter and spring of 1973 undermined living standards as the wage freeze held earnings inflation down. The TUC continued to shout its objections and policy prescriptions from a distance. Yet when the Prime Minister renewed negotiations with the TUC and employers' representatives during the summer of 1973, the TUC General Council again decided to avoid any sort of cooperation that might prove internally disruptive.

It was during the late fall of 1973 that TUC leaders finally learned the cost of their intransigence. The Arab-Israeli war in October produced a sudden fuel shortage, greatly worsening the economic situation. Then the coal miners made matters much worse by refusing to work overtime as a response to their dispute with the Coal Board over a new contract. Prime Minister Heath's announcement that Britain would go on a three-day workweek from December 30 finally jolted the TUC to intervene in the crisis with its full energies.

The scenario of that TUC intervention over the following two months demonstrates the price that the union movement paid in suffering poor access and influence with the Heath government because of its earlier vetoes of a cooperative relationship. The TUC viewed the three-day week with considerable alarm. It lived with the frightening memories of the last fuel shortage in 1947, when unemployment soared to more than three million within just a few days. The General Council believed that the government's plan for a three-day week would produce a similar disaster. Moreover, the TUC criticized the government for overreacting and for being too inflexible in negotiations with the miners. The TUC therefore wanted very much to persuade the government to postpone the three-day week while it helped to resolve the impasse.

The problem for the TUC in dealing with the crisis, however, was that it had failed to develop relationships with the government that it might have used at this moment of crisis. This was especially true of the TUC relationship with Prime Minister Heath. After making his sharp U-turn in mid-1972 toward collectivist politics, the Prime Minister had become embittered at continued union intransigence. Now he was deeply embroiled in the miners' dispute, but distrustful of both the miners' union and the TUC, with which any eventual settlement would have to be worked out. Matters were further exacerbated by the retirement of the one figure whom Heath really trusted in the union leadership, Victor Feather, from the TUC general secretaryship. Heath viewed his successor, Len Murray, as a partisan up to no good.

It was in this poisonous atmosphere that the TUC set out to solve the miners' dispute and end the national emergency, especially including the three-day week. The Prime Minister must take a healthy share of the blame for misperceiving the TUC's peace efforts; he certainly should have shown more flexibility in dealing with the miners' claim and shown more trust in the TUC offers, which would have provided the basis for settlement. But the TUC contributed to its own impotence in dealing with Heath by its earlier rebuff of the Prime Minister's offers of cooperation, which it carried out primarily in order to resolve internal union tensions.

The most telling example in this scenario of TUC impotence and Heath miscalculation occurred at the height of the crisis, between January 9 and 14, 1974. The TUC had reached a point of enormous frustration in the series of discussions with the Prime Minister about ways to solve the dilemma. TUC representatives had simply been unable to persuade Heath either to end the three-day-week order or to provide the additional compensation necessary to buy peace with the miners, who were clearly in no mood to compromise. In response, Heath had argued that he would destroy his entire pay policy, which millions of workers had already accepted, if he settled with the miners as a "special case."

Faced with Heath's stubbornness and obvious distrust, senior leaders of the TUC decided on the morning of January 9 to take a dramatic initiative. Jack Jones, Len Murray, Hugh Scanlon, Alfred Allen, and Sidney Greene, who together comprised the TUC negotiating team, expressed the full range of union attitudes. They decided to offer that "if the government was prepared to give an assurance that it would make possible a settlement between the miners and the National Coal Board, other unions would not use this as an argument in negotiations for their own settlements." It was a bold promise that would give substance to the TUC insistence that the miners were a special case. And these leaders were willing to back up their offer by the promise that they would win the support of all union executives at a special meeting to be called on January 16.

The next day the TUC team met with the Prime Minister to press their offer. It was made in good faith. But the Prime Minister turned it down. He remained skeptical that the TUC would be as good as its word. How could they promise that other unions would not take advantage of the situation once the miners were safely back at work and the three-day week ended? No amount of conversation budged him, and we know now that he angrily viewed the TUC initiative as a cheap trick—part of a collusive strategy with the Labour Party to embarrass his government.

From that point onward, the chance for any sort of negotiated settlement of the miners' dispute slipped away very quickly. The talks did drag on until early February, but ended as the miners voted to call a full national strike, and the Prime Minister on February 7 set the stage for a general election on the last day of that month. The dispute was finally settled, but by the new Labour Government and on miners' terms, during the week after it took office in early March.

Concluding Remarks

This story of missed opportunities and policy frustrations is interesting in itself. Yet its importance lies in the legacies that the experience has left for union–Conservative Government relations in the future. The prospect is that the union movement will suffer from this relationship, and probably suffer more than will future Conservative governments.

The Conservatives and their leader took considerable punishment from their union adversaries between 1970 and 1974. The miners' strike was a real tragedy for Edward Heath. He missed the crucial opportunities for settling the dispute. He could have come to terms with the TUC and saved his painfully constructed income policy. But he completely misunderstood the sincerity of the TUC's offer. He failed to appreciate the TUC's overriding interest in ending the three-day week rather than in putting him out of office.

At the same time, the course of the miners' dispute and, in fact, the whole period from Heath's conversion to collectivist politics in mid-1972 were also a bitter experience for the union movement. The General Council could not agree to accept the role its senior leaders wanted in jointly managing the economy. Though the members of the General Council could well envision the value of protecting their members' economic interests, the prospect of cooperating with the Tory "enemies" proved too divisive. Sabotaging the tripartite talks, whatever their merits, became the only alternative course of action. Later the General Council would regret its lack of access and influence with the Prime Minister and his cabinet. Faced with the miners' dispute, the TUC could not overcome the Prime Minister's mistrust and suspicion. The General Council tried frantically but vainly that winter of 1974 to get its members back to full-time work. But the Prime Minister could not accept the credibility of the TUC's offer to make the miners' case special.

Defeat was traumatic for the Conservative Party, but it was just as traumatic for the TUC. Though the union wounds were salved by the return of Labour to office, the spectacle of the TUC's impotence during the miners' dispute was not lost at Congress House. For the first time, the traditionally hostile and ugly relationship between the Conservative Party and the union movement had worked against the unions as well as the party. Before, the TUC had enjoyed its vetoes of Conservative economic policy and retired from interaction secure in the knowledge that the Tories would still defend the basic economic security provided by the 1944 new economic and social contract. But all that had changed as the TUC learned that the deterioration in the appeal of Keynesian wisdom compelled them to defend their interests by winning influence and access to government policy making. Internal union politics still dictated conflict or at least noncooperation with the Tories, however, even at the price of diminished influence. In 1973 and 1974 the TUC General Council thus learned that Churchill's warning about the dangers of union-Conservative relations now also applied to them.

The problem that the TUC faces for the future is that it will likely suffer from the same dilemma—or worse—during the life of the next Tory government. The General Council will certainly continue to have a vital stake in exercising influence on economic policy in an aggressive manner, but internal union pressure will make such a move difficult. At the same time, if one may judge by current statements, the next Tory government will probably go out of its way to avoid entangling relations with the union movement. James Prior, the shadow employment minister, has said repeatedly that the next Conservative government will not seek conflict with the union movement by legislating a new industrial relations act. Mrs. Thatcher has added that her government also looks forward to administering a monetarist economic policy free of income policies and other sorts of entrapping relationships with the union movement. She promises to consult with the unions but to deprive them of the instruments, such as income policies, which she believes they have used so skillfully to frustrate and paralyze the policies of earlier Tory governments.

Congress House thus faces an unhappy dilemma. It must overcome the force of traditional relations with the Conservatives as they affect internal union politics and overcome somehow the avowed Tory policy to avoid union influence altogether. No wonder, then, that the members of the General Council scurry to support the present Labour government while reflecting on the good old days.

5 | *Britain's Economic Problems: Lies and Damn Lies*

STEPHEN BLANK

I

The notion of long-term economic decline provides a standard explanation for Britain's current economic plight. Such scholars as E. J. Hobsbawm have described Britain's "climacteric" during the last decades of the nineteenth century. In Hobsbawm's view, "this sudden transformation of the leading and most dynamic industrial economy into the most sluggish and conservative, in the short space of thirty or forty years (1860–90/1900), is the crucial question of British economic history."[1] For many observers of the British scene, any number or combination of sociological, economic, industrial, technological, and developmental factors serve to connect this conception of loss of industrial preeminence with the "British sickness" since World War II. Since 1945 Britain has simply been playing out the last act of this sad drama of decline and fall.

What is ironic, as Sir Henry Phelps Brown has recently observed, is that this view "should have gained currency at the end of the quarter century of most rapid and sustained economic advance in our recorded history."[2] Many indicators suggest that Britain's economy has not been in a state of continuous decline since the end of the nineteenth century. Indeed, they suggest instead that beginning in the late 1930s the British economy

An earlier draft of this paper was prepared for a seminar at the Washington Center of Foreign Policy Research, Johns Hopkins School of International Studies. My thanks to Simon Serfaty, director of the Center.

entered a period of revitalization that lasted well into the 1960s. Britain's economic performance, particularly in the first decade after the end of the Second World War, was remarkable by any standards, and might, with only a modicum of exaggeration, be termed Europe's first economic miracle.

Between 1945 and 1950, industrial production increased by 30 to 40 percent, and between 1948 and 1960 the annual rate of real growth in total industrial output was 3.7 percent. The annual rate of growth between 1920 and 1937 was 3.1 percent and between 1877 and 1913 only 1.6 percent. The rise in the rate of productivity was equally impressive. The annual rate of increase of industrial productivity was almost twice as great between 1949 and 1960 as it had been between 1907 and 1924: 3 percent compared to 1.6 percent.[3] Indeed, Phelps Brown observes that "the rise of productivity in British manufacturing on average of 1950–74 was greater than we know ever to have been sustained over any such period before." By his calculations, output per worker-hour during this period increased by nearly two and a quarter times.[4]

Investment, too, Phelps Brown observes, has been high in this period, at least by Britain's historical standards. He writes: "Whereas in 1870–1913 gross fixed investment, other than in dwellings, averaged little more than 6 percent of the gross national product, and in the inter-war years the average was still less than 7 percent, through 1952–75 the average was over 15, and in the last ten years of that span over 17 percent."[5] And the rise in the standard of living has been remarkable as well. For manual workers, real weekly earnings doubled in the years since the war.[6]

Britain's international trade performance also improved dramatically. Briefly, British visible exports increased sharply after World War II, far more rapidly than imports. The net gap (visible imports minus exports) since the war has been much smaller than at any other time in the twentieth century, and the remaining deficit has been more than made up by a surplus on the invisible account. As a result, Britain consistently ran a surplus balance on its private account after the war (at least through the late 1960s) as favorable as that of France or Germany. (Britain's overall balance of payments, including government spending and lending abroad, was normally in deficit, of course.)[7]

In addition, all of this was accomplished against a background of economic stability, the consolidation of the welfare state, a fairly large redistribution of personal income in favor of wage earners, and the maintenance of full employment. It is not at all surprising that Richard Caves, summing up the Brookings team's assessment of Britain's economic prospects in 1968, wrote:

> In many ways, Britain's economic performance since World War II outstrips any earlier period in the past half century. Her rate of growth, her attainment of full employment are, in the perspective of history, fit objects of pride, the more impressive because they were achieved despite the immense problems of postwar reconstruction, dwindling overseas earnings, and increased competition in export markets.[8]

What is surprising, in Sidney Pollard's words, is "that the period appears in much contemporary literature as a period of chaos and failure."[9]

Comparing Britain's postwar economic achievements with its own historical record may disprove the long-term-economic-decline thesis, but in doing so it establishes a much more interesting and puzzling research question. A comparison with other advanced industrial nations reveals Britain in a much less favorable light, with lower rates of growth of output and productivity.[10] Despite impressive gains over its earlier record, Britain remains at the bottom of the Western European league tables for most indicators of economic success. The annual rate of growth of per real output in Britain between 1950 and 1970 was only slightly more than half of the Western Europe average, and by 1976 per capita GNP in Britain was only about three-quarters of the average of the nine members of the EEC. Once the richest nation in Europe, Britain is presently in danger of becoming one of the poorer.

The more interesting question, therefore, is, given this pattern of economic resurgence in the early postwar years, why Britain's economic performance has been so mediocre compared to that of other nations and to its own growth potential. If the "British disease" isn't the result of long-term economic decline, what is its cause?

One can fairly easily dismiss another explanation—that Britain's economy is overburdened by a massive social welfare system, far more extensive than that of any other country. Even the most insular Little Englander can no longer claim that this is true. As one student of Britain's welfare system has recently observed, "Among comparable nations, Britain's welfare provisions are apt to seem relatively stingy."[11] Data compiled by *The Economist* show that public expenditure in Britain on social security and health is not only considerably below that of Sweden and Holland but also less than that of France and Italy.[12] Except for the National Health Service, which still is more comprehensive than similar programs elsewhere, "in social programs as well as in economic growth, Britain now finds its European compeers in the two least industrialized nations, Italy and Ireland."[13]

In terms of the proportion of total personal income taken by taxes on income and social security contributions, Britain ranks sixth of nine countries analyzed by *The Economist*: a greater percentage of total personal income is taken by tax in Britain than in France but less than in Germany. To be sure, income tax in Britain is heavy. The maximum tax rate on earned income is high and it comes into effect at a low level of income; the maximum rate on "unearned" income is very high and it, too, begins at a very low level. Still, the national profile of taxation and public expenditure on social security and health in Britain is not all that different from that of the other Western European nations, certainly not different enough to explain the much greater variance in economic performance.

II

There is no dearth of other concepts or theories about Britain's recent hard times. Several have achieved fairly wide currency. "Overload" is one such concept. In Richard Rose's terms, overload occurs when expectations are greater than resources plus institution plus outputs plus impact. Overloading arises from one or many sources: "a shortage of national resources, an excess of expectations, deficiencies in governmental institutions, inadequacies in the outputs of government, or government outputs having less impact upon society than either governors or governed would wish."[14] This is obviously a handy framework and

Rose provides us with a neat term, but, at this stage at least, it doesn't tell us much about Britain.

Tony King has gone somewhat further along these lines. British government is overloaded, he says, for two reasons: "the range of problems that government is expected to deal with has vastly increased, and its capacity to deal with problems, even many of the ones it had before, has decreased."[15] Certainly the world is more complex today and made more so not only by the double advance of technology and government responsibilities but by the increasingly dense web of interdependence, internally and externally, which all nations face. But has the capacity of British government to exercise its responsibilities *declined*? This may be a definition of "overload," but it is scarcely an explanation of it—even if it were possible to measure relative capacity in such a dynamic environment as King describes.

Rose and, to a rather greater extent, King seem to focus on suboptimal or even actually declining performance by governments as the key element in overload. But if this is the case, we still want to know why—in this world of heightened complexity and interdependence—British government seems to work even less adequately than other governments. In a world in which no one is doing all that well, the Germans, the Japanese, and the Swiss, for example, seem to be doing better than most, and most seem to be doing better than the British. I am not sure that British government has undertaken (or has had thrust upon it) more responsibilities than governments elsewhere, or that the British environment is necessarily more complex.

Others emphasize a factor that Rose and King note: rising expectations. In this formulation (most often advanced by economists) governments and parties seek to maximize public support by escalating public expectations. For some people (for example, Samuel Brittan) excessive expectations are generated by the very nature of the democratic system, which rests upon a competitive struggle for the people's vote. This is one of "the economic contradictions of democracy."[16]

This argument, which is representative of efforts to apply economic analysis to political phenomena, deserves more attention than can be given it here, and a brief response will have to suffice. In the first place, although "bidding up" is one element in the democratic political process, it is really quite untenable to suggest that arousing expectations—especially economic expectations—is the critical element in that process, let alone that it dominates. An examination of neither government policy, party manifestos, nor, more important, voting behavior lends credence to the idea that party appeal or voter choice rests primarily on perceptions of economic self-interest.

We have lived since the end of World War II in a world of increasing expectations. Having witnessed dramatic leaps in our standard of living and, for the most part, in the quality of our lives, we have become accustomed to this pattern of upward change. And we have tended to react poorly when that change cannot be sustained. Political parties and governments in the advanced world have been a part of this environment and it has been both a blessing and a curse for them: a blessing when things are going well and a curse when they are not. Affluence has tempted governments to accept responsibilities that they may regret deeply in periods when growth rates level out. But "economic man" does not inhabit the polity, and voters' expectations are by no means limited to material well-being. Besides, there is some doubt as to whether expectations are in fact continuously escalating. Peter Jenkins recently suggested that Britain may be experiencing a "counter-revolution of diminishing expectations" and that this "mounting disbelief in steady and continuous material improvement" might be a factor in "undermining the patience and restraint necessary in a mixed-economy democracy."[17] Indeed, a sense of diminishing expectations—a zero-sum game in which the stakes get smaller and smaller—may be far more corrosive of democracy than escalating expectations.

Brittan suggests that the generation of excessive expectations among voters by the process of political competition is a less serious "contradiction" of democracy than the "disruptive effects arising from the pursuit of self-interest by rival coercive groups," in particular the trade unions. The basic difficulty, Brittan says, is that "the benefits from restraint in the use of group market power are 'public goods' . . . while the costs are incurred by the group which exercises restraint. It is therefore in the interest of each union group that other unions should show restraint while it exploits its own monopoly power to the full."[18]

The unions have played the heavy role in British politics for more than a decade; the climax, of course, occurred early in 1974, when Heath asked the electorate to decide "who governs Britain." But the union argument has to be made with care, with far more care than it is usually accorded by conservative journalists and politicians or by foreign observers. In the first place, although there was an explosion of strikes in the early 1970s, Britain is—and remains—a low-strike nation. The image of strike-prone Britain is simply inaccurate. Second, it is not at all easy to calculate the economic impact of trade union activity. As a recent study on British inflation concludes, "Investigations into the extent to which the trade unions have played an independent role in the acceleration of inflation during the 1970s have been dogged by continued controversy."[19]

What about the unions' political power? *The Economist* not long ago observed: "The most dramatic change in Britain's decision-making process in the past 10 years has been the astonishing growth in the political power of the trade unions."[20] The unions have been more involved in politics since the late 1960s than they were at any other time since the years immediately after the war, and their visibility has been heightened because they now oppose government policies more frequently than they have done at any other time since the 1930s. But it would be difficult to support the contention that the net effect of their activities has been politically destabilizing. I have described elsewhere the defensive and conservative goals of trade union activity in the late 1960s and early 1970s. Another student of British politics writes:

> Despite their influence, the unions have, since 1974, consented to an effective reduction in the real wages of their members, levels of unemployment which are extraordinary for the post-1945 period, a decline in social and public services and an increase in user fees, and have not sought to pressure the Labour government toward implementation of the Party's 1974 election manifesto commitment for "a fundamental and irreversible shift in the balance of power and wealth." To the contrary, the unions have acquiesced in repeated assertions by the Prime Minister and the Chancellor of the Exechequer that corporate profit margins must be allowed to increase in order to provide further funds for investment even while real wages decline.[21]

A close examination of the relationship between the trade unions and the Labour Party and Labour governments between 1964 and 1977 strongly suggests that the overall role of even the militant union leadership has been to maintain continuity and cooperation with the government.

III

What, then, are the causes of Britain's current economic problems? In my view they are primarily political rather than economic, and for the most part they represent the failure of successive British governments to formulate policies and create institutions appropriate to Britain's needs and resources in the postwar world.[22]

The single most important factor in Britain's economic difficulties lies in the decisions taken by post-1945 governments about the nation's role in the world and in the domestic and international policies that resulted from these decisions. Commitments made in the 1940s and '50s to restore and protect Britain's role as an international power dominated domestic economic policies and objectives. Domestic policies served primarily to support international aspirations and responsibilities, and the result was to lock Britain into a low-growth situation.

Briefly, British efforts after 1945 to play the role of a global power—in the financial and economic spheres if not in political and military terms (although here, too, British commitments were enormous)—were excessively expensive and well beyond the nation's resources and capacities. Britain often acted with great responsibility to support the postwar international political and economic systems. The rearmament program in 1950, the decision to maintain a British army in Europe in 1954, and the rush to restore full convertibility of the pound in 1957 were highly responsible actions, at least from the perspective of the postwar international order. Yet the reference point for each of these decisions was Britain's role as a world power, not the costs that would be borne by the domestic economy. No calculation of Britain's actual ability to bear these costs ever seems to have been carried out. At times, it appears, Britain was lured or pressured into taking similar steps (to support the U.S. dollar in the Johnson era, for example) by the manipulation of the "special relationship" with the United States, but this behavior too reflected the overwhelming desire of British leaders to walk in the corridors of global power and to play Greece to the American Rome.

The result, especially after 1955, was that British citizens were told again and again that they were living beyond their means and that they would have to accept higher taxes, cutbacks in public services, and slower economic growth if the nation was to remain solvent and to maintain its international competitiveness. The government resorted to more violent attacks on the domestic economy, raising interest rates and restraining investment, in order to support Britain's international position. To an ever increasing extent, domestic economic policy was determined not by the needs of the local economy but by the movement of international confidence in the pound, a situation that one of the most acute observers of Britain at the time found "both tragic and absurd."[23]

Severe deflationary packages were imposed on the domestic economy in 1957, 1961, and 1966—although from 1965 until 1970 the economy was in a state of almost continuous retrenchment. Domestic investment was cut or held back by direct government action and indirectly influenced by high interest rates, credit restrictions, and cuts in investment allowances. Business expectations were depressed by the continuing stop-go cycles, efforts to expand output were limited, and investment was less productive than it should have been. Frequent deflation (whether or not the economy was actually overheated) and continuous uncertainty reinforced traditional tendencies toward restrictive practices and inhibited more aggressive management practices.

The indirect effects on the economy were equally serious, and perhaps more dangerous in the long term. There had been little disagreement among Britain's leaders after the war about the need to maintain the country's international role. By the early 1960s, however, the policies of the past decade were viewed as increasingly anachronistic by substantial segments of Britain's leadership, and some began to urge a reevaluation of national goals and policies, especially as they affected economic growth and performance.

The result was the attempt in 1961 to create a new approach to economic policy making involving a tripartite commitment to greater coordination in the economy (although the word "planning" was much used, what was devised could scarcely be called a planning system) in order to enhance domestic economic performance and create the conditions for more rapid economic growth.[24] The collapse of this effort in 1964 had very serious implications. In the first place, it showed that the priorities of the leaders of the government had not changed and that the preservation of the existing rate of exchange would take precedence over the domestic economy. Moreover, the government was forced to assert even more strongly that the pound would never be devalued. Second, the opportunity to gain the support of a substantial segment of British industry (and, more important, to mobilize a cadre of Britain's brightest younger businessmen) for the planning experiment was lost. No Monnet, Wilson might still have played the role Cripps had played in the early postwar years and established a more effective and productive working relationship with leaders of British industry. Third, when devaluation did take place, it was too late to achieve many benefits. Instead of freeing the economy from external constraints, the 1967 devaluation forced economic policy makers to squeeze the economy still more vigorously and to keep their attention focused even more rigidly on external confidence in the pound.

The failure to increase economic growth rates and, even more, the need after 1967 for still more deflationary policies significantly exacerbated relations with the trade unions. In Britain, as elsewhere in Western Europe, generational changes in the composition of the work force and changes in workers' attitudes were bound to heighten tensions over the allocation of the national income, the organization of labor, and the operation of the social welfare system. The rising material expectations of a new generation of workers who had not passed through the stern experience of the depression and war came into violent conflict in the late 1960s with economic policies that resulted in higher unemployment, a decline in the growth of real income, and, for many, an actual fall in real net income. Confrontation with the unions strengthened the hands of radical leaders, politicized union demands, and undercut the fragile foundations of an effective policy on prices and incomes. It helped weaken the authority of the

Trades Union Congress and heightened the level of social conflict in British society.

The failure of the National Economic Development Council (Neddy) experiment aggravated a second major political dimension of Britain's postwar economic difficulties, the weakness of institutional development. Britain has suffered severely from an inability to evolve institutions appropriate to the advanced industrial-social welfare mixed economy of the second half of the twentieth century. In particular, British institutions in both the private and the public sectors have been poorly developed in those areas where the borderline between the private and public sectors has become blurred and in which there has been an extensive interpenetration of public and private power. To maintain full employment, rising growth rates, and stable prices—if it is possible at all—requires a fundamentally different relationship, both institutional and informal, between the public and private sectors than has existed in Britain. Moreover, not only have successive British governments failed to support and facilitate institutional development to meet these new needs, they have worsened the problem through their lack of sensitivity to the requirements of institutional change.

As others have observed, the British government, and its administration in particular, is highly effective as a crisis manager. Certainly this was one heritage of the war. The plucky make-do-and-mend attitude, the commitment to muddling through, and the belief that courage is an adequate substitute for planning were reinforced by the war experience. To be sure, wartime methods were impressively successful in the early postwar years. Britain experienced none of the institutional shock that engulfed France, for example. The same individuals who had led during the war led during recovery. They relied on the same network of personal contacts, and the wartime experience stood them in good stead.

But attitudes remained invariably short-term and efforts in institutional innovation, even in this period, were barren. The Treasury regained responsibility for economic management and bitterly resisted any attempt to share that responsibility more widely within the government. Yet the Treasury seems to have given little thought itself to the long-term economic problems Britain would face. In retrospect, it seems that the Treasury never wished to take the helm. On one hand it sought some fixed point, such as the state of sterling in the world economy, against which direction could be determined automatically.[25] On the other hand, its officials worked dutifully, even heroically, in the bilges, manning the pumps to ensure that the ship stayed on an even keel, no matter where it was sailing. But no one steered.

The British have been terribly willing to jeetison programs, plans, and institutions long before there has been an opportunity to see what will work and what will not. Both parties seem impressively ignorant of the conditions and requirements of institutional development. Achievements in institution building were in fact not negligible. The development of Neddy from 1961 to 1965 and the experiments with the Prices and Incomes Board remain impressive. But their long-term impact was limited. Successive governments, dominated by a short-term mentality, persisted in seeing each new initiative or institution as the immediate remedy for Britain's continuing economic crisis. Each new agency was created in the flare of battle, rushed to the front, and thrust into the thick of the struggle. As each was bloodied in turn, enthusiasm and political support evaporated. Little thought was given to the needs of long-term institution building or to the coordination of economic policy. Instead of a process of gradual institutional development, there was a parade of tentative and partially organized vehicles. The result was to degrade the policies, demoralize the participants, and in the end strengthen the position of those institutions, especially the Treasury, traditionally responsible for the conduct of economic affairs and the policies with which they were identified.

The most worrisome development, however, has been the politicization of the entire process of institution building. Lacking an adequate sense of long-term policy and its requirements and faced with declining popular support, the major parties have responded by promising merely to undo what the other has done. Government policy with regard to incomes, investment incentives, and industrial coordination has had more stops and goes than the economy.

Earlier in this essay I wrote that the charge that the parties generated excessive expectations among the voters did not seem borne out by the facts. But the parties have, I think, been guilty of irresponsible opposition, an unthinking and mindless sort of opposition that attacks government actions or policies to make momentary political hay, without realizing that it will one day depend on the very same policies or institutions. This is what Michael Stewart has called the increasingly Jekyll-and-Hyde side of British politics:

> In a world of limited resources and virtually unlimited wants, any government must make many hard and unpopular decisions. If the opposition regularly tries to cash in on this unpopularity for electoral reasons, by condemning such decisions, however justified and necessary, and promising to reverse them, a different kind of threat is posed to the democratic system. The electorate will be encouraged to believe that there is an easy way out, that hard choices can be avoided, and that all their problems stem from the mistakes of a confused and incompetent government.[26]

Heath's government was determined to wipe the slate clean of institutions created during the previous Labour government. Within a year and a half, however, almost every one had re-emerged, although with a new name. They were again largely demolished by the Labour Government early in 1974, but most again have reappeared in a new form. Mrs. Thatcher seems likely to attempt once again to undo what has been done before. Thus the credibility of policies has declined, although in fact the same policies are maintained, and any sense of overall economic strategy is lost. The result here, too, has been to heighten the sense of fragmentation, conflict, and frustration that is one of the foundations of the present economic crisis.

IV

What all of this suggests is that we may be observing in Britain a wider process of institutional disintegration. If, following Boulding, we define modern industrial society by the "organizational revolution," then what we may be witnessing in Britain is the decline of several critical organizations in modern British society: the political party system, the civil service, and the trade union movement. The complex web of relationships among these great organizations has provided both the structure and the sub-

stance of British politics since the end of the nineteenth century.
The rise of these bodies at the end of the nineteenth century
disturbed, angered, and frightened liberal England, and the remarkable facility with which they have interacted—their coherence—made the British political system so uniquely effective in
the twentieth century.

Perhaps the most fundamental and portentious changes are
taking place in the image and functions of the parties and party
system. In the British system of politics in the twentieth century,
the function of representing the national interest, which was once
attributed to the sovereign and later to Parliament, was performed in large measure by the political party. Party, Samuel
Beer has written, echoing Herman Finer, "is indeed 'king.' "[27]
Although the efficient operation of the political system was frequently, and erroneously, attributed to the two-party system
(which never really existed), the critical issue was the capacity of
the party system to (in functional terms) aggregate the interests of
the political system into two relatively coherent frameworks or
points of view. Because of their capacity to do this, the pattern of
representation changed in British politics with the rise of the mass
parties, but the pattern of government did not. Government was
still carried on essentially by the cabinet (and increasingly by the
prime minister), with the support (at least tacit) of a majority of
the members of the House of Commons, in the form of a continuing dialogue between government and Parliament. Thus, because
of the capacity of the party system to aggregate interests into two
fairly coherent groupings, the essential quality of government-by-
dialogue was maintained in the new era of "party government."

The alignment of issues and organizations was a vital dimension
of this capacity. From the 1880s onward, and particularly from
the First World War, a new set of issues, associated with industrialization and expressed in terms of the ownership of the means of
production, dominated British politics. With the rise of the
Labour Party and the emergence of a new Conservativism, there
was a clear coherence among the organizations and issues that
increasingly dominated the political system.

Thus in Britain the rise of the new political organizations—the
mass parties—facilitated and channeled the expression of the
major political issues of the day. This situation was quite unlike

that in France, for example, where major political parties of the Third Republic continued to be dominated by issues (such as clericalism) less and less relevant to the interests of French society, and thus acted as barriers rather than bridges to political involvement and expression.

Today, however, the British parties and the party system are in a state of advanced crisis. The evidence is compelling. There has been a gradual "partisan dealignment" since 1950, but these tendencies were dramatically advanced in the February 1974 election. Both parties did exceptionally badly: the two-party share of the vote fell to 77 percent, lowest since the war, and to barely 61 percent of the electorate. The Conservative share of the vote was the lowest it had received since 1906, Labour's its lowest since 1931. The pendulum in British politics simply stopped swinging.

This is not only an electoral phenomenon. Again and again it was noted during Heath's and Wilson's governments that as public confidence in the government fell, there was no corresponding rise on the side of the opposition. Indeed, public confidence in both dropped at times simultaneously. What is perhaps most interesting—and most ominous for the future of the major parties—is that despite the apparent resurgence of ideological and class conflict in the 1970s, the dealignment of major-party support intensified.

Whether the elections of 1974 mark a crucial turning point in British party politics or whether the elections will be seen instead to represent a continuing gradual decline in major-party support, the alignment of party and issue that characterized British politics throughout most of the first half of this century seems no longer to exist. On the one hand, neither party seems capable of presenting clear and acceptable positions on the major economic and industrial issues of the day. Rather, the major parties constantly seem to reverse themselves so that policy development has taken on a characteristic U-shaped configuration. Despite an increasingly ideological rhetoric, the public has little confidence that either party offers a distinctive (and potentially successful) set of policies to deal with Britain's economic difficulties.

On the other hand, many issues that have aroused intense interest and concern—economic policy, race and immigration, devolution, Europe, civil rights, and capital punishment are examples—have cut across and divided both major parties. Thus we see a further dealignment: a dealignment of party and issue and a consequent inability of the major parties to speak coherently and convincingly on many of the most important issues of the day. This inability to aggregate interests effectively and to state issues clearly on these matters is, of course, especially serious in Britain, where the major parties have performed these functions so successfully in the past.

The great organization of government, the administration, is also in a state of crisis today. The achievements of the British civil service—the Rolls-Royce of civil services—have, of course, been numerous. It has been the governmental institution with the key responsibility in the era of party government for maintaining a continuity of policy. It has been and for the most part has been perceived to be politically neutral and thus has served extraordinarily well to resolve conflicts among interests in British society. These factors and others have made it one of the primary symbols of the legitimacy of British government. The British civil service has responded well to crises, such as the two world wars, and has a deserved reputation for a capacity for ad hoc measures. In all, the administration has been a highly effective stabilizing force in the British political system.

We are familiar with the many criticisms of the civil service that have been made for more than a decade. I do want to suggest that there is no obvious correlation between the scale and complexity of the tasks facing the civil service and its ability to perform successfully. The sheer magnitude and complexity of its responsibilities was never greater than during the world wars, particularly World War II, and yet the administration is universally given extraordinarily high marks for its efficiency and effectiveness in those difficult days. Thus the problems are far more qualitative than quantitative.

The problem lies in the inability of the administration to meet certain key demands posed in contemporary society. In many cases, the excess of its virtues is the source of its vices. For example, the members of the British civil service have never constituted the same sort of government-within-a-government as the members of the *grandes corps* in France. The British administration, even at its highest levels, has been organized almost entirely by departments with a strong "departmental view"; their perceptions of their own roles have emphasized maintaining continuity, resolving conflicts, and preserving departmental interests. The political value of these attitudes is clear. But, in the world as it now exists, these attitudes are also the source of difficulties.

The British administration seems to have particular difficulty dealing with issues that demand long-term planning and the coordination of the activities of many departments. Its commitment to political neutrality does not mean that the British civil service has not had deeply ingrained political values. Indeed, in certain policy areas, the British administration emerges as remarkably unpragmatic and deeply committed to certain types of policy. One such area involves the relationship between the public and private sectors. The civil servants did not (as many Labour politicians feared they would) reject socialism or the social welfare policies of the 1945 Labour government. British public corporations have been fairly impressively well managed, and the positive role of the administration in creating the postwar welfare state is fully acknowledged. The Treasury absorbed Keynesian notions of demand management rapidly, although assimilating them into its own particular world view. The point is that so long as government policies recognized and reinforced a clear demarcation between the public and private sectors, and so long as policies for dealing with the private sector were global, things worked well. But British civil servants have responded poorly to the need to develop more discretionary policies and to operate in environments in which the border between the public and private sectors was increasingly unclear.

Finally, the administration has been highly oriented to Whitehall and to London, and the development of new relationships and policies between the center and periphery have been accomplished only with great difficulty. In the face of these new demands, pragmatism seems to have turned to rigidity, and the conviction that one can muddle through in the end has obscured the need to produce meaningful long-term policies and to evaluate the long-term consequences of existing policies and commitments.

Thus the administration has failed to acquire the very skills most required by the present environment of British politics. One

result has been endless efforts to evaluate and repair, and consequent demoralization and loss of credibility. More important, as
we have seen, has been the record of failure in institutional innovation. Since the early 1960s the British government has undergone more reorganization than at any other period in modern
history. But the general impression is of indecision and failure,
especially in those areas related to the management of the economy. From Neddy and all the little Neddies to the DEA, the IRC,
and MinTech and the ups and downs of ten more years of al-
phabet soup, institution creation can easily be perceived as a substitute for significant change and development.

The British administration has failed to adapt to an environment characterized by the interpenetration of public and private
powers, an environment in which power must be shared on a
continuing and intimate basis between public- and private-sector
actors. These failings have been compounded by the inability of
the parties to develop coherent economic programs and the consequent politicization of policies and institutions. The task has
been made still more difficult by increasingly intense centrifugal
tendencies within the British trade union movement (and, similarly, within the employers' organizations).

The national organizations of neither workers nor employers
have had much centralized authority in Britain, and the decentralization of authority has increased in recent years, particularly
in the trade unions. This growing loss of authority at the center
has produced two particularly significant results.

In the first place, it has been more and more difficult for leaders in the TUC and even in individual national unions to struggle
effectively against local or shop-floor militants. Pressures for
more radical or more militant action have percolated up in the
unions, and national leaders have found it harder and harder to
resist. To a very great extent, the crisis in labor-government relations in the late 1960s and early 1970s was really a crisis within the
unions, a struggle for power between the center and the shop
floor and the local unions. Strikes have occurred against the
wishes of union leaders and represent assertions of local authority
within the union. Union leaders, even those on the left, have
faced an increasingly difficult task in balancing the requirements
of government policy, even the policies of a Labour government,

and the demands of their own membership, over whom they have precious little control. The same holds true on the employers' side with regard to prices and wages, except that the decentralization is substantially greater. Except for a series of short-term "bargains," the central associations of employers have had little influence in price setting or dividend policy, and even individual industrial federations have rarely coordinated wage policies beyond basic bargaining with their unions.

Second, this lack of central authority has made it still more difficult for governments to develop long-term economic and industrial strategies. If the only way to maintain full employment and stable prices is through either the creation of some sort of income policy or at least a new mechanism of wage negotiation, then some kind of centralized bargaining structure is required. One can think in terms of sharing power: "Government is finding that it can govern only by sharing power with other representative institutions, notably the Trades Union Congress. For wages and prices policy to be effective, it will be necessary in the end for the trade unions themselves, acting as representative and democratic bodies, to legislate rules and enforce them"; or in terms of forcing the unions to recognize the inevitable: "The opportunity has now come to confront the union movement with the real choice, namely unemployment or a new wage negotiation machinery"; but in either case, representative, credible, and authoritative central institutions will be a necessity.[28] Existing institutions, however, fulfill none of these criteria, and their trend is toward less, not more, capabiiity in the future. Samuel Beer, in the Preface to my book on the Federation of British Industries (FBI), described this dilemma:

In the days of a less active state, the weakness of central authority in the TUC and FBI relieved government of comprehensive pressures that were potentially more formidable. But as government came to depend more and more upon the cooperation of producers' groups, this weakness was less and less of a virtue from the point of view of the needs of government. One of its major needs was precisely for bodies that could speak with "one voice" respectively for industry and labor on such large, economy-wide matters as the question of prices and incomes.[29]

V

Britain's postwar economic problems have rested ultimately on that nation's inability to define satisfactorily the relationship between the international and domestic political and economic systems. British leaders were unable, especially in the first postwar decade, to devise an acceptable international role that the nation could afford. Moreover, the British have been less capable than the French (who have had their own commitment to international *grandeur*) of formulating a long-term strategy that focused initially on domestic recovery and growth as a basis for an international resurgence. Such are the penalties, in Britain's case, for winning a war.

The global economic order that emerged after 1945 was not what the British had sought, and many of Britain's leaders were well aware that their country's interests might suffer severely under this regime. But they felt compelled to give that order their wholehearted support, both because they feared the consequences for international peace and prosperity if they refused their support and because such support was (they believed) the ticket that identified them as a leader in the postwar world. More to the point, opposition seems never to have been seriously contemplated.

Compared with other nations, Britain suffers from significant disadvantages in seeking to improve domestic economic performance and still maintain international competitiveness. One, its dependence on international trade is greater than that of other major states and it is therefore more vulnerable to international disturbance. Two, Britain lacks the central capacity of France or Japan to influence domestic price levels, to allocate capital, and in other ways to guide internal economic development. Finally, Britain has both a strong trade union movement and a highly outmoded system of industrial relations, which, like the trade union organization on which it rests, remains thoroughly embedded in the nineteenth century, and which—worse—even as it collapses seems incapable of modernization.

In my view, the British political system provides two key resources for coping with these problems: strong executive leadership and the voluntary tradition. At the present time, however, the first is lacking and the second is decidedly out of fashion. Britain's leaders have cried Dunkirk so many times in the past fifteen years that political credibility is severely damaged. The entire process of institution building, particularly in the area of economic policy, has become so politicized that successive governments feel obliged to wipe the slate clean before they can begin to seek their own remedies for Britain's problems.

Both front benches seem to agree that by continuing to squeeze demand and to attack public spending, they will—ultimately—solve Britain's economic problems. It seems to me, however, that the consensus on which Britain's rather impressive early postwar achievements rested represented above all commitments to full employment and the welfare state, and therefore that policies that implicitly and explicitly attack the roots of this consensus are unlikely to succeed. Without a credible reaffirmation of the commitment to full employment and to rising standards of living, which includes the enhancement of the welfare state (although it does not necessarily exclude some fairly substantial alterations in welfare policies), I don't think the unions will accept major reforms in union structure or in industrial relations. Given the available instruments of government policy and the values of British political culture, if such reforms cannot be accomplished voluntarily, I doubt that they can be accomplished at all.[30] And, this, I believe, remains the basic dilemma of the British situation.

Notes

1. E. J. Hobsbawm, *Industry and Empire* (London: Penguin Books, 1968), p. 178.

2. Sir Henry Phelps Brown, "What Is the British Predicament?," *Three Banks Review*, no. 116 (December 1977), p. 3.

3. K. S. Lomax, "Growth and Productivity in the United Kingdom," in *Economic Growth in Twentieth-Century Britain,* ed. Derek Aldcroft and Peter Fearnon (New York: Humanities Press, 1970), pp. 12 and 26. See also E. H. Phelps Brown, "Labour Policies: Productivity, Industrial Relations, Cost Inflation," in *Britain's Economic Prospects Reconsidered,* ed. Sir Alec Cairncross (London: George Allen & Unwin, 1971).

4. Phelps Brown, "What Is the British Predicament?," pp. 3–4.

5. Ibid., p. 4.

6. Ibid.

7. W. A. P. Manser, *Britain in Balance: The Myth of Failure* (London: Penguin Books, 1973).

8. Richard E. Caves and associates, *Britain's Economic Prospects* (Washington: Brookings Institution, 1968), p. 3.

9. Sidney Pollard, *The Development of the British Economy, 1914–1945,* 2d ed. (New York: St. Martin's Press, 1969), p. 375.

10. Angus Maddison, *Economic Growth in the West* (New York: W. W. Norton, 1967), provides the best comparative assessment of economic growth rates up to the early 1960s.

11. Leslie Lenkowski, "Welfare in the Welfare State," in *The Future That Doesn't Work: Social Democracy Failure in Britain,* ed. R. Emmett Tyrrell, Jr. (Garden City, N.Y.: Doubleday, 1977), p. 147.

12. *The Economist,* April 8, 1978, p. 100.

13. Lenkowski, "Welfare in the Welfare State," p. 147.

14. Richard Rose, "Overload Government: The Problem Outlined," *European Studies Newsletter,* December 1975, p. 14.

15. Anthony King, "The Problem of Overload," in *Why Is Britain Becoming Harder to Govern?,* ed. Anthony King (London: BBC Publications, 1967), p. 25.

16. Samuel Brittan, "The Economic Constraints of Democracy," *British Journal of Political Science* 5 (1975), reprinted in *Why Is Britain Becoming Harder to Govern?,* ed. King.

17. Peter Jenkins, "Britain's Troubles," *Trialogue,* Fall 1976, p. 3.

18. Brittan, "Economic Constraints of Democracy," pp. 120 and 112 (in King).

19. P. J. Curwen, *Inflation* (London: Macmillan, 1976), p. 102.

20. "Do the Unions Govern Britain?," *The Economist,* November 29, 1975.

21. Robert Lieber, "Labour in Power: Problems of Political Economy," unpublished paper prepared for CUNY conference on the New Left, November 1976, p. 40. See also Lewis Minkin's work on New Left unionism and the Labour Party.

22. A good deal of this section is based on my article "Britain: The Politics of Foreign Economic Policy, the Domestic Economy, and the Problem of Pluralistic Stagnation," in *Between Power and Plenty,* ed. Peter J. Katzenstein (Madison: University of Wisconsin Press, 1978).

23. Andrew Shonfield, *British Economic Policy since the War* (London: Penguin Books, 1958), p. 218. Susan Strange, *Sterling and British Policy* (London: Oxford University Press, 1971), is the best recent study of these issues.

24. In addition to the well-known sources on the planning experiment, notice should be taken of a recent study by Michael Shanks: *Planning and Politics: The British Experience, 1960–76* (London: George Allen & Unwin, 1977).

25. Maddison, in *Economic Growth in the West,* briefly reviews Treasury efforts to create an automatic link between the state of the pound inter-

nationally and domestic economic policy. He characterizes the episode as "another case of wishful hankering after the will-of-the-wisp of automatic devises, which springs from a desire to abandon the heavy responsibility of formulating policy" (p. 188).

26. Michael Stewart, *The Jekyll and Hyde Years: Politics and Economic Policy since 1964* (London: Dent, 1977), p. 244.

27. Samuel Beer, *British Politics in the Collectivist Age,* 2d ed. (New York: Vintage Books, 1969), p. 88.

28. Jenkins, "Britain's Troubles," p. 4; Wilfred Beckerman, "Inflation and the Unions," *New Statesman,* March 7, 1975, p. 296. For a violently opposed view, see Samuel Brittan, "The Political Economy of British Trade Union Monopoly," *Three Banks Review,* September 1976.

29. Samuel Beer, Preface to Stephen Blank, *Government and Industry in Britain: The Federation of British Industries in Politics, 1945–1965* (Farnborough: Saxon House, 1973), p. xii.

30. See Shanks, *Planning and Politics,* chap. 5, and Peter Parker, "A New Industrial Polity," Stamp Memorial Lecture, University of London, 1977.

6 | Britain's Relative Economic Decline: A Reply to Stephen Blank

ROBIN MARRIS

Economists seldom agree with anyone else and I am no exception, for I see recent British economic history in a quite different light from the one in which Stephen Blank sees it. We disagree most profoundly over what I take to be his underemphasis on the significance of Britain's relative economic decline compared to the performance of what he refers to as Britain's neighbors.

The postwar pattern of economic development among rich countries has seen those countries that at the end of World War II had relatively low levels of income per capita catching up with the United States; the farther behind they were, the more they have caught up. The one exception to this rule—basically the outstanding exception among OECD countries—is the United Kingdom.

The countries labeled rich are essentially the members of the Organization for Economic Cooperation and Development, which is all of North America and Western Europe plus Japan, New Zealand, and Australia. One must remove from that group, however, the countries that are basically anomalies: such developing countries as Spain, Portugal, Greece, Ireland, Turkey, and Yugoslavia, which have data that just do not fit the pattern of the other countries in population and the like. We are left with nineteen countries that are generally advanced and rich. From the end of World War II to the present day they have had a growth rate of real gross national product per head of 3.5 percent. Among those nineteen is a subgroup composed of countries that were founded by Anglo-Saxons, that is to say the United Kingdom, the United States, Canada with the exception of the province of Quebec, Australia, and New Zealand, which one can call the Anglos. This group of Anglo countries has had a growth rate of only 2 percent. If we remove the Anglos and look at the remaining countries, not all of which are by any means dominated by data comparable to those for Germany and Japan, we find they have a growth rate of 5 percent. That is a rather startling statistic and suggests that something about economic maturity or political maturity or social maturity may be involved here.

One should also note that at the end of World War II, the United Kingdom had a much lower level of income per capita than any of the other countries in the Anglo group. This calculation is based on rather sophisticated methods of dealing with international cost-of-living differences and exchange rates, which are now available to us. Roughly speaking, at the end of World War II the U.K. GNP per capita was about 60 percent of that of the United States. All Britain has done in the intervening period is to get up to about 65 percent, barely improving its relative position. It's just not true that the only other countries to have done better are Germany and Japan. There is, after all, the outstanding example of France, which may well now have a GNP per capita which is not much more than 10 percent below that of the Anglo-Saxon countries excluding the United Kingdom. The French GNP per capita is now about 85 percent of that of the United States. And this is not the country that one usually thinks of when making comparisons of that kind.

Other data can be invoked to refute Blank's argument that the conventional idea of a long-term economic decline is misconceived. Recent thinking of economists studying economic growth in developed countries suggests, for example, that since World War II international "technology gaps" have tended to even out through the migration of knowledge, the activities of multinational companies, increasing trade, and similar forces. So it is expected that a country's growth rate will tend to be faster the farther it is behind. This means that Germany, France, and Italy, for example, should have begun by growing faster than the United Kingdom after World War II. But it does not mean that they should have overtaken Britain!

This theory works well against the data. For convenience, let us call it Robin Marris's law: the relative growth rates (per capita) of any two industrialized countries at any time should be inversely proportional to their relative per capita GNPs. Of the real-life situations I have tried my law out against, the only two where it breaks down are the United Kingdom in the decade 1960–70 and West Germany in the decade 1950–60. So the idea that there was something special about the good German performance of the first postwar period and about the bad British performance of the second is rather precisely confirmed. In the earlier period, Britain's growth rate, though not exceptional, was almost exactly as predicted by my law. If only it had continued merely to follow this law since 1960, Britain's real GNP today would be no less than *one-third* higher than it actually is. This is an enormous failure. What I'm suggesting is that this kind of calculation and others like it do tend to support the idea of a genuine relative decline in the British economy which I actually happen to believe, along with Hobsbawm, goes back to about 1890.

Let me suggest some other indices of decline that go back to that period. Look, for example, at the share of each of the countries in the total manufactured exports of the nineteen rich countries that I mentioned. In 1935 the United Kingdom had 25 percent of that trade, the United States had 15 percent, and the remaining countries had 60 percent. By 1955 the United Kingdom, despite its having been in a very strong position in the immediate postwar period to take the markets of such countries as Germany, had fallen to 20 percent. The country that had taken those markets was the United States, which in 1955 had gone from 15 percent to 25 percent. It had replaced the United Kingdom as the world's manufacturing supplier, and the rest of the world was just slightly down because, of course, it was still the period of postwar recovery. What has happened between 1955 and 1978? The United Kingdom now has under 10 percent. Its world trade in manufacturing has absolutely collapsed. What is also interesting is that something very similar has happened to the United States. The only thing that one can say is that the United States until recently was still above its 1955 figure, although I doubt that this will be the case in two or three years' time. What has happened is that the rest of the world, which in this case does mainly consist of Germany and Japan (but with a lot of support, oddly enough from Italy and France, although not quite to the same extent), has now 75 percent of that trade. This is a fairly shattering indicator.

To what extent can we clarify this situation by conventional explanations? The most often heard is that Britain has been more prone to inflation and has therefore had rising relative export prices and has not devalued the pound fast enough to cope with it. Dealing with that argument requires a good deal of complicated data that I think would indicate that the United Kingdom has been less inflation-prone than Japan, for example, and although it has not been less inflation-prone than Germany, the devaluations, by and large, have been quite sufficient to meet that point. The devaluations themselves, of course, have made Britain more inflation-prone and created other problems, but they have been sufficient to maintain the competitive position on formal figures of competitiveness. I also don't believe the other conventional explanation that Britain has been crushed by the welfare state. I do believe, however, that had I known in the fifties what was going to happen to Britain industrially, I wouldn't have been an enthusiastic supporter of its attempt to be first in this particular field. And had I known what I now know about some of the problems of the background of British industrial management, I might have been less in favor of high taxation on earned incomes, marginal earned incomes, of successful industrial managers, which really is a main feature of the United Kingdom's problems.

I believe that what we have at work here is a kind of technological and commercial backwardness or decline. The British are always one step behind what the market is doing technically and commercially. When one is not selling the thing that people want, no amount of price cutting will make any difference, or to put it another way, the price cutting is going to be pretty expensive to have much effect. This has been argued by a good many people, and the more it has been looked at, the more they seem to confirm this idea. I also believe, basically, in the conventional sociological and political interpretation. The Industrial Revolution was created by the lower middle classes, who, once they became rich, had only one ambition, not to go back into commerce but to provide country estates for their children. The British educational system is also partly responsible for the economic decline. It is an attractively elitist educational system, particularly at the higher level. What is appalling, however, is that in this system a quite startlingly low proportion of British middle and upper-middle management, even as late as the middle sixties, had had any higher education at all, as compared with Germany and France, let alone the United States.

Having inherited its industrial problem from the late nineteenth and early twentieth centuries, why did Britain fail to take the opportunities for recovery that presented themselves after World War II? It would have been rather surprising if it hadn't done rather well after World War II. What one has to explain is why it didn't do a great deal better. It is certainly true that English people of all classes do not appear to achieve as much in a working day as their opposite numbers in competing countries. They are prone to reject tasks they consider tedious. A gentleman may work in the style of the gifted amateur but should not appear to enjoy making money as such. If money is short, he should either marry wisely or go into the City. At all costs, he should not go to Birmingham, the industrial heart of England, because as any superficial international comparison of the life-styles will show, the British have a distinct comparative advantage in the business of spending money (as against producing it) and Birmingham is not the place for that.

What Britain suffers from is, in fact, a lack of commercial adaptiveness, an inadequate sales drive, a dislike of traveling abroad to sell things, despite the fact that British governments ever since the end of World War II have put more emphasis on exports than any other country. It was the British weak point, and that is why the government has emphasized it. No other country has a Queen's Award for exports.

The principal source of British decline, however, is its managerial malaise. Throughout the postwar period, British second-class graduates—people without the top degrees, whose equivalents in the United States, Germany, and Japan make up the ranks of middle and upper-middle management, where dogged bureaucratic efficiency is the key to modern industrial success—continued to avoid industry in favor of finance and similar occupations. In pure inventiveness, where small and medium-sized firms are important, Britain has, to be sure, done quite well. It has failed in development and marketing, where a disciplined and more highly educated corporate bureaucracy is particularly important.

In the late 1950s only a quarter of all British managers had any higher education, compared with proportions three times as high in America, Germany, and France. The typical British manager of the 1960s and 1970s has been a self-made person inadequately prepared for the commercial and technological conditions of the modern world. I cannot remember any pupil—anybody I had taught in Cambridge personally—in the twenty-five years I was there who has actually gone into industry. Many of my best pupils have finished up not doing economics, but are in the BBC, which all would agree is excellent. There are certainly positive aspects of modern British society, such as the BBC. But that my economics students go there and not into industry is itself symbolic and symptomatic of Britain's relative industrial decline.

PART III ::

The Modern British State

7 | *Was Guy Fawkes Right?*

JORGEN S. RASMUSSEN

Back in the dark ages, when the United States still was in Vietnam and Nixon was in the White House, the humor editor of *The Economist*, seeking to prove the House of Commons' ineffectiveness, used to regale its readers with stories of the great power of the American Congress. I began to believe that parallel universes did exist; clearly, he was writing about a United States other than the one in which I lived. In my United States, Congress was trying to find out whether we were bombimg Cambodia—not, mind you, trying unsuccessfully to stop it, but simply to discover whether we were doing it. The Congress I knew was having no great success in achieving even the limited objective of getting the executive to tell them what was happening. In London, however, someone was proclaiming the ability of Congress to control American policy making. Such articles certainly provided a bit of comic relief.

More seriously and in historical perspective, that a Briton should think an American political structure superior to a British one was remarkable. For years Britons had told Americans that our political institutions were deficient; a judgment we accepted readily. Lord Bryce and Woodrow Wilson are merely the best known of a long list of such writers on both sides of the Atlantic. As late as 1950 the Committee on Political Parties of the American Political Science Association argued that American government and politics could be improved significantly if only American parties were made to be more like British ones. Although that prescription was based on an almost total misunderstanding of the

97

British party system, it illustrates, nonetheless, that the belief that British is better was a long time adying in the United States.

Ironically, not long after the Committee on Political Parties report, Britons increasingly were becoming disillusioned with their political system. Perhaps to be hailed as a model polity, a nation needs not so much sound political institutions as world power. In its obvious international weakness, Britain seemed less worthy of emulation. While the origin of a shift in values never can be dated exactly, Michael Young's *Chipped White Cups of Dover* at the start of the 1960s certainly was one of the earliest critiques. A veritable flood followed—books whose titles clearly revealed their authors' belief in Britain's decline: *The Stagnant Society, Great Britain or Little England?, Suicide of a Nation,* and the remarkable series of books from Penguin, *What's Wrong with . . . ,* proclaiming the failures of virtually all the major structures of British society.[1] Britain's economic and political problems of the late 1960s and 1970s served only to validate these gloomy portraits. (It is reassuring to have the word of the American ambassador to Britain that no matter how discouraged the British may be, they at least haven't lost their appetite.)

American doubts about British political virtues were slower to appear in print, although J. Roland Pennock's comparative study of agricultural policy was a harbinger.[2] Pennock concluded that special interests could convert their goals into authoritative policy more easily in Britain than in the United States. Here was the first hint of the theory of pluralistic stagnation which was to become such a prevalent theme in American analyses of British politics as a result of Samuel Beer's classic summation of the interplay of politics and ideas in Britain.[3] Shortly after Pennock's paper, a more extensive study by Kenneth Waltz argued that the process of formulating foreign policy was performed more effectively in the United States than in Britain; surely, given Britain's reputation for effective diplomacy, the unkindest cut of all. "Massive continuity, painfully slow adjustment, response to crises only when they have almost hopelessly deepened"—this was not a description of Third Republic France but Waltz's view of post–World War II Britain.[4]

Thus, that a major critique of British political institutions should appear in *The Economist* in November 1977 is not surprising.[5] The specific reforms it advocated are not so extreme, although it is notable that the positions of the two countries have so altered that *The Economist* almost recommends that Britain adopt the American constitution in its entirety. What is unexpected is the virulence of the attack. Suggesting, even figuratively, that Parliament should be blown up seems in questionable taste for a respected newspaper, especially given the bombing of Westminster Hall only a few years earlier.

Such vehemence from an influential journal demands close consideration of its critique. This is appropriate as well because the critique includes many of the most significant charges made by others in recent years. After the validity of the diagnosis has been considered, the appropriateness of the remedies proposed can be assessed. Should the diagnosis be mistaken, the prescription is hardly likely to be effective, may indeed be harmful.

The Economist argues that the British political system operates so inefficiently and is so unrepresentative that it drives citizens to political cynicism. The system generates mediocre leaders (shades of Bryce's "Why Great Men Are not Elected President") who, on the basis of a party tyranny, exercise autocratic power.

Parliament has ceased to be effective because leaders use ritual and formal procedures to avoid doing anything new. The Commons is dominated by ideologues, since each of the leading parties is controlled by its extreme wing. Therefore, each government devotes most of its efforts to undoing what its predecessor just did; parties fight the same old battles over and over. The resultant failure to deal effectively with public problems alienates the citizens. Parliament's unrepresentativeness increases their cynicism further. The electoral system converts electoral pluralities into legislative majorities; low turnout makes the allocation of seats an even less accurate reflection of popular desires. This unrepresentativeness is unmitigated, given the absence of a federal system to decentralize power.

Even unrepresentative MPs might be of some use if they did not let party discipline turn them into lobby fodder. Since they vote as they are told, however, special corporate interests have replaced the Commons as the real policy makers. The Commons now is so irrelevant that the popular standing of politicians turns more on how they perform on television than on what they say and do in the House.

The prevalence of docile MPs does not produce dynamic leaders who have a free hand to act decisively. Even the top leaders are an uninspiring, mediocre lot, lacking national vision. They are brokers of the worst sort of compromise, compromise not between parties but within them. Their central concern is to hold their party together; those who become prime minister are those who have proven best at not offending their party.

Despite their unfitness, these leaders are made autocrats. The typical prime minister "has unfettered executive power beyond an American president's dreams." The payroll vote and the ambition of back-benchers assures the prime minister of firm support. Therefore, the executive is able to prevent the Commons from controlling public expenditure, adequately investigating the subject matter of proposed legislation, obtaining information about executive plans and actions, even from controlling its own legislative timetable. The Commons' inability to check the executive is serious especially because the judiciary can do little to protect people from the partisan legislation that the cabinet rams through Parliament.

In summary, this is an undemocratic system that lacks even the virtue or the justification of making the trains run on time. Clearly, the time has come for "blowing up a tyranny."

The most apparent defect of this all-warts portrait is its lack of logical consistency. Reconciling the picture of the prime minister as a mere broker of intraparty compromise with his characterization as an autocrat is difficult. Nor is it clear how MPs can be lobby fodder, supinely following voting orders, and constitute party wings sufficiently powerful to force governments, apparently against their better judgment, to reverse previous policies.

Spotting a second defect requires only a little reflection. Some of the specific examples chosen to flesh out the portrait have been wrenched from context. The ability of the Commons to compel the executive to divulge information about the start of the Crimean War before it was over occurred well before the nuclear age. Wars hardly involved questions of national survival then. The much higher international stakes prevailing now help to explain why executives are more reluctant than in the past to provide information.

The considerable control of the British executive over the parliamentary timetable should not be mentioned without a reminder of the way this control came about. The executive obtained this power to prevent a militant minority—the Irish Nationalists—from subverting the parliamentary process by preventing any action until they had coerced the government into granting their desires. These rules were introduced so that the Commons could regain the power to transact its business. This historical point suggests that these rules may have special contemporary relevance. To this point the Scottish Nationalists have operated within the system. Should devolution not be implemented and should the Scot Nats win thirty-five to forty seats in the Commons, however, they might well decide to block all legislative action until they secured independence, were the executive not able to control the timetable.

Even apart from this hypothetical situation, control of the Commons timetable has some virtue, as *The Economist* itself has recognized in one of its noncrusading moments. Not much more than a year before its Guy Fawkes Day critique, it had written:

> Despite their malign reputation, guillotine motions have normally had a beneficial effect on the quality of scrutiny of government bills. Before guillotines, much time is wasted on debating at length the more inessential clauses, on procedural arguments and party dogfights, while government supporters take virtually no part in the debate for fear of holding up progress. Afterwards, there is a deliberate concentration on the more important clauses, a minimum of time-wasting, and government supporters are just as likely to participate as opposition MPs ... a good way to improve the parliamentary examination of bills would be to submit all of them to a guillotine procedure.[6]

Executive control of the timetable, therefore, helps the Commons perform more effectively.

A denunciation of MPs for failing to be "Burkean inquisitors of government and all other centres of power" has an impressive ring until one recalls the historical context. The unpalatable fact is that Burke for much of his career sat for a pocket borough; so long as he pleased his patron he had no need to worry about reelection, a situation that greatly facilitates independence. As Sir Lewis Namier wrote of the early stage of Burke's parliamentary career, "Edmund Burke was yet to learn by experience how much freer an Opposition Member was when sitting for a pocket borough than as a representative of Bristol."[7] The freedom of a member sitting for a pocket borough hardly was absolute, however; sometimes the leash was less slack than at others. On important issues such members were lobby fodder for landed aristocrats. Why that state of affairs should be preferable to being subject to the policies of the leaders of mass political parties *The Economist* does not make clear.

A third inaccuracy in the portrait is due to a tendency to exaggerate the size of the warts. Certainly, governments do repeal some of their predecessors' programs, but to claim that they spend the bulk of their time undoing virtually everything is plainly inaccurate. The Labour government of 1945–50 is one of the two most reformist governments of twentieth-century Britain. Despite the breadth of Labour's welfare and economic initiatives, the Conservatives accepted the great bulk of them. Apart from major social reform, even in a matter clearly of partisan interest, the Conservatives did not try to alter the financial relation between the unions and the Labour Party, but accepted the return to contracting out.

Some MPs can be classified as ideologues, but the claim that they are the ones that dominate the Commons and control the government simply cannot be squared with the findings of research. This is obvious especially in a comparative context. Having interviewed close to two hundred national legislators in Britain and Italy, Robert Putnam found that the bulk of British MPs were low to medium on both ideological style and partisan hostility.[8] Their striking contrast in this regard with the Italian deputies, most of whom scored much higher, was one of the clearest findings of the study.

Of course, any political party does contain a diversity of views, and party leaders must spend some time attempting to reconcile those views if they are to maintain themselves as leaders. To move from this fact, however, to the assertion that one gets to the top of the slippery pole only by not offending people contradicts the experience of the last third of a century. Half of the last eight prime ministers had been party rebels, and two of them even had resigned from ministerial positions. Looking ahead, the prospects in the next-prime-minister-but-one derby of Anthony Benn have, if anything, been enhanced by his reputation for opposing his party's leadership.

Popular opinion of politicians probably is not as high as it was in the past. But except for entertainment celebrities, few elite figures have the status that was enjoyed in a more deferential age. To call this political cynicism is an overstatement; the available evidence is ambiguous. For example, a 1973 poll did find that about two-thirds of the respondents agreed that most politicians will promise anything to get votes.[9] But only 39 percent thought that politicians were in politics for what they could get out of it (33 percent disagreed), and almost half believed that "politicians *do* care what people like me think," a proposition rejected by less than a third of the respondents. Furthermore, over 40 percent of those surveyed thought that an ordinary MP was very valuable to the community, more than granted this virtue to either trade union leaders (28 percent) or senior civil servants (24 percent). In April 1978 a MORI poll that asked people to rate eighteen political leaders as honest or dishonest found that in every case more people considered them honest (frequently a substantially greater proportion) than thought they were dishonest. And only five of the eighteen were felt to be out of touch with ordinary people by more respondents than the number thinking that they were in touch.

The Economist, like most of those who view with alarm, argues not only that things aren't what they used to be but that they are better elsewhere—primarily, as we have seen, in the United States, but also in Germany. The desire to learn from others, while commendable, can degenerate all too easily into a grass-is-always-greener attitude. Only a few months after *The Economist*'s critique, which noted that the Bundestag was more effective than the Commons, Annemarie Renger, a vice-president and former speaker of the Bundestag, warned that the German parliament was in danger of becoming superfluous: its public debates were inadequate and it lacked the power to participate effectively in the planning work of the executive. In short, the Bundestag had become a mere "backdrop" for the government in a manner that was "intolerable."[10] Perhaps Germany is not such an appropriate model for reform after all.

As for the United States, the contrast of the Commons with Congress may not be so impressive as *The Economist* assumes, nor are the results of the American executive-legislative relation necessarily beneficial. Since 1953 the *Congressional Quarterly* has calculated a "presidential support score," which indicates the president's ability to get Congress to agree with him on those issues on which he clearly indicated a preference through messages and public statements before each legislative vote. In the quarter of a century through 1977, this score has varied considerably.[11] In three separate years presidents were able to obtain congressional support only about half of the time, certainly an unheard-of situation in contemporary Britain. A meaningful comparison, however, must exclude those years in which Congress was controlled by a party different from that of the president, since in Britain the same party normally controls both the legislative and the executive branches or at least is the largest legislative party. In the United States the same party controlled both branches for eleven years during the period 1953 through 1977. During those years the presidential support score ranged from 75 to 93 and averaged 83. American presidents can hardly count on automatic support in Congress, but when their party controls the legislature, they are quite successful in getting their legislation through; the contrast with the success rate of the British cabinet is not that striking. Representatives are not whipped through lobbies like cattle, but arm twisting before a roll call is not unknown or ineffective on Capitol Hill.

Furthermore, that the country is better off when Congress refuses to support the president's policies is debatable. President Carter's proposals for an energy policy would seem to be motivated by a concern for the national interest, a concern the lack of which in Britain *The Economist* deplores. At the very least, one hardly would devise such a program to try to curry favor with the voters or to reconcile factions within the majority party. Precisely because in the United States governmental action has to overcome so many obstacles, the eventual energy policy is not likely to be coherent and integrated or to meet the nation's needs effectively. If, as *The Economist* alleges, government is inefficient in Britain because the executive has too much power, in the United States not infrequently it is inefficient because the executive has too little.

To this point I have dealt mainly with the details of *The Economist*'s critique without considering the central theme that the cabinet, and the prime minister in particular, is an autocratic executive tyrannizing over the Commons because MPs are mere lobby fodder. Except for the hyperbole of the language, this is a commonplace, widely accepted description of the British political system. But precisely because this is what we all know, it is essential to examine the changes that have taken place in the relation between the Commons and the cabinet during the last decade.

In the quarter of a century from the end of World War II to 1970, no government ever was defeated in the Commons because of intraparty dissension.[12] This is not to say, however, that the Commons could not have had a decisive effect upon major government legislation during this period. In 1965 the government decided to drop its plan for a compulsory wage freeze when enough back-benchers threatened to abstain to defeat the legislation.[13] The government had to abandon its legislation to reform labor relations in 1969 when it became clear that the bill would not get through the Commons. The government was not defeated only because it gave in to dissident MPs so as to avoid losing a Commons division. Richard Crossman's account of the key cabinet meeting at which the government decided to surrender has a livid Harold Wilson shouting at the cabinet, "I won't, I can't, you can't do this to me!" before finally conceding that he would have to drop the bill. Similarly, the government had to forgo its plan to reform the House of Lords because it lacked sufficient support in the Commons to pass the bill.

From 1970 to 1974 the government was defeated six times in the Commons because of intraparty dissent.[14] In two instances the results of the defeat did not survive into the final bill. And only one of the defeats could be said to be on a truly significant subject. That one occurred when the Commons defeated the Home Secretary's rules to implement the 1971 Immigration Act. The majority against the government—thirty-five—is the largest post–World War II defeat suffered by a British government.[15]

Many Conservative MPs opposed their home secretary's rules because they felt they restricted too greatly immigrants from the "white" Commonwealth. As a result of the defeat, the Home Secretary rewrote the rules and met all of the objections of the dissidents. Except for this case, the defeats weren't major matters; nonetheless, all but one occurred on whipped divisions and half were on three-line whips.

During 1974 the government's only defeats occurred because, as a minority government, it was vulnerable to being outvoted by the combined opposition.[16] Nonetheless, that this happened fifteen times in less than a year is some evidence of the ability of the Commons to check the government and contrasts sharply with its image of a latter-day Balfour's poodle.

Intraparty dissent defeated the government three times during 1975.[17] The subjects were backdating of value-added tax (VAT) on TV rentals, the electoral disqualifications of the Clay Cross councillors, and the earnings rule under which pensioners lost part of their pensions if they continued to work after retirement. Despite the government's wish to keep at its current level the amount that could be earned without reducing pensions, the Commons voted to increase the sum by stages over several years. In yet another instance, the Commons forced the government to expand the pension system to include disabled housewives, who up till then were entitled to nothing. The government gave way to the Commons on this issue without a vote so as to avoid the embarrassment of a defeat.

The following March the government suffered what was to that point its most significant defeat since World War II. The Commons voted against the government's white paper on public expenditure; it refused to accept the program of cuts that the government had devised in attempting to solve Britain's economic problems. While this vote was not the cause, it seems relevant that within a week Harold Wilson had resigned as prime minister. Although he claimed to have planned months earlier the time of his departure, one may at least wonder whether the defeat may have been the final frustration that persuaded him not to change his plans.

By now defeats for the government had become almost commonplace. In July 1976 the government was defeated when the

Commons voted to reduce taxes on war widows. Then in November the government suffered a major reverse on the Dock Work Regulations Bill. The House of Lords, in what clearly was a wrecking amendment, had altered the area to be affected by the bill so as to eliminate precisely those facilities that the legislation was intended to cover. The government's plan to eliminate this amendment when the bill returned to the Commons was thwarted when Labour back-benchers Brian Walden and John Mackintosh abstained and the Commons voted to sustain the Lords' amendments.

The docks bill was not the only instance of government difficulties with the Lords. The Lords amended the Aircraft and Shipbuilding Industries Bill to exempt ship repairers from nationalization. Uncertain of its ability to get this change reversed in the Commons and pressed for time, the government abandoned the bill rather than give in to the Lords. The following session it reintroduced the bill, intending to enact it under the provisions of the Parliament Act of 1949. Whether the bill was a hybrid, which would require a more laborious and time-consuming legislative process, was a key issue. The government's inability to avoid this problem finally led it to concede that the ship repairers would be excluded from the legislation. Thus the government had to settle for the situation it had found unacceptable some months earlier.

The government had to retreat on another matter of lesser significance during 1976 because of opposition in the Commons. It had introduced a public lending right bill to pay authors royalties for library circulation of books. The strength of dissent in the Commons persuaded the government to abandon this proposal before it was defeated.

Perhaps the major political story of 1977 was the government's defeat on its devolution proposals. In February the government lost a guillotine motion in the Commons, which thereby killed the bill for all practical purposes for that session. Major as this defeat was, the government almost could have rejoiced in it had it guaranteed that no other reverses would occur. The government already had been defeated on the Reduction of Redundancy Rebates Bill. In June it was defeated in standing committee on increased tax allowances for lower income groups. So tenuous was its control of the Commons that it did not feel able to seek to reverse this defeat when the bill returned to the floor. In July the Commons amended the Criminal Law Bill, contrary to the government's desire, to provide that a suspect had a right to contact someone after being arrested and taken to a police station. The government also had to forgo its plan to increase the petrol tax since it lacked the votes to get this portion of its budget through the Commons. The Commons voted against the government's plan to close four of the ten Scottish colleges of education because of low enrollments.[18] As a result of this defeat, the government announced the next month that one of the four would not be closed and that it would reconsider the position of the other three. By the end of the year it conceded that these colleges would remain open as well.

The government's fortunes failed to improve in the new session, which began near the end of the year. Almost immediately the Commons defeated the government on a matter of full disclosure of information. Although the government had planned a semisecret investigation of the huge financial losses of the crown agents, the Commons forced them to concede that there would be a public inquiry. By now it was the government's weakness, not the Commons', that was an occasion for jokes. The Labour Whips' Office was reported to be thinking about changing the wording on the whip from "Your attendance is essential" to "It would be awfully good of you if you could spare the time to pop in for just a moment, if you haven't got anything else to do."[19]

The government reintroduced its devolution legislation, providing for increased autonomy for Scotland and Wales, having conceded some of the demands of opponents and having split the proposals into separate bills for the two territories. Straightaway the government lost two divisions. In a symbolic gesture of opposition the Commons removed the first clause of the Scottish devolution bill, which had declared that the bill did not "affect the unity of the United Kingdom." More significantly, the government also lost the clause that would have required the Scottish Assembly to take account of any national pay policy.

Even the latter defeat paled into insignificance in January 1978, when the government lost another three divisions on devolution. In one instance the bill was amended so that the Orkney and Shetland islands would be excluded from devolution should they, as was expected, vote against it in the referendum. The other two defeats altered the bill to provide that the devolution proposals could be implemented only if they were supported in the referendum by 40 percent of the total Scottish electorate. Should the Scottish turnout be about what it was for the EEC referendum, little over 60 percent, then instead of just a favorable simple majority, devolution would require nearly a two-to-one positive vote.

So damaging was this amendment that the government sought to reverse the defeat the following month in a later stage of the bill's progress through the Commons. The government tried first to eliminate the provision but failed. Then it attempted to reduce the required percentage of support; again it was defeated. Not content with their success, the opponents of devolution sought to make their victory certain by denying to the government a tactic that would have been likely to gain the maximum turnout. They amended the bill to provide that the referendum could be no closer to a general election than three months—both could not occur on the same day, as the government was thought to be planning so as to get a turnout of around 75 percent.

Devolution was not the only cause of government defeats in early 1978. On a division that was a matter of foreign policy as much as domestic policy, the Commons defeated the government on revaluing the EEC's green pound. Although the government had proposed that the green pound be devalued, the Commons, in two separate votes, supported a 50 percent greater devaluation than that the government wanted.

In May the government had to give up its plan to make the use of metric measures compulsory in all shops by a certain date. It was not defeated in the Commons, but rather was forced to abandon its plan to bring the matter up when it became clear that to do so would mean almost certain defeat. In this case it was not a matter of the government's inability to get the Commons to pass the legislation it wanted; it was a question of issuing statutory instruments and the government's inability to prevent the Commons from voting them down.

This survey provides at least one example of almost every type of conflict between the Commons and the government—amendment of legislation and defeat of statutory instruments, foreign as well as domestic matters, preventing government secrecy, and voting against government policy proposals. It includes even an instance—the 1977 loss of the intended petrol tax increase—of a financial matter, an area in which the government's power and authority normally are thought to be virtually unchallengeable.

The petrol tax defeat was as nothing, however, compared to the government's setback on the following year's budget. The Conservatives managed to get the Commons to vote to cut a penny in the pound off the standard rate of income tax. Although this sounds trivial, it means a loss of £370 million a year in tax revenues. The government also lost on an amendment that raised the threshold at which higher rates of taxes are paid. It is estimated that this change will cost somewhere between £40 million and £105 million. Thus even on extremely significant financial matters the Commons is able to defeat the government.

In summary, this survey would seem to suggest that the analogy of dogs' being threatened with the loss of their licenses should they bite too frequently more accurately describes cabinet-Commons relations than the old cliché of sheep or cattle. Since most of the incidents mentioned occurred during the last few years, however, someone will object that this period is unusual, that Britain "normally" has a majority government. The accuracy of this demur depends on one's time frame and whether "normal" means almost always or simply more often than not. The quarter century from 1945 to 1970 hardly is the statutory benchmark for British politics; taking broader time perspectives can be instructive. During the entire twentieth century thus far, close to a third—29 percent—of the twenty-one general elections have failed to produce a House of Commons majority for one single party (see Figure 1). Taking a very lenient definition of working majority—one party has at least twenty seats more than its combined opponents—only about half of the elections have produced such a result.

Since general elections occur irregularly, perhaps a more accurate measure of normality in Britain is the number of years of one-party majority control of the Commons (see Figure 2). During about a quarter—24 percent—of the twentieth century, one party has not controlled the Commons, a situation clearly necessitating some compromise, some check on the cabinet's ability to

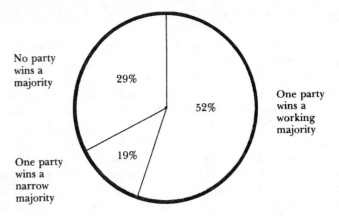

Figure 1. Results of 21 elections in the twentieth century

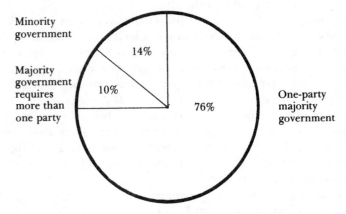

Figure 2. Types of twentieth-century governments

dominate the Commons. Perhaps the latter part of World War I should be excluded from this total, as the national government then in office, although a coalition, was not a minority government. The same is true of the 1918–22 government. During these times some interparty compromise could be **expected to occur** within the executive, but the cabinet would not lack control of the Commons. Even when these times are excluded, however, during 14 percent—a not insignificant proportion—of the years of the twentieth century Britain had minority governments. The cabinet hardly can be thought to have dominated the Commons during these periods.

Thus, minority and multiparty governments are not so uncommon in Britain as those who focus only on the third quarter of the twentieth century believe. Nonetheless, one-party majority governments have been the most prevalent type in the twentieth century. Therefore, at the heart of the Commons-cabinet relation is the frequency of intraparty dissent, the question of party cohesion. Again we must realize that what we have grown accustomed to has not always been the case. R. T. McKenzie began his classic study of British parties with Lord Holland's 1830 observation, "Party seems to be no more."[20] By this he meant, as McKenzie notes, that this was "a particularly confused and fluid moment in the history of British politics." Majorities in the House of Commons were ephemeral and shifting.

Assessing the period more precisely many years later, A. L. Lowell defined a party vote as one in which nine-tenths of a party voted on the same side in a division in the Commons. He found that in 1836 opposed party votes occurred on only 23 percent of the divisions.[21] By 1860 this proportion had dropped to what now seems the even more incredible level of 6 percent. Early in the twentieth century, however, parliamentary behavior had become much more "normal" from our perspective: Beer found that party voting had risen to 88 percent for the Liberals in 1906.[22] Furthermore, the coefficient of cohesion rose from about 60 in 1860 to around 90 in 1906.[23]

Explaining what had happened in little more than a third of a century to produce such a striking change in political behavior is one of the principal themes of Beer's prize-winning study of British political values. Beer sees the growth of the socialist view of democracy, a view that required unity in order to represent and defend class interests, as the basis for increased party discipline and cohesion. Breaking with one's party was no longer "the simple task of disassociating yourself from certain other free individuals who, in your opinion, have mistaken the common good. It is rather to break with your class, an objective social fact. . . . The basis of his party allegiance is not so much that he *agrees* as that he *belongs*."[24]

Since Labour still was only a small party in 1906, the growth of this socialist view was not the only relevant political value. Also conducive to party cohesion was the Tory view that order required hierarchy and authority.[25] This Tory view probably applied more fully to relations between political leaders and the electorate than between the cabinet and the Commons. While the Tories hardly favored a weak executive, McKenzie did find that Conservatives have been more likely than Labourites to drive their party leader from power. Thus in parliamentary matters the Tory view would be to allow leaders a free hand, but to monitor their actions and call them to account as necessary. Cohesive parliamentary behavior would be the norm but would not entail acceptance of an irresponsible executive.

Despite this qualification of the Tory view, the basic point remains that party cohesion was derived from and supported by a class-based value system. Failing to appreciate this fully, *The Economist,* like many others, tends to see party cohesion as based primarily on a system of sanctions. MPs are said to be terrorized by party whips. A variety of studies have found little evidence to support this view.

The national party organizations, which in any case are not synonymous with the parliamentary organizations, have only a limited role in candidate selection. What power they do have is rarely used against dissidents and is not very effective when it is exercised.[26] The decision of parliamentary leaders to attempt to impose some sanction on dissident MPs is affected by such factors as direction and frequency of rebellion.[27] Even those who have rebelled toward rather than away from their party's opponents have managed at times to do so with impunity. Furthermore, those MPs who might seem most vulnerable—ones with relatively short service in the Commons and small majorities—are not inhibited from dissent and may be able in fact to ignore the whips more easily.

In perhaps the most comprehensive study of party cohesion, Robert Jackson not only studied the incidence of dissent over a twenty-year period but also interviewed many whips and those who had violated party discipline. Although he found MPs fully aware of the troubles they could bring on themselves by excessive dissent and able to weigh realistically the potential costs of such behavior, he concluded that "rebels and whips . . . agree that there are very few devices for punishing dissidents which can be effective in practice."[28] What keeps MPs loyal? "Generally speaking whips believe that there are no specific means of preventing rebellion other than by the use of persuasion."[29] Given that the pork barrel is an American, not a British, phenomenon, one is inclined to conclude that more effective means of "persuasion" may be available in the United States than in Britain.

Nonetheless, party cohesion is greater in Britain than in the United States. This obvious fact unfortunately has led many to conclude that parliamentary dissent, and certainly cross-voting, is virtually nonexistent in the House of Commons. Philip Norton's catalog of post–World War II rebellions demonstrates how greatly this belief varies from reality. He found MPs of the party in power more likely to vote against their party than were MPs of the party out of power to vote against their party.[30] Since the party controlling the government presumably has more sanctions to employ against dissidents, this finding contrasts sharply with the picture of party tyranny.

During the 1950s and from 1964 to 1966, votes against the government by members of the majority party were extremely rare, occurring in 2 percent or less of all divisions[31] (see Figure 3). Dissent was more frequent during the Labour governments of 1945–50 and 1966–70, as some MPs voted against their own party's government in 6 and 8 percent of all divisions. The Conservative governments of 1959–64 and 1970–74 had even more trouble controlling their followers. Rebellions occurred on 12 and 18 percent of all divisions during these periods.

Since these figures average several years together, they tend to disguise the high points of dissent. During one session of the 1970–74 government, some Conservative MPs voted against their own government on 36 percent of all divisions and in another session did so in 26 percent. By the time the Heath government left office, two-thirds of the Conservative MPs had voted against their own government at least once and about 8 percent— twenty-six MPs—had voted against it ten or more times. This hardly sounds like a group of terrorized sheep.

Labour behavior is similar. Over half—55 percent—of the Labour MPs elected in 1945 voted against their government at least once from 1945 to 1950 and almost a fifth—19 percent—did

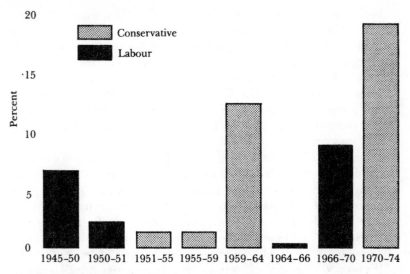

Figure 3. Proportion of all divisions in which some MPs of the governing party cross-voted against their own government

so five times or more.[32] More recently Labour MPs have shown themselves willing to vote against their own government even when its minority status makes it more vulnerable to defeat. It has been alleged that Labour MPs were more willing to wound than to kill, that rebellions were nicely calculated to frighten the government with a near run without actually defeating it. Labour MPs now seem willing to inflict nearly mortal injury. On the February 1978 division in which the government attempted to eliminate the 40 percent requirement for the devolution referendum, some fifty Labour MPs voted against their own government. On the subsequent effort to reduce the percentage, some thirty-seven dissented. The previous month, when the government was seeking to pass a guillotine motion limiting debate on legislation for direct election to the European Parliament, almost half of the 137 MPs that voted against it were Labour.

Examining the actual parliamentary behavior of MPs in some detail is essential because would-be reformers of the British political system must be made to understand that institutional changes are not required to modify political practices and, conversely,

altering institutions by no means guarantees a reform of procedures. The specific reforms proposed by *The Economist* reveal a
touching faith in the utility of legal tinkering. It seems to believe
that one need merely declare something to have been reformed
for reform to occur. After describing how it would reform the
House of Commons, *The Economist* proclaims, "Once in session,
such a legislative parliament would take on much of the power
over the executive, and of authority in the land, enjoyed by
America's congress." Indeed? By fiat?

Were *The Economist* a German publication, this obsession with
institutional reform would be understandable; for a British publication it seems strangely shortsighted. *The Economist* longs for the
golden days of the past when the Commons was effective. Yet in
those days the British system lacked the institutional arrangements that *The Economist* now deems essential to a healthy parliamentary system. The issue is not structure but behavior. Are
MPs now willing, as they were in the past, to cross-vote? If so, the
Commons can check the cabinet effectively; if not, no package of
legal reforms will increase executive responsibility.

The Economist cites as one of the reasons for great party cohesion pressure from constituency parties. This is in keeping with
the findings of both Austin Ranney and Leon Epstein that local
selection of candidates contributes to cohesion because the local
leaders are committed to supporting the national party line and
thus do not need to be persuaded to discipline rebels.[33] While this
was generally true in the past, it is becoming less so. Some evidence from the early 1970s suggests that the power of local parties to disown a sitting member is not so absolute as had been
thought.[34] More important, the power of local selection, especially
in the Labour Party, is beginning to undercut parliamentary
cohesion. MPs are more likely to run afoul of their local parties
for voting as their parliamentary whip instructs them—since this
not infrequently conflicts with what the local activists want—
than for voting against the whip to represent the local party's
policy preferences. Although many factors were involved, the
troubles Reg Prentice, Frank Tomney, and Sir Arthur Irvine, for
example, have experienced with their local parties recently came
about in large part because these MPs were too moderate for the
local activists. Furthermore, the inability or unwillingness of La-

bour's National Executive Committee to defend MPs from their local parties has become increasingly clear. The NEC will deal only with matters of procedure, not of policy preferences. This stance will be even more significant should Labour opt for automatic reselection of sitting MPs, a procedure that has been headed off for the moment but is by no means dead.

Thus, even if MPs were motivated solely by career prospects rather than by principle or the national interest, they would be better advised to defy the whips if necessary to ingratiate themselves with their local parties. In fact, if MPs live in terror of anyone, it is not the whips but the local party leaders. The impact of the power of local selection on parliamentary party cohesion has changed significantly. Writing after the government's 1978 budget defeat, Geoffrey Smith argued in the *Times* that not only has discipline had to be relaxed in both the government and the opposition parties, but local parties are less likely to regard failure to support the government as a crime since defeats do not bring the government down as they did in the past. "So two of the principal restraints upon revolt have been at least weakened if not removed. There is no longer much danger of losing the whip and much less of being disowned for that reason in the constituency."[35]

As our many examples have shown, in recent years MPs have seemed more willing to vote against, even to defeat, their own government. In his introduction to Walter Bagehot's *English Constitution,* Richard Crossman wrote, "There can be very few studies of our parliamentary system that were so rapidly overtaken by events. . . . As an account of contemporary fact, the book was out of date almost before it could be reviewed."[36] Given Bagehot's association with *The Economist,* it seems especially fitting that this comment should apply so well to *The Economist*'s Guy Fawkes critique. The critique denounces a system that rapidly is ceasing to exist. Fundamental political change has outpaced *The Economist.*

I have noted Beer's insight that the basis of cohesion was a system of class values. But what still was an "objective social fact" thirteen years ago, when Beer wrote, is ceasing to be so. A number of studies are beginning to find evidence that the class basis of British politics is dissipating. A residue lingers on, but largely as an emotional attachment to an outgrown myth. David Butler and

Donald Stokes's voting studies plainly show that class voting is declining.[37] Class and education are less important in structuring voting choice than they were in the past; childhood socialization influences the electorate's behavior less than it did. Almost a decade ago 44 percent of those interviewed said that class differences either were "not very wide" or did not exist at all.[38] Butler and Stokes conclude that "the electorate has become progressively less inclined to respond to politics in terms of class . . . the class appeals of the parties themselves have become much more muted."[39]

Other studies have reached similar conclusions.[40] On the other hand, another study—admirably thorough and sophisticated—suggests that to some extent the apparent decline in class voting is an analytical artifact.[41] It argues that class remains an important variable in any effort to explain British voting behavior. Yet even this analysis grants that "there has been an indisputable decline in the ability of class to structure voting choice in Britain" and that the "decline in the predictive power of class is beyond dispute." The major theme of Arthur Cyr's recent interpretation of Liberal Party politics in Britain is the declining dominance of two well-disciplined parties and the growing importance of a political individualism more akin to that which existed in the nineteenth century than to the political collectivism that has thus far characterized the twentieth century.[42]

Changes in electoral behavior are not without significance for cabinet-Commons relations. Nonetheless, when these relations are the issue, the primary concern must be with the political elite. What evidence suggests a decline of class-based politics at that level? That class is less of an objective social fact than it was in the past is obvious from the Nuffield studies. Public school education does continue to be much more important for Conservative than for Labour MPs.[43] Attendance at the most elite public schools, however, has declined among Conservative MPs.[44] In Britain university education is not so dramatic an index of class differences as secondary education. Nonetheless, that Labour and Conservative MPs no longer differ greatly in this regard seems notable.[45]

As for occupational background, the change, though gradual, has been noticeable over the years.[46] The proportion of workers among Labour MPs has declined while the proportion of professional people has risen even more. Professional people have become the most common occupational type in the Conservative Party as well. The chief difference is that the Labour professional tends to be a teacher while the Conservative is a lawyer. Class differences have not been eliminated but are much less sharp than they were in the past. The effect of those that remain upon parliamentary behavior seems likely to be limited to those MPs who continue to believe that striking a man-of-the-people pose offers some political mileage. The rewards for such a pose seem likely to decline as the electorate moves away from class-based political behavior.

Thus, the current objective social facts appear to be moving Britain away from the highly cohesive parliamentary parties that characterized the 1950s and 1960s. Less automatic, more flexible electoral behavior has a greater potential for producing minority governments. Ostensibly, behavior during minority governments establishes no precedents for practice under majority governments. Yet these experiences cannot be erased from the mind. In the last few years MPs have become well acquainted with the previously unthinkable idea that a government can be defeated even on major items of legislation and still remain in power. Only should the defeat occur on a motion of confidence would a government be forced to resign. Speculating on what would happen were the government to be defeated on the 1978 budget, the *Sunday Times* disagreed with its parliamentary authority, Ronald Butt, that the government would have to resign. "That theory no longer holds good. A reverse in a matter of financial management is quite another thing from a defeat on a question of confidence."[47] And after the defeat had occurred the *Times* commented, "There is no constitutional principle that requires a government to regard any specific defeat as evidence that it no longer possesses the necessary confidence of the House of Commons."[48] Such categorical statements of the relation between the government and the Commons would have been very difficult to find even ten years ago.

Offering a convincing reason why only minority governments should be expected to tolerate such defeats is difficult. Of course, what is happening now will not automatically alter constitutional practices. But many people are beginning to think seriously about the implications of current departures from past practice. Geoffrey Smith, for example, observes, "If there is another hung Parliament, then the habits of mind engendered in what now seem exceptional circumstances could become more lasting."[49] Future majority governments may well find that they will have to accept occasional defeats because this is what MPs have become used to. MPs may continue to shout "Resign!" when the results of close votes on legislation are announced, but this will be even more a case of political bantering than it is now.

Thus even should minority governments become no more common than they have been in the twentieth century (which is to say, more common than they were in the 1950s and 1960s), government control over the Commons seems likely to decline from the level it reached during the third quarter of the twentieth century. This certainly is not to say that the Commons will come to exert the power over the Cabinet which the Congress usually does over the president. A fusion-of-powers system, after all, differs basically from a separation-of-powers system. The point—to broaden the comparative context—is that Canada demonstrates that a cohesive British two-party system cannot be linked with a federal system approaching in diversity that of the United States. Britain is not so diverse as Canada, so party fractionalization or discohesion need not proceed as far as it has in either Canada or the United States. Britain is not so politically homogeneous, however, as it was twenty years ago. Thus some movement away from the 1950s British pattern of legislative-executive relations in the direction of the Canadian and American pattern should be expected. In so far as this movement occurs and MPs express more fully the diverse views of various parts of the United Kingdom, proposing a constitutional federal system becomes rather irrelevant, since the country will have moved in that direction in practice.

Although parliamentary party cohesion is a key element in the relation between the Commons and the cabinet, concentrating on cohesion alone presents an incomplete and distorted picture of the Commons' functions. *The Economist* seems almost to suffer from a macho orientation with its great concern over whether the Commons is able to vote things down. It is as though the Commons can display power only by defeating or destroying the government's proposals. *The Economist*'s specific proposals for reform deliberately seek to build conflict into the system, conflict between legislative and executive, conflict between center and region. In almost an aside *The Economist* grants that "the commons [*The Economist* recently has adopted a rather peculiar stype of capitalization in which many governmental institutions, apparently because of their insignificance, no longer require upper case letters] can still stage good clashes between the parties . . . What it can do is to orchestrate the political case for and against such legislation once the proposals have been agreed upon." *The Economist* fails to recognize how essential this function is, nor does it link it with its proposed reform of televising Parliament.

The basic function of the Commons is not so much policy making as it is political communication, political education. This function must be performed well if a democratic system is to be sound; no political institution in Britain is better equipped for this task than the Commons. The complexity of most current political issues means that there are no pure rights and wrongs, only potential benefits and associated costs. The objective of political communication is to clarify for the public the implications of one course of conduct compared to another, to make unpalatable political truths swallowable without sugar coating. Unless this function is performed effectively, the gloomy predictions of such people as Willy Brandt and Peter Jay about the future of democracy may well prove to be true.[50] This is what the House of Commons must be about and it need not be perpetually voting things down to do it well.

Televising Parliament may well be a considerable help to effective performance of the political communication function. Reducing the number of members of the Commons might well make debates more manageable. But this step also would mean increasing the number of constituents per member and might make Parliament seem even more remote to the average person. The political communication function is performed not only on the floor of the Commons but also by personal contact in the local constituency. Essential to the political communication function, whatever the size of the constituency, is adequate office and staff facilities for MPs, a reform overlooked by *The Economist*. Adequacy entails not only Westminster facilities but also full-time staff and an office in each constituency. Saturday-morning surgeries are not enough. Expanded contact with citizens through such enhanced facilities would help to encourage a greater respect for and interest in the Commons. It would ensure that even carpet-baggers had extensive knowledge of local problems and desires. This knowledge in turn would encourage MPs to fight harder for subnational interests even when this involved voting against and perhaps defeating their own government. The ombudsman or welfare worker role need not be confined to making contacts with aloof administrators; it involves legislative policies as well.

Another reform strangely overlooked by *The Economist* is primary elections. One would think that those who believe that MPs are beholden to local extremists and/or national party tyrannies would want to take the candidate selection process out of party hands at whatever level and give it to the electorate. One does not need to believe these things, however, to recommend primary elections as a means of ensuring that MPs are interested in appealing to a broadly based local electorate and representing their views in the Commons. Adopting a system of primary elections would eliminate the concern expressed by many in the Labour Party that reselecting MPs will cause the party to lurch to the left. It also would be a means of moving toward a federal system in practice without instituting it constitutionally; certainly it would be a means of representing more adequately the more politically diverse Britain of the last quarter of the twentieth century.

Over the years Britain has amply proven that the most effective method of political reform is to retain the structures and modify the procedures. And, without embracing Burke entirely, many students of British politics have come to understand that those reforms are most likely to endure that have grown out of developing practices. Extensive institutional reform now is both inadvisable and unnecessary. Political practices and behaviors in Britain are changing in fundamental ways, and only limited additional action is required to support and facilitate these positive trends.

Notes

1. Michael Shanks, *The Stagnant Society* (Harmondsworth: Penguin Books, 1961); John Mander, *Great Britain or Little England?* (London: Secker & Warburg, 1963); Arthur Koestler, ed., *Suicide of a Nation* (London: Secker & Warburg, 1963); The most overtly political book in the

Penguin series was Andrew Hill and Anthony Whichelow, *What's Wrong with Parliament?* (Harmondsworth: Penguin Books, 1964).

2. J. Roland Pennock, "'Responsible Government,' Separated Powers, and Special Interests: Agricultural Subsidies in Britain and America," *American Political Science Review* 56 (September 1962): 621-33.

3. Samuel Beer, *British Politics in the Collectivist Age* (New York: Knopf, 1965).

4. Kenneth Waltz, *Foreign Policy and Democratic Politics: The American and British Experience* (Boston: Little, Brown, 1967), p. 304.

5. "Blowing Up a Tyranny," *The Economist*, November 5, 1977, pp. 11-16.

6. *The Economist*, July 24, 1976, p. 20.

7. Lewis Namier, *The Structure of Politics at the Accession of George III*, 2d ed. (London: Macmillan, 1957), p. 89.

8. Robert Putnam, *The Beliefs of Politicians: Ideology, Conflict, and Democracy in Britain and Italy* (New Haven: Yale University Press, 1973), esp. pp. 31-90.

9. Random sample of 2000 carried out by National Opinion Polls for the Granada TV series "State of the Nation," reported in *The Guardian*, July 23, 1973, p. 15.

10. *Frankfurter Allgemeine Zeitung für Deutschland*, January 24, 1978, as reported in *The German Tribune*, February 12, 1978, p. 5.

11. *Congressional Quarterly Weekly Report*, January 7, 1978, p. 9.

12. Philip Norton, "A Note on the Government Defeat: 10 March 1976," *British Politics Group Newsletter*, no. 4 (Spring 1976), p. 2.

13. David Butler and Michael Pinto-Duschinsky, *The British General Election of 1970* (London: Macmillan, 1971), p. 4.

14. Norton, "Note on the Government Defeat" and *Dissension in the House of Commons: Intra-Party Dissent in the House of Commons' Division Lobbies, 1945-1974* (London: Macmillan, 1975), pp. 440-41, 505-7, 515-17, 523-25, 560, and 582-84.

15. Norton, "Note on the Government Defeat."

16. Philip Norton, "The Guillotine Motion and the Government Defeat: February 22, 1977," *British Politics Group Newsletter*, no. 8 (Spring 1977), p. 13.

17. Ibid.

18. For a fascinating account of how the campaign for this defeat was organized see Edith Cope, "Consultation or Confrontation?: The Campaign to save the Scottish Colleges of Education," in *The Scottish Government Yearbook*, ed. Henry Drucker and Michael Clarke (Edinburgh: Rowman & Littlefield, 1977).

19. Peter Hillmore in *The Guardian*, December 13, 1977, p. 15.

20. R. T. McKenzie, *British Political Parties* (London: Heinemann, 1955), p. 1.

21. A. L. Lowell, "The Influence of Party upon Legislation in England and America" (Washington, D.C., 1902), pp. 326-27, cited in Beer, *British Politics in the Collectivist Age*, p. 50n.

22. Beer, *British Politics in the Collectivist Age*, p. 185.

23. Ibid., p. 257.

24. Ibid., p. 85. For the development of the argument see pp. 69-91.

25. Ibid., pp. 91-102.

26. Austin Ranney, *Pathways to Parliament: Candidate Selection in Britain* (London: Macmillan, 1965), esp. pp. 42-51, 81-90, 154-66, 183-85, 191-93, 272-73, 280-82.

27. Leon Epstein, "British M.P.s and Their Local Parties: The Suez Cases," *American Political Science Review* 54 (June 1960): 374-90, and *British Politics in the Suez Crisis* (London: Pall Mall, 1965), chap. 6; Jorgen Rasmussen, *The Relations of the Profumo Rebels with Their Local Parties* (Tucson: University of Arizona Press, 1966) and "Party Discipline in War-Time: The Downfall of the Chamberlain Government," *Journal of Politics* 32 (May 1970): 379-406.

28. Robert Jackson, *Rebels and Whips: Dissension, Discipline, and Cohesion in British Political Parties since 1945* (London: Macmillan, 1968), p. 200.

29. Ibid., p. 301.

30. Norton, *Dissension in the House of Commons*, p. 609.

31. The figures in this paragraph are calculated from the information in the table on p. 609 of Norton, *Dissension in the House of Commons*. The information in the following paragraph comes from p. 610 of the same book.

32. R. K. Alderman, "Discipline in the Parliamentary Labour Party, 1945-51," *Parliamentary Affairs* 18 (Summer 1965): 294.

33. "In short, the national leaders do not need to control local candidate selection in order to maintain party cohesion in Parliament; the local activists do the job for them" (Ranney, *Pathways to Parliament*, p. 281); "Assuredly the local organizations were not taking action, and probably could not take effective action, against M.P.s who merely disagreed with local leaders while following their national leaders. This is not to deny what is a principal point of the analysis: that association pressure on Suez was partly if not largely self-generated and by no means dependent on orders from the national party. The pressure was *both* self-generated and in line with the national party" (Epstein, *British Politics in the Suez Crisis*, pp. 135-36).

34. Austin Ranney, "Selecting the Candidates," in *Britain at the Polls: The Parliamentary Election of February 1974*, ed. Howard Penniman (Washington, D.C.: American Enterprise Institute, 1974), pp. 54-60.

35. Geoffrey Smith, "The Heyday of the Party Rebel," *Times* (London), May 12, 1978, p. 16. My thanks to Harry Lazer, one of the participants in the Cornell conference, for calling this article to my attention.

36. The Fontana Library edition published by Collins in 1963, p. 1.

37. David Butler and Donald Stokes, *Political Change in Britain*, 2d college ed. (New York: St. Martin's Press, 1976), pp. 122-52 and 273-90.

38. Ibid., p. 140.

39. Ibid., p. 139.

40. For example, Richard Rose, ed., *Electoral Behavior* (New York: Free Press, Macmillan, 1974), pp. 523–33.

41. Mark Franklin and Anthony Mughan, "Decline of Class Voting in Britain: Problems of Analysis and Interpretation," *American Political Science Review,* forthcoming.

42. Arthur Cyr, *Liberal Party Politics in Britain* (New Brunswick, N.J.: Transaction, 1977), esp. pp. 38–41 and 281–96.

43. Seventy-five percent of the Conservatives elected in October 1974 had been educated at a public school, while only 18 percent of the Labour MPs had been (David Butler and Dennis Kavanagh, *The British General Election of October 1974* [London: Macmillan, 1975], pp. 213, 214).

44. In 1964 almost 100 Conservative MPs, 32 percent of the parliamentary party, had been educated at Eton, Harrow, or Winchester, while 10 years later the number had dropped to 65, which was less than a quarter of the party (ibid., p. 213).

45. The October 1974 election returned only eight more university-educated Conservative MPs than Labour MPs; the proportions of such members in the two parliamentary parties were 69 and 57 percent, respectively) (ibid., p. 214).

46. In 1951 well over a third of all Labour MPs were workers, while not quite a quarter of a century later only somewhat more than a quarter were. The proportion of professional people among Labour MPs rose from 35 percent in 1951 to 50 percent in 1974. At the later time 46 percent of the Conservative MPs were professional people (ibid., pp. 214–16).

47. *Sunday Times* (London), April 30, 1978, p. 16.

48. *Times* (London), May 10, 1978, p. 17.

49. Smith, "Heyday of the Party Rebel." See also *Sunday Times* (London), April 30, 1978, p. 16.

50. Peter Jay, "Englanditis," in *The Future That Doesn't Work: Social Democracy's Failure in Britain*, ed. R. Emmett Tyrrell, Jr. (Garden City, N.Y.: Doubleday, 1977), pp. 167–85.

8 | *Women and Equality in Britain*

BARBARA CASTLE

My discussion of women in British life will deal with two dimensions of the issue. There is first the role that women play in politics—in the parties, trade unions, and Parliament. Here I shall draw heavily from my own experience. The second involves questions of public policy. What legislative and social reforms with respect to women are occurring in Britain today? How is the status of women in the broader social context evolving? Here I shall describe in detail some recent parliamentary legislation. What we shall find is by no means discouraging. Change is in the air, but we must keep at it. To my first concern, then.

Women in Political Life

Britain has a reputation for having pioneered women's rights, a reputation that somehow rather curiously sticks with us. There was, indeed, a marvelous beginning with the suffragists, women who in the nineteenth century struggled against sweated labor and appalling conditions for women workers. They fought the battle for civil rights for women generally. I think that today women in Britain have probably gone further than in any other country in the holding of top responsibility. We now have, for example, a woman as leader of the Conservative Party, which is epoch-making judging from their historical position on the issue of women's rights. But her position does mark the change in attitude that has taken place in Britain toward the acceptance of women in positions of top responsibility.

126

Yet there is a serious vacuum below the one or two high flyers, such as Margaret Thatcher. There is a glaring underrepresentation of women in positions of leadership in Britain's political life today. Of the 635 members of the British House of Commons, only 27 are women. Eighteen of those 27 are Labour, 2 are Scottish Nationalists, and 7 are Tory. In the trade union movement also there is a scandalous lack of inclination to give women anything like the representation that their numbers in trade unions would otherwise dictate. The Trades Union Congress, for example, has managed to come up with only thirty full-time women organizers. Even more shocking is the sight of only 60 women among the 1000 delegates at the TUC annual conference. This is all in a nation where it is the rule rather than the exception for women to go out and work.

This underrepresentation of women exists also in industry. Once as secretary of state for employment and productivity I had the unusual pleasure of being asked to address the Institute of Directors at their annual conference. These were the top boys of British industry. It was apparently a daring move, as I was the first woman to address them in their history. What I also discovered was that of 36,000 members of the Institute of Directors, only 900 were women. This is another example of how far we have to go in improving the role of women in our political, industrial, and public life in Britain.

Why haven't women made more headway in British public life? The answer lies to some extent in women's own attitude. They don't yet instinctively feel "the world's my oyster." For those who do, nothing can stop them. Much more important, however, is that society has not yet organized services to enable women to combine happily and fruitfully marriage, home, and a career. Society still makes it very difficult for women to have both. I never had any doubt that I was going to be a member of Parliament. Who was going to stop me? Men have managed to retain power in the past by telling women—as they used to tell me when I was a young woman pining to get into politics—that they ought to be in the House of Commons, but women just won't vote for women. Quite to the contrary, in fact, it is the women who are rooting for women in public life. I represent an industrial constituency in the north of England in which married women normally go out to work because the family needs a two-wage income. These women want a woman representing them and they like to see more women entering political life. Nothing can justify that women, the larger section of voters, have got 5 percent representation in the House of Commons.

There have been some attempts to correct this imbalance in representation. Some of these solutions raise the issue of "affirmative action." "Affirmative action" or discrimination on women's behalf will require men to realize that women exist. As an example of useful positive discrimination, it would be obligatory in the Labour Party for a woman to be on every selection list. She will still have significant prejudice to overcome, but at least she will be getting a hearing. We might even combat this imbalance in representation by having a double vote in every constituency, one man and woman as MP in each.

One particular form representation of women has taken in the history of the Labour Party is less clearly helpful in raising the status of women. Under the Labour Party's constitution, the National Executive is made up of three parts: one, the largest, is elected by trade unions; another is elected by the local Labour Party; and another is a women's section, which is elected by both the rank and file and the trade unions. The women's section has been traditional. It comes out of the early battles of women to get any kind of recognition in the Labour Party at all. When the Labour Party's Labour Representation Committee was formed in 1900, and Ramsay MacDonald was leader of the Labour Party, there wasn't a single woman delegate. And it wasn't until women got together and formed the Women's Labour League that any of the men in the Labour Party became aware of the political existence of women. Unfortunately this form of representation raises the issue of separate and unequal. Given a special little niche of their own, women are not going to enter the mainstream of political activity. A women's section of a political party represents that particular danger.

While there are certainly too few women in public life in Britain, when they do enter political life, women have significant influence. Women who reach positions high in political life in Britain seem to be accorded more esteem, status, and recognition than women in American political life, for instance, perhaps because in Britain politics is a prestigious business. To be a member of Parliament is to occupy an honored position. To be a member of a cabinet is, in most people's minds, an apotheosis.

If too few women have shared in this apotheosis, or have entered business, engineering, or professional occupations, more than their own attitude has impeded them. To get more women into these strata and to make it possible for them to come forward, we need to create the kind of conditions that make it possible to combine careers. Support services for women are woefully lacking in Britain because cuts in public expenditures have undermined, for example, our policy supporting the expansion of day nurseries and the provision of trained and registered child minders. Considering the lack of support services, it is a miracle that so many women do work and manage to combine any kind of public life with the home.

Working-class women in particular are affected by this lack of services and prevented from being more active in public life. The mass of working-class women cannot ever combine a job and the home unless there is a day nursery for their children, a tax system allowing them to charge their child-minding bill to taxable expense, a better provision for maternity. When these women do become active in politics, they are often active at the local levels, raising the issues of the needs of women. The only steps toward instituting these reforms in Britain were taken by working women getting into political life themselves. Politics has been the key to their own emancipation, not only through the vote but through the extension of all these public services, such as the provision of school meals and pithead baths, for example. These services have lightened the working woman's burdens so she can be more than an absolute drudge. The increasing number of women in politics and the expansion of these support services are linked to each other. The former depends on giving political priority to the latter.

One example of dramatic change brought on by women in politics can be drawn from recent history in the House of Commons. It is a political reality that if a woman is going to reach the top in politics, she has to enter the House of Commons at a reasonably early age, what would still be childbearing age for most women. We have got a new young intake on the Labour side, particularly in the House of Commons, young women of childbearing age, in whom we see great promise. One of them had a baby only a year ago, and it caused enormous excitement in the House because we were then a majority of three. Every vote could be crucial. The great question was whether this baby would arrive on the same night as a three-line whip, in which case the government might have fallen. The whips would do all the necessary calculation about when the baby was expected, and try to keep the vote, as much as they could control it, off the danger point. Nothing, of course, can stop the opposition from putting a motion of censure on the government, and if a party is defeated on that it has to resign.

Never before in the House of Commons had a woman expecting a baby walked through the division lobby night after night, sometimes until two in the morning. The whips sent her home when they could, but when a party's back is to the wall with a small majority, every soldier has to be on the battlefield. She timed the birth beautifully, just avoiding missing a crucial vote. Within days of the birth she was back with a nurse, making do without a creche or appropriate facilities in the House of Commons for feeding a baby. We lady members put at her disposal a small retiring room that we have, and she arranged to have the nurse watch the baby there, dashing in between divisions, feeding the baby, dashing out again. She managed and she coped. In fact, we were so touched we got a whip around and we bought her a pewter goblet, engraving on the back "To the baby who saved the day, from the Labour women MP's." These are literally the kinds of condition in which women have to try to build a career. Now this woman has changed history. It will soon be as natural as daylight for pregnant women to be members of the House of Commons. One can't imagine why motherhood and politics should not be combined naturally if the proper facilities are provided.

Although attitudes are changing gradually, even in the House of Commons, traditions, particularly those that make the atmosphere there male, linger on. The House, although it is much less class-bound than it was, is still overwhelmingly monastic. Although the men are courtly and cordial to the women who do make it, the House is epitomized by a sort of clubby male atmosphere in which all the men on the front row, where the leaders are, sit with their feet up on the table in the center, a posture that, as one visitor observed to me, women can scarcely adopt.

Legislation and Public Policy

As for the particular legislative reforms that will assist women to find their political independence, one must ask of each what it can do. One of the reforms that I have carried through is the family allowance plan, the cash payment to the mother based on the number of her children. This particular reform is, I think, quite revolutionary because it recognizes the beginning of the wage for the mother. Britain has had a family allowance, although a modest one, ever since 1945, part of the great national insurance reform of the time. In addition to the family allowance, however, the husband was entitled to tax relief for his children. The husband would realize a higher weekly salary with increased deductions. Our reform was to combine the man's tax relief with the cash payment into one large cash payment and pay it to the mother. This reform meant necessarily a reduction in the man's take-home pay in favor of the wife's benefits—quite a reversal of the usual societal assumptions about who should control the family's money. Instead, this mother's wage recognizes that she is the one who is going to feed the family. The working man often won't tell his wife what he earns, and she has no right to any proportion of his salary even though she pays the food bills and manages most of the family budgeting. She depends entirely on his will. If his wage goes up, it is up to him to give her more money. This reform, however, ensures that she will have a steady income coming in the middle of the week, just when the money's running low, to help buy the food. This reform also gives her a certain amount of independence, which in itself creates a climate of self-reliance. The child-benefits move was strikingly unpopular with many Labour men MPs, however. Their attitude was that a man's wage is his own affair, as is what he decides to give to his wife.

Attitudes such as these which don't recognize a woman's right to control money her work at home has earned and has entitled her to make women think in terms of dependence on men, a dependency they are conditioned by the whole of society to accept. Legislation can help to weaken this dependency. I have worked closely with two of the three acts of Parliament we have carried through to promote equality for women. The first was the Equal Pay Act, which as secretary of state for employment I carried through in 1970 and which came into full operation in 1975. Women's organizations said of the act, and rightly, that the right to equal pay must be supported by an act outlawing discrimination against women in such areas as education, training, and promotion. In response, Roy Jenkins, as home secretary, put the Sex Discrimination Act on the statute books.

The Sex Discrimination Act provides for the setting up of an equal opportunities commission with a woman chairman and a woman vice-chairman. The thirteen part-time commissioners are drawn from the trade unions, from industry, from the academic world, and from women's organizations. When they feel discrimination is taking place, as in the field of employment, promotion, and so on, these commissioners carry out investigations. If they find discrimination is taking place, they can issue an antidiscrimination order, which is enforceable. A woman can also bring her own claims of discrimination before an informal local industrial tribunal, in certain fields, representing both sides of industry under an independent chairman. It is possible, however, that the commission is not operating as effectively as it could be. Women in Britain have said that not enough of these investigations are being carried out, that there's not been a single antidiscrimination order, and that there is no legal obligation in our legislation to institute affirmative action. If it is clear, for example, that an equally qualified woman is being passed over in favor of a man in a university, English law does not extend as far as American legislation to protect her interests.

The issue of protective legislation for women and equal rights, in light of this issue of discrimination, is an interesting one. I interpret women's rights in terms of the whole of society. I don't interpret them in a narrow sense of an equation of rights between men and women, which is too rigid an idea. But if it is in the interests of society for women to refrain from certain work, such as heavy coal mining, that is not a reason for denying women equal pay. It is in the interests of the whole of society, if a woman has a childbearing function, to protect this capacity from the work

that would endanger it. It is important to emphasize I don't necessarily equate physical feebleness with women, but there might be
certain situations in which it is better for the family as a whole that
a woman should have certain protection. For example, she might
be protected from being forced to do night work—although it is
actually men, not women, who did not want women to do night
work in the past, partly because night workers got a higher rate,
which the men wanted for themselves, and because the men
wanted the women at home when they came back there. One of
the protections still retained in my equal-pay legislation was to
provide maternity leave for women without the threat of their
losing their jobs or receiving lower pay. Protective legislation must
be judged on its merits by the women through their trade union
organization.

A third important act reinforcing women's equality came into
operation in April 1978, a new pension act, which as secretary of
state for the social services I put on the statute books in 1975. This
act not only gives women equality of treatment in pension rights
in Britain but actually gives them preferential treatment in such a
way that the needs of the whole society are being taken into
consideration.

Our Conservative predecessors introduced a pensions bill that
they almost got on the statute books, in which they would give
women a lower pension than a man's in spite of their having made
the same contribution out of their salary. Their reasoning was
that women should receive a lower pension because women committed two crimes: one was that they lived longer, the second was
that they retired earlier. One could argue that if a woman draws
her pension earlier than a man, she should get a lower pension.
But how can we penalize the sex for living longer than men? My
legislation, on the other hand, goes a little in the opposite direction, providing that a woman who contributes the same percentage of her wage will receive the same percentage of her earnings
as the man would, except that she will get it five years earlier than
he. There was opposition to this provision. Men argued that if
men retire at sixty-five, at which age they are urged to retire, and
not before, a certain lack of equity exists if women, retiring earlier, receive the same pension. Actually my response to this is a
social one. It would have been wrong to put the retirement age at

sixty-five for women who have been working and contributing all their lives on the assumption that they would retire at sixty. Nor could we financially afford to bring the man's retirement age down to sixty. Gradually over time we will work toward a common retirement, perhaps a flexible retirement age for both sexes between sixty and sixty-five. But in the meantime, women cannot live in an impoverished old age because they retired earlier than men.

One aspect of our new pension scheme works to help a married woman working outside the home to obtain some measure of financial independence she didn't have before, although I had been warned that this new provision might prove unpopular at first. Under the pension scheme, married women going out to work used to have the right to opt out of paying the full national insurance. They could pay a very small amount that would cover themselves for industrial injury and depend on their husbands' insurance for their pensions. Of course, they saved money immediately in their wage packet, but when they retired, which they of course did earlier than their husbands, there was no compensating pension until the husband retired. Under our new scheme, we've given women equal rights but equal responsibility by phasing the married women's option out. We chose to phase the option out rather than abruptly end it so as not to alter what some women have become used to, but anybody new coming into employment has got to pay the full contribution. They'll then have a pension in their own right as an individual, not as an appendage to the husband or a second part of a marriage.

In addition, our new pension scheme not only greatly improves the widow's benefit but also introduces a widower's benefit. If marriage is a partnership and both have gone out to work and the husband has had to forgo the convenience and comfort of his wife's presence every time he came home, it is only right that if she predeceases him he should enjoy the benefits of her contributions, just as she enjoys the benefits of his. As a member of Parliament, I am outraged that while I have had equal pay with my male colleagues and contributed similarly to a pension scheme for thirty-three years, if I predecease my husband he receives no automatic entitlement to what I have been taking out of the family, although when my male colleagues die, their widows will inherit. My husband would have to prove that he was incapable of self-support before he got a penny. Payment for the widow and a means test for the widower? The widower's benefit will correct his inequity.

There is one final arena where policies affecting working in public life are undergoing change: the schools. There is in Britain a new drive in the direction of encouraging girls at school to look beyond some of the traditional careers they've always sought. Secretary of State for Education Shirley Williams has been encouraging schools to offer a much better range of opportunities for girls in schools, and also in training and apprenticeships. Of the children who leave school at sixteen and don't go on to any kind of further education, nearly half the boys and less than a tenth of the girls go on to apprenticeships. And when the girls do go on to apprenticeships, they usually are in catering or hairdressing. We're trying to alter this imbalance; because we're desperately short of skilled engineers, we're trying to encourage girls to take up engineering. Recently I was going around the factory in my constituency and met a group of skilled women engineers working on quite sophisticated machinery. I asked them if they enjoyed their work. They enthusiastically replied in the affirmative and added they also loved the salary they were receiving. Again we are reminded that work that is seen as traditionally male is also often more highly paid.

The educational system is also partly responsible for the traditions that pertain to class as well as to sex. These attitudes die hard. But inequalities based on class must be redressed before we will fully solve the inequalities based on sex. The channel to all the highly paid, prestigious jobs in Britain is through the school, from the private school up to the university. As far as these high-status jobs are concerned, it has long been recognized that it is who you are rather than what you know that will give you access to them. The labor movement is committed to change that privileged connection. The Labour Party and the Labour Government promote comprehensive education and try to weaken the grip of selective education and prestigious fee-paying schools on the handles of the doors to power in Britain. We are working to strengthen the idea of a school that breaks down the social barriers and snobbism that have been a curse in Britain.

Change is slow. I don't pretend there's any one answer to the social and economic questions raised by the quest of women for full public and political representation. But I do agree that providing the necessary conditions through legislation and improving our schools are ways to make changes. I dedicate my life to inciting women to believe in themselves and to make these changes.

9 | *The Americanization of British Politics*

IRA KATZNELSON

I

If intellectual fashions are to be our guide, Britain is in a fundamental economic crisis. It must be difficult for readers of *The Public Interest,* the *Wall Street Journal,* or even *The Economist* to think of Britain other than as the scene of a morality play teaching the perils of social democracy. Conveniently ignoring Scandinavia, the new wisdom on the right uses the British example to demonstrate the ineluctable connections between state interference in the market and economic stagnation and decline. Nor is it easy for followers of the much more theoretically rewarding debates conducted in neo-Ricardian and Marxist terms to think of the current situation other than in terms of the contradictions of advanced capitalism.

This economic crisis, caused by either too much democracy or too much capitalism, curiously mocks so much scholarship of the recent past which had a rather different emphasis. More than any other capitalist democracy, Britain was understood by admirers as the paragon of democratic stability. Mainstream social science, codified in virtually every major textbook on British politics published in the 1960s and early 1970s, venerated the British experience for having "solved" (presumably once and for all) the main problems associated with the simultaneous reproduction of capitalism and liberal democracy. Especially in the United States, as Dennis Kavanaugh has shown, a "science of British politics" sought to draw appropriate lessons for America from Britain's balanced formula of "gradualism, stability, consensus, deference, and *élitism.*" The British system at the time of the American tumult of the 1960s seemed "to blend liberal and conservative values in its institutions and provide safeguards against populism by virtue of the character and culture of its élites."[1] Corresponding discourse on the left did not so much break with the description mainstream social science provided of the British polity as focus on the countertheoretical reformism of the working class. The most important explanations usually developed one variant or another of a theory of the labor aristocracy.

Right, left, and center, intellectual discourse was dominated by attention to the related issues of class formation and links between the state and the working class, themes that have been obscured by more recent treatments of the crisis of British capitalism. Yet these are precisely the issues that must be brought again to the fore if we are to understand the current situation and possibilities ahead. For in fact the economic situation in Britain today hardly constitutes a crisis in the medical sense, which connotes the indeterminacy of life and death for an individual, and thus of basic social, economic, and political structures in a social formation. British capital has performed poorly, to be sure. Growth has been relatively slow (compared to that of the Germans, French, and Scandinavians, but not of the North Americans), stagflation persistent, unemployment high, and investment low. Yet it would be folly to think that British capitalism has exhausted its possibilities. Further, although the share of national income commanded by capital has fallen in the postwar decades as a result of militant working-class activity, no class-conscious proletariat in Lukács' (not in the looser) sense of the term exists, nor is a mass movement for socialism, as opposed to social democracy, on the horizon. Only a very gifted seer would hazard the prediction that the inherently tension-ridden joining of a liberal democratic polity based on mass suffrage to a staunchly capitalist economy modified by a social democratic program will not persist for quite a long time to come.

The current condition, in short, does not constitute a crisis in the core relations of British capitalist democracy. Rather, I argue, there is a weaker but significant crisis of indeterminacy in what

Gramsci called the "trenches" of society that protect this core. There is today a more fluid and fragmented politics of class than has existed for nearly a decade and a half. The coexistence of a very strong and global understanding of class by workers with a gradualist political formula has been called into question, not by the imminent possibility of revolutionary change but by what I metaphorically call the Americanization of British politics.

II

With the publication of landmark works by Marx and Bagehot in 1867, Britain moved to the very center of intellectual debate about the contradictory impulses of capitalism and democracy and the prospects for their stable simultaneous existence. Both Marx and Bagehot shared an understanding of the tenuous character of this relationship. Marx, impressed above all by the relative purity of capitalist development in Britain and by the starkness of its class structure, concluded in 1867 that "the process of social disintegration is palpable." Bagehot, by contrast, argued that capitalism could be made stable with an apposite mix of values, institutions, and mystifications.[2] Subsequent events appeared to confirm Bagehot, not Marx. Class struggles, with one partial exception, have been directed into entirely constitutional pursuits. What Hobsbawm calls "high classness"—a keen sense that society is structured in all its dimensions along class lines—has proved to be compatible with a very high degree of regime stability.

Some analysts explained this outcome by stressing Britain's unusual political culture. A well-known study of value systems and democracy in five nations praised what it described as Britain's delicate, well-balanced psychological orientations and political attitudes this way:

> What emerged was a third culture, neither traditional nor modern, but partaking of both; a pluralistic culture based on communication and persuasion, a culture of consensus and diversity, a culture that permitted change, but moderated it. This was the civic culture. With this civic culture already consolidated, the working classes could enter politics and, in a process of trial and error, find the language in which to couch their demands and the means to make them

effective. It was in this culture of diversity and consensualism, rationalism and traditionalism, that the structure of British democracy could develop.[3]

This portrait, which echoes a Whiggish conventional wisdom, was taken up by the majority of observers to explain the transition from the patterns of political institutionalization portrayed by Bagehot to those of the twentieth century. The political crisis of the early years of the century, when the country faced substantial labor unrest and class cleavages appeared to threaten the transformation of the polity and economy, was overcome, in this view, when, to paraphrase George Woodcock, the labor movement moved out of Trafalgar Square into the committee rooms. The parliamentary Labour Party was absorbed into the regular political system as it assimilated traditional political attitudes and broadened its class base. The unions similarly developed into a "rational" interest that could be tolerated, consulted, and conciliated. This labor movement of party and trade unions provided the key element of linkage between the working class and the state, which made possible a stable, coherent, and manageable politics of class.

Two views, not mutually exclusive, were presented to account for this result. The first, associated mainly with students of modernization and political development, but also taken up in modified form by Perry Anderson and other Marxists, stressed macro-historical considerations. The sequence of crisis resolution in the British past had taken a special path that cleared the deck for the patterns of class relations fashioned in the nineteenth and twentieth centuries. National unity, Otto Kirchheimer wrote in his analysis of the "pristine beauty" of the British case,

> brought about in the sixteenth century consolidation of the establishment, followed by a seventeenth century constitutional and social settlement allowing for the osmosis between aristocracy and bourgeoisie. The settlement happened early enough to weather the horrors and concomitant political assaults of early nineteenth century industrialism. The fairly smooth gradual incorporation of the working classes was accomplished late enough so that the unnerving cleavage between the political promise and the social effectiveness of democracy lasted only a couple of MacDonald-Baldwin decades...

The impact of constitutionalism slowly unfolds in the eighteenth century, then follows the acceleration of middle class and the beginnings of working class integration during the nineteenth century . . .[4]

The second explanation, taken at a more micro level, has been the theory of a labor aristocracy. This relatively privileged stratum of the working class—more skilled, better paid, benefiting from the bounty of imperialism, more likely to be in leadership positions (precise definitions of the group vary from theorist to theorist)—has been incorporated into the regime in ways that deflect the dispositional potential of the working class to be a militant, revolutionary proletariat.

These traditions of explanation are at best only partially satisfactory. Both avoid crucial issues of working-class culture and class-state relations, and both sidestep treatment of the period of early class formation I consider critical. Further, the macro and micro traditions make greater causal claims than the most sympathetic readings of their interpretations allow.

The past, of course, limits and conditions the present and the future. But the tradition represented by Kirchheimer goes further, in imputing a happy teleological trajectory to the British experience. The "smooth incorporation" of which Kirchheimer writes would not have been recognizable to participants or witnesses of nineteenth-century working-class movements. On the eve of the first reform bill, England was rocked by the Captain Swing riots in the countryside, the mass pressures of industrial workers in the manufacturing areas of the Midlands and the North and West, and by the interclass movement, based in the cities and suburbs, for political reform. One need not wholly share E. P. Thompson's judgment that in 1832 as in 1819, the year of Peterloo, "a revolution was possible" because "the government was isolated and there were sharp differences within the ruling class"[5] to recognize that the issue of reform or revolution was hardly settled in 1688.

Not that the regime problems solved before the early nineteenth century did not have an important conditioning effect on the pattern of early working-class formation. For the resolution of questions of national integration, church-state ties, and peasant-landlord relations excluded these issues from the nineteenth-century agenda, opening the way for class relations to occupy center stage. The past informed the context for the making of the working class in other ways as well. The landed dominant classes provided the key link in the eighteenth century between capitalist development and parliamentary institutions and traditions. This class emerged after 1688 to control Parliament and build the nation-state; Britain was *their* state in the early nineteenth century. J. H. Plumb rightly stresses their sense of possession and the "naturalness" of their rule.[6] The long eighteenth century of their governance has been seen as a period of political stability. Yet this stability, married to a social order governed by an elaborate code of paternalism, coexisted with, or rather overlay, major structural change in the economy and in the life of the peasantry, which disappeared as a major social force. This juxtaposition made for a society characterized by what Thompson recently has called "class struggle without class," a world of resistance and rebellion with a moral economy of its own.[7] Together with artisan traditions of independence this agrarian inheritance fashioned a series of resources for the new working class.

The state was integrated in the eighteenth century by patronage. In a period of rapid growth of government in the mercantile ministries of the Treasury and Foreign Office, the central issues of politics were concerned with the possession of office rather than the structure of the regime or patterns of class relations. Politics was a politics of intraclass competition, within a class widening its membership, becoming more variegated in its functions, and thus potentially rent by more and more divisions and conflicts. Questions of class and the regime were politicized in the nineteenth century within the framework provided by this inheritance, but by no means was the outcome determined in a narrow or rigid sense in advance.

The micro-level labor-aristocracy explanation accepts the contingency of nineteenth-century developments. But apart from problems of identifying the aristocrats with precision, some logical problems have been noted by H. F. Moorhouse. If, as he rightly suggests we should, we take the precise value and institutional elements of working-class culture to be the main problem, then "it is difficult *a priori* to accept the special significance of any aristocratic group within it." And if at issue is the role of working-class leaders in the unions, local organizations, and the Labour Party, then it is imperative that we divorce the analytically separate issues of professionalized leadership from questions of a labor aristocracy into which they are often collapsed. The search for the roots of reformism in the working class, he proposes, should point to no particular stratum but to "the much wider and infinitely more difficult question of the development, negotiation, and constant renegotiation of culture, of the myriad processes of social control, and so on."[8]

Implicit in this suggestion is the understanding of class as a historical category, conditioned, to be sure, by the inheritance of the past and by structural imperatives of production and the regime, but subject to historically specific experiences of class formation which of necessity do not follow preconceived sociological blueprints. The central issue in the analysis of class relations in various capitalist societies is understanding whether and how class exists at the cultural level of dispositions.[9] These questions cannot be skirted by recourse to historical teleology or to such preconceived theoretical notions as that of a labour aristocracy. Nor is the kind of analysis of political culture provided by Gabriel Almond and Sidney Verba a meaningful substitute. Individual responses to survey questions aggregated together are not the same as a culture, understood as a collective way of life and thought; neither is it sensible to read back into the past attitudes recorded in the present.

III

The British working-class experience is contrasted most often with a too simple but serviceable portrait of a "Continental pattern" of class relations. In this comparative universe it is the reformism of the British working class that demands explanation. The macro and micro analyses discussed above claim to explain this special outcome. This traditional problematic, however, overstates the peculiarities of the British. More striking than the differences with the Continent in this respect are the similarities: nowhere in the West has a revolutionary proletariat or situation emerged. All workers in all the capitalist democracies share broadly a history of political and social incorporation on reformist terms, in spite of important differences in party and trade union histories, regime formations, and ideological understandings.

A comparison with the United States, however, raises other questions. For in the United States, too, workers have eschewed class struggle outside of a gradualist, constitutional framework. But the U.S. and British variants of working-class reformism differ widely, and the differences, crucial to an understanding of the current political crisis in Britain, are bound up with the relations of workplace and residence community.

The newly emerging working classes of Western Europe and the United States in the nineteenth century had to come to terms with a type of massive social upheaval for which no precedent existed. Among the most significant changes was the separation, in space and by role, of the workplace from the residence community. Working-class responses to this new situation in their formative period everywhere in the West established patterns that account to a considerable extent for their subsequent development. A comparison of common features and variations in the situations faced by working classes at this time, as well as common features and variations in their responses to these situations, therefore provides a focus for penetrating questions of what is distinctive about national class cultures and the ties of workers to the state.

As a consequence of the separation in space and by role, two new kinds of links were fashioned between the subordinate and dominant classes: those between capital and labor at work and those between the state and workers as citizens in the communities where they lived. The vocabularies and institutions that workers fashioned to understand and manage these links shaped the features of class relations in Western Europe and the United States for subsequent generations. By the end of this period, each society had developed a political class culture that mediated between the new industrial political economy and citizens' dispositions. These political cultures that made sense of the separation of work and community were not simply automatic results of past regime developments, nor were they the exclusive preserve of one group or another within the working class. Rather they defined the broad limits of common sense in each society experiencing capitalist industrialization.

In the period preceding rapid industrialization, capitalism's merchant-dominated development was sustained by patterns of social control that depended on the very close relations of the classes, which bound the worker into the cultural group of the employer not only in the market but in production and living space. This pattern could not survive the spatial dynamics of industrial capitalism, of which the separation of work and residence was an integral part.

Everywhere in the West, when confronted with these new challenges, the state responded in pursuit of order in unprecedented ways. Although not identical from place to place, they did always have three constituent elements: an attempt to regulate, and often proscribe, combinations of workers at the point of production; the use of the franchise to regulate the political rights of workers to secure social cohesion; and the development of a new nexus of political relationships of representation and service delivery that linked residence communities to government.

Collectively, these responses by the state replaced traditional "private" forms of social control with public authoritative activity. One consequence was the displacement of much of the emerging dynamics of conflict between capital and labor onto relations of state and citizen. The ways in which this displacement occurred, the ways workers came to think and talk about these spheres of collective activity and of their interrelationship, and the nature of the institutions they fashioned—unions, parties, churches, voluntary associations—came to define distinctive national patterns of class association and conflict.

At this level of analysis critical differences between the U.S. and British experiences of class formation in the first industrial revolution become apparent. In the United States, by the outbreak of the Civil War, an "exceptional" pattern of class relations had been established in comparison not only with that of Britain but with those of other Western societies. The connections between conflicts at work and conflicts in residence communities became increasingly tenuous. Each dimension of social life came to have its own distinctive idiom and set of institutions: community groups and local parties, churches, and secondary associations; work class and trade unions. In the former set of relations, ethnic and racial markers came to define the units of political action more than those of class. Outside of the workplace pluralism flourished. But at the workplace, the working class became "labor." "Class" conflicts came to be comprehended as workplace conflicts; and unions—not political parties—were the appropriate vehicles for organizing workers as labor. In this formative period, in short, class came to be lived and fought as a series of *partial* relationships, and was experienced and articulated as only one of a number of competing bases of social life.

By the time of the Chartist movement in the 1830s a recognizably modern working class had been "made" rather differently in Britain. Class came to be lived, understood, and fought not as a series of partial relationships but in terms that connected politics, economics, and society. The exclusionary franchise and statutory attempts to control workplace combinations had pressed economic and political demands together and forced the dynamics of work grievances onto the terrain of the new class-homogeneous neighborhoods of industrial cities. The class political culture that was developed used an inherited radical Jacobin ideology to fashion a coherent, presocialist interpretation of class that comprehended the new society as divided along a single class cleavage at work, in politics, and in community life.

In short, by the end of the first major formative period of modern class relations, working-class dispositions and images of society, fashioned in response to very similar objective circumstances in Britain and the United States, differed in the two societies with respect to understandings of the relations of work and community. Many of the subsequent differences in the ordinary politics of the two societies and in the character of their reformist, distributive politics may be traced to this initial divergence. The institutionalized class-based party competition in Britain in the twentieth century, however mild its terms and conduct, has depended on a *global* rhetoric and analysis of class, and on the joining together of workers' concerns where they labor and where they live. In the United States, by contrast, the linguistic, cultural, and institutional meanings given to the differentiation of work, community, and state relationships have continued to take a serial character. The political separation of workplace and community relations—with the party system based on the latter—has thus defined for nearly a century and a half the "exceptional" pattern of the politics of class in the United States.

Somewhat paradoxically, it might be said that the American pattern, so long discussed in terms of "American exceptionalism," might in fact be the more "natural," at least in situations of juridical permissiveness. For where the law permits autonomous organization by workers at work and in their communities, the phenomenal separation of these worlds is likely to be mirrored in ideology and practice. The British pattern is thus largely the result of early nineteenth-century state policies of repression and exclusion which made the residence community the sole possible locus of class development. When at last, in the first two decades of the twentieth century, the juridical restraints on the workers' franchise and trade union organizations were eliminated, a coherent labor movement was in place to continue the by now traditional global traditions of class. It was this movement, of course, that had the capacity to institutionalize the class division in the reformist fashion so admiringly chronicled by students of "democratic stability."

IV

In the years since the Second World War—or, one might say, in the years since the Attlee government brought the modern British welfare state into being, thus exhausting Labour's program for creating a more egalitarian, socialist society—this pattern of a single working class joined to the state through the single linkage of the labor movement has been so eroded that today the British political scene has come more and more to resemble some features of American practice. Consider the following changes in British politics and society.

Under the impact of massive urban redevelopment, geographical mobility, and the standards of the national media, traditional working-class communities that were the key units of political life and which had combined a marked sense of political grievance with socially and politically conservative values have largely disappeared. The structurally rooted grievances remain, but the insular value constraints that misleadingly have been called "deference" have been replaced by more instrumental values. J. H. Westergaard remarked over a decade ago on the implications of this development:

> The character of individual classes as 'quasi-communities', as partially separate sub-cultures each with its own fairly distinctive set of norms, standards, and aspirations, will be loosening. Parochial tradition-bound ceilings on hopes and demands in the various strata and groups of the working class will be in process of replacement by a common 'middle class' yardstick of material achievement . . . while the common 'middle class' yardstick is continually being raised, the levels of material achievement which it prescribes are perpetually, and by definition, beyond the reach of the bulk of the population. The persistent economic inequalities thus guarantee built-in tension between goals and the objective possibilities of achieving them.[10]

This shift to a more instrumental and less communal politics of class does not, as John Goldthorpe and his colleagues have shown, produce less collective modes of political conflict; on the contrary, instrumental aspirations require collective activity at work and in interaction with the state to maximize individual and family income.[11] But as the impulse to act collectively has grown, the disciplining capacity of the labor movement has declined. Basic changes in the Labour Party have been masked by its continuing electoral viability. From ward to cabinet the Labour Party, aside from its contentious trade union base, is not really a working-class party but rather more resembles the middle-class Liberal Party before its decline. Constituency party membership has been declining steadily since the war; even the low official estimate of 687,000 individual members is grossly inflated. Grass-roots organization has withered. The Conservative Party employs 350 full-time agents, including one in every marginal constituency. The Labour Party has 77, about a 50 percent reduction since 1973. Most marginal seats have no Labour organizations at all, and even such staunch Labour voting areas as Liverpool have no local organizations to speak of.[12] This organizational incapacity is only one indicator of the loosening of ties between British workers and "their" party. The unprecedented volatility of by-election swings, decreasing turnout rates, and the general failure of the party to evoke much public enthusiasm even in the face of a sharp

Conservative lurch to the right also demonstrate that the Labour Party no longer commands the intense and assured solidarity of the mass of working-class voters, even as it still receives a majority of their votes.

In large measure, this shift in the place of the party within the working class is the result of its contradictory position as a movement party and as a governing party. This tale has been told many times and need not be repeated here. But the consequences should not be discussed, as they usually are, principally in electoral terms. Far more important is the party's loss of the capacity to direct with confidence and authority the behavior of British workers and to maintain the traditional formula of high classness and gradualism. For without the Labour Party's integrative capacity, high classness has been heightened at work; and in residence communities new bases of action have been fashioned on extraclass identities outside of the framework of the Labour Party and the labor movement.

Shop-floor behavior has become more and more militant and less and less disciplined by national trade unions. Established bargaining relationships between national union leaders and corporate managements have been challenged effectively by shop-level militancy. More than nine of ten strikes are now unofficial. Wage drift virtually doubles the size of nationally negotiated pay settlements. This double system of trade union organization more than any other single issue has dominated the headlines and the concern of political elites for the past decade. As labor at work, the working class is more militant than ever.

But outside of the workplace the erosion of party strength has been accompanied by diffuse, variegated, persistent challenges to authority on extraclass communal bases. Clients of the welfare state, for example, have organized on issue-specific platforms largely outside of party and union structures. Their political independence and ephemeral character have made it difficult for local and national elites to establish enduring, predictable patterns of bargaining. Tenants, claimants, and other community action groups have heightened the noise of British politics but, even more important, have increased its uncertainty. So too has the introduction of race into political life. The rejection by most blacks of the institutionalized apparatus of the Community Relations Committees, the development of militant black-controlled vehicles of protest, and the confrontations of such neofascist organizations as the National Front and anti-Nazi mobilizations have taken place outside the traditional class political pattern. So too have the country's movements for sexual equality and for regional and national identity and independence. Outside of the workplace a new pluralism of ad hoc movements and discontents now defines political conflict. Ties between the community and the state are more direct, unmediated by the unitary labor movement. A more American-style pattern prevails.

But whereas in the United States such a pattern is a mark of continuity and stability, in Britain it connotes change and uncertainty. The metaphor of Americanization thus has obvious limits. For not only does the present character of class relations in Britain differ from prewar relationships in the respects discussed above, but the inheritance of high classness and the long experience of indigenous working-class organization give current conflicts a greater potential to affect core relations of the political economy in Britain than they have in the United States.

But this heightened uncertainty is also a crisis for the British left, as its accustomed conduct is in disarray. While one possibility is the emergence of a more militant and capable socialist movement, other outcomes are at least equally likely: a more pluralist, fragmented politics; openings on the right at the level of the residence community of the kind already seized with respect to race by the National Front and many members of the Conservative Party; a further weakening of the capacity of the trade unions and the Labour Party to resist incursions by a more laissez-faire capitalism; the triumph of regional and national identities over those of class.

The working class, in short, and its relations to the state are being formed anew. These changes and this fluidity are understood best not in economistic terms but by a return to the agenda, if not necessarily to the conclusions, posed in 1867 by Bagehot and Marx.

Notes

1. Dennis Kavanaugh, "An American Science of British Politics," *Political Studies* 22 (September 1974): 252.

2. Walter Bagehot, *The English Constitution* (London: Collins, 1971); Karl Marx and Friedrich Engels, "Preface to the First Edition," *Capital*, vol. 1 (New York: New World Paperbacks, 1968), p. 9.

3. Gabriel Almond and Sidney Verba, *The Civic Culture* (Boston: Little, Brown, 1965), p. 6.

4. Otto Kirchheimer, "The Transformation of the Western European Party Systems," in *Political Parties and Political Development*, ed. Joseph La Palombara and Myron Weiner (Princeton: Princeton University Press, 1966), p. 177.

5. E. P. Thompson, *The Making of the English Working Class* (London: Penguin Books, 1968), p. 737.

6. J. H. Plumb, *The Growth of Political Stability in England, 1675–1725* (London: Penguin Books, 1973).

7. E. P. Thompson, "Eighteenth-Century English Society: Class Struggle without Class?," *Social History* 3 (May 1978).

8. H. F. Moorhouse, "The Marxist Theory of the Labour Aristocracy," *Social History* 3 (January 1978): 73.

9. See Ira Katznelson, *City Trenches: Urban Politics and the Patterning of Class in the United States* (New York: Pantheon Books, forthcoming), chaps. 1, 2, 4.

10. J. H. Westergaard, "The Withering Away of Class: A Contemporary Myth," in *Towards Socialism,* ed. Perry Anderson and Robin Blackburn (Ithaca: Cornell University Press, 1966), p. 87.

11. John Goldthorpe et al., *The Affluent Worker,* 3 vols. (Cambridge: Cambridge University Press, 1968, 1969).

12. Stephen Kelly, "Withering Away at the Grass-Roots," *New Statesman,* September 29, 1978, pp. 400–401.

10 | *A State of Desubordination*

RALPH MILIBAND

I

In time to come, the seventies in Britain may well be seen as an uneasily transitional decade, in which what I will call the settlement of 1945 slowly came apart under the pressure of forces and tendencies which pushed the country in new directions. My purpose here is to discuss some of these forces and tendencies and the directions in which they may be leading.

The settlement of 1945 was made up of a number of familiar elements. Among the most important of them was a commitment by the state to full employment and economic growth, with a much higher level of state intervention in economic life than hitherto in peacetime. After the nationalization measures undertaken by the Labour Government after 1945, this state intervention was largely conceived in terms of fiscal and budgetary measures designed to help an enfeebled British capitalism; and this, it was thought, would achieve both full employment and economic growth. The settlement also involved a commitment by the state to a much enlarged system of welfare and social service provisions, most of them on a "de-commodified" basis, by way of non market and collective assurance of various supports and guarantees. The prevailing wind was in the direction of egalitarianism; and while this indeed mostly remained little more than wind, aggressive inegalitarianism tended to be intellectually and politically unfashionable, and was therefore somewhat muted.

Economic interventionism and social welfare were intended by different people to achieve different goals. But one goal which

152

was crucial and which was shared by the leaderships of both the Labour and Conservative Parties was the prevention or at least the drastic reduction of social and industrial conflict. The two men whose names are most closely associated with the main lines of the settlement of 1945—Keynes and Beveridge—were dedicated and self-conscious seekers after social pacification within the ambit of capitalism, soon to be renamed "the mixed economy." Much the same purpose was at the very center of the policy orientations which came to be known as "Butskellism": the idea was not of course to do away with class society, only with class struggle. The trade unions, or rather trade union leaders, were expected to play an important part in this enterprise, which would also involve business leaders and the state in a "partnership" that had both formal and informal, institutionalized and unofficial aspects. Much of this was a continuation of earlier trends, but in a much more definite, explicit, and structured form.

As for the political part of the settlement, it envisaged or rather took for granted the domination of national politics by the Labour and Conservative Parties, linked in a quasi-monopoly of parliamentary politics, on the basis of an electoral system which, however wayward and "unfair," was acceptable to the two parties, since it greatly strengthened their position against possible competitors. Also, the two front benches might differ on broad and ultimate social goals (though this should not be exaggerated); but such differences as there might be usually found no greatly divisive expression in actual policy terms. Suez, but only up to a point, was the only notable exception. Both in home and foreign affairs, there was a very high degree of consensus among the people who were in charge of the British state in those postwar decades. Also, the continued territorial unity of the United Kingdom was naturally taken for granted: the very idea that this was not settled for all time would then, at least in England, have appeared perverse or eccentric.

In one sense, the settlement of 1945 was a remarkable success. Of course, it cured very few if any economic or social ills (though it did produce or at least witness the disappearance of chronic mass unemployment). Deprivation on a large scale endured, and the "affluent society" remained more of a slogan and an aspiration than a reality. But important improvements in most aspects of daily life for most people did occur, and the all-important purpose of social pacification was to a substantial extent achieved. From the point of view which was common to the Conservative and most Labour leaders, this was a critical test of success. Notwithstanding the radicalization produced by the war and the promise held out by the election of a Labour government backed for the first time by a massive majority in the House of Commons, an economic and social system was perpetuated and even consolidated in which the working class remained an effectively subordinate class and where there endured a vast inequality of access, as well as an inadequacy of access, to the resources which determine the texture of life; and this was achieved at relatively small cost to the main beneficiaries of the system.

The people who were in charge of affairs over this period of a quarter of a century or so appeared to believe that the settlement of 1945 would endure indefinitely, with minor ups and downs. They were encouraged in that belief by a multitude of academic and nonacademic ideologues, overwhelmingly dominant in the field of what Marx called "mental production," who assured the men of affairs and everyone else that crisis and conflict, at least on any serious and sustained scale, were things of the past for the "postcapitalist" societies, of which Britain was one.

This confidence has now been thoroughly dissipated: its erosion began in the sixties and has gone on ever faster since. It would be easy but I think mistaken to attribute this loss of confidence to a new awareness of Britain's economic problems or of its poor economic performance. Of course, economic problems form the backcloth to all else. But then it has been so for a very long time. One way and another, Britain has been in economic trouble for a hundred years, ever since it lost that industrial supremacy which made it for a time the "workshop of the world." There has not, naturally, been any time since then when it was not in a situation of relative decline. This is no matter for complacency, particularly since the rate of relative decline has accelerated in recent years. But aggravated economic problems, however important a part of the story they obviously are, do not provide a sufficient or adequate explanation for the generalized sense that the settlement which had been thought permanent in the decades following 1945 has ceased to be viable.

Economic problems do not produce major difficulties or crises unless they find translation in political terms. Often, they do not find such translation. Thus, Britain has been the country above all others which has experienced chronic economic problems *and* great political and social stability. Even where economic problems do find political translation, the resultant political events may do no more than touch the surface or fringes of the political system, and leave it basically unimpaired. An economic crisis such as the one of the summer of 1931 produced a political "crisis" of some consequence, but there was never any question of the political system itself coming under challenge, even less the economic and social system. Nor was there any such question in the "crisis" of the General Strike of 1926. In fact, there has not been a really serious institutional crisis in Britain in this century, and for a long time before that either. This in itself should induce a certain caution in speaking of crisis. Nevertheless, some of the changes which have been occurring in Britain over the years do pose a challenge of unusual dimensions for the political system, and may in time produce what could be called a genuine crisis.

II

It has traditionally been assumed that any serious challenge to the normal workings of the political system must be the result—intended or not—of a coherent and programmatically far-reaching movement on the left, not only committed to the thorough transformation of the capitalist system in socialist directions but also able and willing to embark upon it. No such movement has ever existed in Britain, which is why the political system has not been unduly strained or overloaded; but it was and remains perfectly reasonable to think that the emergence of such a challenge would impose a very great strain upon the system, with consequences that are unpredictable.

On the other hand, it may well be that this kind of projection is much too narrow, and that a clear-cut and coherent socialist challenge is not the only way in which the political system may be brought under great pressure: other possibilities need to be explored.

My starting point is that there is at work in Britain a process which I will call *desubordination* for want of a better term to convey what is involved. Desubordination means that people who find themselves in subordinate positions, and notably the people who work in factories, mines, offices, shops, schools, hospitals, and so on, do what they can to mitigate, resist, and transform the conditions of their subordination. The process occurs where subordination is most evident and felt, namely at "the point of production" and at the workplace in general; but also wherever else a condition of subordination exists, for instance as it is experienced by women in the home, and outside.

In relation to work, desubordination is of course a very old phenomenon and has assumed a wide variety of expressions, from Luddism and sabotage to go-slow, strike action, sit-ins, work-ins, and various forms of political protest, engagement, and action. It also involves—and this is one of its most common forms—a refusal to do more than the minimum that is required, or less.

But while desubordination is a very old phenomenon, it seems to me that it is, in many manifestations, a much more accentuated and generalized feature of life in Britain now than at any time since the first decades of the last century; and that even though it is not a unilinear process and may be less acute in some years than in others, it is more likely to grow than to diminish. It may be a more thought-out process, or less. It may take the form of collective action or of individual action which may turn into collective action. It may be one expression of a larger phenomenon of "delegitimation," but it also may be many steps behind it, and lack clear political dimensions. But whatever form and content it assumes, it does at least denote a certain rejection of the validity of one or other or all of the multiple subordinations which are part of capitalist society, and particularly of the subordination at work which is an essential part of capitalism. (Incidentally, the rejoinder that the problem of subordination arises under socialism as well is not, in this context, particularly relevant, though it may help to explain why many people who accept this argument practice desubordination but are not interested in socialism.)

Marxist thought on this phenomenon has always been rather thin, with a traditional dichotomy between revolutionary consciousness on the one hand (itself by no means an unambiguous concept), and 'trade union consciousness' (i.e., limited, economic, sectorial, "corporate" demands and perspectives) on the other. The distinction poses many problems, not least because the two forms of consciousness may intersect. But it does not in any case do justice to this complex and diffuse phenomenon, which greatly affects the "relations of production" of capitalism, and all other social relations as well. The fact that it can assume such a wide variety of forms, and that it does not require premeditation and organization to find *some* expression, is itself a contributory element to its pervasiveness.

The question of the relationship of desubordination to socialist purposes and prospects is obviously important. But the more immediate question is what impact it has in, so to speak, its own right. For the fact that it does not easily fit into familiar ideological slots ought not to obscure the powerful force which, in its "detotalized totality," it represents, or the degree to which, in its own way, it constitutes a repudiation of notions of integration of the working class into present-day capitalist society. It is precisely this nonintegration which is the central problem for the political system, one of the main tasks of those who run it being to contain, deflect, and defeat the pressures which desubordination generates.

To do this requires the main institutions of the labor movement, and notably the trade unions, to play an enlarged role, which in turn underlines the dual and necessarily ambiguous role they play in the system. On the one hand, they are subject to powerful pressures from many sides—and never more so than when a Labour government is in office—to moderate their demands, to control and restrain their members, to act "responsibly," "in the national interest," and so on. At the limit, which is a long way from having been reached, this must involve trade union leaders in a "corporatist" integration into the state, which drastically curtails if it does not altogether abolish the freedom of trade unions to act in defense of their members. On the other hand, there is the pull to the militant assertion of demands emanating from the rank and file, which trade union leaders are unable to ignore or dismiss, and which they do not in any case necessarily want to ignore or circumvent. One of the most important features of the seventies in Britain has been the strength of that pull from below, though it would be wrong to underestimate how much

there was of it in earlier years—after all, the wage freeze which
had been part of the Attlee government's purpose and policy
after 1947 eventually went awry because of the pressure from
below which exceedingly "moderate" trade union leaders, however powerful and well entrenched in their organizations, could
no longer contain. But that pressure is now far greater and more
sustained than in earlier decades.

As the last few years have shown, in this context as well as in
others, rank-and-file restiveness has also enhanced the importance of the role which Labour governments play in curbing and
countering the demands of labor and the expectations of activists.
It is significant that one of the main claims to office which Labour
now advances or has is that a Labour government is better able
than a Conservative one to "handle" the unions, meaning in effect
that it is better able to contain and defuse pressures and demands
from below; and it may well be true that such a government is in
present conditions more likely to be successful in the relatively
smooth management of class conflict than a government of the
right. But it is worth stressing that, in so far as the claim has
strength, it does acquire that strength by virtue of a pressure from
below that is a permanent fact and whose containment is a permanent problem.

There are many Conservatives and other partisans of the status
quo who know full well that trade unions, or rather trade union
leaders, now have a much enhanced role in the resolution or at
least in the attenuation of the difficulties presented by desubordination; and they are also well aware that Labour governments too
have their definite uses in this respect. But even the most clear-
sighted such people are unlikely to view trade unions as much
more than necessary nuisances, to be kept so far as possible strictly
in check; and Labour governments remain, for the same people,
undesirable alternatives to Conservative ones. After all, even the
most moderate Labour government can only be an effective
agency of containment and control if it manages to persuade organized labor and others that it is also, at a minimum, an agency
of improvement and reform; and it must at least provide *some*
evidence to that effect.

But this, not surprisingly, is a matter for anger and alarm for
those people who feel that improvement and reform—of the kind

that have come to be associated with the settlement of 1945—have already gone much too far; who also believe that the trade unions are running—and ruining—the country; and whose traditional fear of "the workers" has been greatly increased by the spread of desubordination. This fear has always been an important (if often furtive and deflected) element in middle-class and lower-middle-class thinking—and for that matter in the thinking of some parts of the working class as well. But it now seems to be more prevalent than at any time in this century. If there is deep and widespread desubordination on one side, so is there deep resentment of it on the other, which spills over onto the political system which allows it.

III

A number of features mark off the present period from previous ones. One of them is an apparently strong conviction held by many people that something like a counterrevolution is essential and overdue. What they want is to reverse the trends of policy and thought which have dominated British politics for thirty years in regard to state intervention, welfare, the growth of trade union influence—all that might, in this context, be subsumed under the label 'Labourism' and which Conservatives are wont to call "socialism." It is this "socialism" which they take to be responsible for Britain's economic decline, and which they want to see pushed back.

This ambition is now powerfully fueled by a steady flow of reactionary ideas from a vast and disparate army of propagandists and pamphleteers. Some of them are traditional Conservatives who speak with a new stridency; others are ex-Labourites now in the business of warning all and sundry of the horrors to come at the hands of totalitarian trade unionism; and some are professional antisocialists, who find in the crimes and derelictions of Soviet-type regimes an excellent excuse for denouncing anyone on the left who advocates anything beyond the most tinkering kind of piecemeal social engineering.

Such people proclaim not only that the Labour Party may one day be captured by subversives, Marxists, and what not, but that the capturing process is already far advanced. This political science fiction has a ready access to all the means of communication, commands a wide audience, and injects a pronounced paranoid streak in the political culture. It also helps to heighten fears of the future; and it may also help to create a climate of thought in which the most reactionary "solutions" to the dangers which are being evoked and denounced come to appear as by no means unreasonable. The evolution of the debate on "immigration" provides one instance of this process, that on "law and order" another.

Conservative forces need leadership in the political realm proper—pamphleteering is not enough. The kind of leadership which the Conservative Party has been getting is another feature of the present period which needs to be noted, for it marks a definite shift from the Butskellism of the postwar decades and is much more in tune with the mood of the rank and file of the party than was the case earlier. Previous leaders served Conservatism well enough, but that was not quite the same as serving the Conservative rank and file. The latter has always had its own impulses tempered by its leaders, who tended to belong to the One-Nation, Keynesian-interventionist current of thought in the party. Conservatives in the constituencies went along with this, and followed the precept enunciated by Burke in a different context, that "we must venerate what we are unable presently to comprehend." But their hearts were a good deal further to the right: hence the popularity of Enoch Powell, despite everything, at the Conservative grass roots. Edward Heath sought to give expression to the we-won't-stand-for-any-nonsense-from-the-trade-unions current of Conservative thought; yet he also remained encoiled in the One-Nation tradition, which helps to explain the uncertainty and incoherence which marked his period of office.

The present leadership of the Conservative Party is clearly concerned to move away from the "consensus politics" of the last three decades and to assert a much tougher kind of Conservatism, which would try to undo some at least of such gains as organized labor has made in that time, and which would seek to implement more markedly inegalitarian, antiwelfare, antiunion policies than previous Conservative leaderships thought it prudent or were keen to attempt.

In this sense, it is true, as has sometimes been said in recent times, that there has occurred a reversal of roles between the

Labour and Conservative parties, or at least between their leaderships. It is the Labour party which is now the party of consensus and continuity, and which accuses its opponents of preaching dissension and spreading divisiveness; while it is the Conservative Party which seeks to make an appeal on the basis of a definite break with 1945 and after.

Making such an appeal presents many problems. For one thing, the Conservatives must at all costs appeal to a working-class electorate which is not greatly drawn to the attractions of "free enterprise," private health, fee-paying education, and the "recommodification" of many collective services and provisions. For another thing, the people who run the most important and powerful sectors of British capitalist enterprise are by no means unequivocally in favor of "free enterprise." On the contrary, they very much want the state to help them, in a permanent and extensive system of intervention which would yet leave them free from state control; and the same people have long found that this could be got from a Labour government as well as from a Conservative one. Moreover, they are in a good position to appreciate to the full the role which trade unions play as control agencies of organized labor; and they have no great wish to create conditions in which confrontation becomes likely or inevitable. They may, on the whole, prefer a Conservative government to a Labour one; but unlike many Conservatives at the grass roots and in the political leadership of the party, they are not at this point bent on counterrevolution.

No doubt, most Conservative leaders do not actually want confrontation with the trade unions either. But their policies, positions, commitments, and purposes nonetheless make confrontation a very distinct possibility for a Conservative government; and there are probably some people in the Conservative leadership who do believe that a confrontation with the trade unions, from which the government must at all costs emerge successful, is a necessary condition for the reversals of policy which they and some of their colleagues would want to see such a government carry out.

"Some of their colleagues" because there is a Conservative left as well as a new right which is in varying degrees committed to earlier trends of policy, and which remains influential. For the first time in a very long while, the Conservative Party is now deeply divided, not only on issues of personality and tactics but on more fundamental issues of policy and position; or rather, Conservative leaders are thus divided. These divisions no doubt reflect the uncertainties of those people in business and politics who are in charge of the long-term management of British capitalism; and one additional—and major—factor of uncertainty is precisely the existence and spread of desubordination, and how to deal with it in the given context provided by the political and institutional system. In the end, it may not be too much to say that all else comes back to this.

A further complication is presented by the emergence of a fascist right as an independent political presence. The potential for growth of this tendency is a matter for surmise; but it would not be safe to assume that a fascist movement could not exercise a greater attraction than is now the case over various sections of the population, including members of the working class who see no hope of relief from an exceedingly bleak future through the traditional organizations of the working class. In a suitably charged social climate, and in conditions of considerable economic, social, political, and cultural malaise and uncertainty, propaganda based on chauvinist, anti-black, anti-Semitic, xenophobic, anti-left, and other assorted slogans is likely to have some resonance, to put it no higher. Organizations that peddle such stuff are not "respectable," but this may easily turn into a strength rather than a weakness. Indeed, fascist slogans may well have an appeal to some people—for instance, young workers and unemployed youths—who are deeply alienated from the existing system, yet who are also "unpolitical" and hostile to all forms of traditional (or what are taken to be traditional) affiliations. Desubordination takes many forms and can have many expressions. This is one of them.

The impact that fascist organizations (such as the National Front) may make on the Conservative Party is impossible to gauge precisely, but it seems reasonable to suppose that it must have some. The appeal of such organizations is directed at many of the same people that the Conservatives need to attract. Until recently, Conservative leaders did not need to concern themselves greatly with competition from this quarter, at least at the national level. But it may no longer be or remain so; and even if extreme right-wing movements fail to achieve a really significant presence on the political scene, they may well be able to act as a pressure group upon the Conservative Party and help to push it further to the right, and not only on the issue of "immigration."

IV

At a superficial glance, it might seem as if any projection of class relations and political developments in the years immediately ahead must take North Sea oil as providing a certain element of balm. Even on pessimistic calculations, there will for some years to come be an attenuation of some of the problems which have beset the British economy since the end of World War II, and for that matter earlier, notably in relation to the balance of payments. This being the case, it would be easy to assume that the oil revenues will bring out an economic sun under whose comforting rays economic, social, and political tensions will also be much reduced.

There is not much warrant for this view. Even if the possible exacerbation of Scottish nationalism because of North Sea oil is left out of account, with all the vast consequences this would have throughout the political system, the assumption that the oil revenues will ease class tensions rests on the antecedent—and mistaken—assumption that these revenues will be used for economically and socially desirable humane and progressive purposes. But this is akin to the fallacy that was being advanced not very long ago that economic growth would take care of poverty, structural problems in the economy, and all else that was socially divisive, to the point where class conflict would be only a bad memory of an epoch irrevocably and mercifully gone.

What this notion ignored, among other things, is that economic arrangements are a political question. The same applies to North Sea oil. Given the balance of political forces that are brought into play in regard to the oil revenues, the likelihood is that the proceeds will do very little to strengthen the infrastructure of collective services on which the vast majority of people depend in very large measure for the quality of their daily existence, and that even the opportunity to strengthen the structure of the British economy in any significant way will also be missed.

The oil revenues are in a way comparable to the foreign aid given to underdeveloped countries. Such aid occurs in a context that is unfavorable to its use for the benefit of the mass of the people. The economic, political, and administrative structures of the countries concerned are neither suited to nor intended for this purpose. Such benefits as may accrue to the mass of the people are almost incidental—a fallout of the benefits that accrue to the well-to-do and privileged minority. The point is also relevant to the ways in which the oil revenues will be used. Capitalist priorities will be in command: other needs will trail a long way behind. The labor movement is at this stage too uncertain in its purposes, too incoherent in its policies, and too greatly undermined from within to be able to impose different priorities on the disposal of the revenues of North Sea oil, whether a Labour or a Conservative government is in office. Whatever else they may achieve, these revenues will not reduce the level of desubordination.

V

Desubordination, however, is by no means sufficient to bring into being a socialist movement able to shape the policies to be adopted in the coming years. Such a movement does not now exist in Britain. The Labour Party has long ceased to be—if it ever was—an effective agency for the propagation of concrete socialist alternatives to an enveloping capitalist reality, not to speak of the actual implementation of such alternatives by a Labour government. The Labour Party could hardly be such an agency, since most of its leaders are utterly determined to keep it on the path of marginal social reform, at the most; and in this, at least, they may be expected to succeed.

Nor can any other party or grouping on the left realistically hope to make a substantial impact on policy in the relevant future. The great paradox of political life in Britain is precisely the existence of a strong and pervasive sense of desubordination on the one hand and on the other the absence of significant political agencies which could give to that sense coherence and shape. It will not always be so, but it is so now.

This being the case, the prevailing circumstances seem to point in the direction of a considerable reinforcement of state power for the purpose of containing pressure from below. This is not to engage in prophecies of the coming of an authoritarian regime. The reinforced state does have authoritarian characteristics in so far as it is marked by a further inflation of police powers of a discretionary sort; but this can be accommodated without too much difficulty within the constitutional shell of the existing political order. A Conservative government in particular would in the present period be tempted or driven to try to reinforce the state and be firm with greedy workers, picketing strikers, presumptuous trade unions, subversive teachers, noisy students, tiresome blacks, welfare scroungers, sinister Marxists, misguided libertarians, and everybody else standing in the way of national renewal by way of "free enterprise" and the worship of the market.

But this could hardly provide the basis for a new settlement to replace that of 1945. Nor is the less abrasive approach of a Labour government likely to achieve this. In this perspective, the period ahead, whichever government is in office, appears destined to be marked by much greater social tension, class conflict, and political instability than has been the case for many a year past.

PART IV : :

One Britain?

11 | *From Scotland with Love*

JACK BRAND

"The establishment of a Scottish Assembly is the first step toward the breakup of the United Kingdom." This was one of the constant arguments put forward by opponents of devolution, and if it is true, Scottish politics must be a major component of the British crisis. This paper is devoted to what has happened in Scotland over the last twenty years to bring this situation about. We shall look at the rise of national feeling in its modern form in Scotland and the reasons it has taken a political form. Two major topics will be covered. I shall look first at what has happened in Scotland and then at the impact of Scottish developments on politics in Britain.

The Changes in Scotland

Three generally known features of the Scottish scene are pertinent to our inquiry. One is the rise of the Scottish National Party (SNP) vote, the second is the decline of the economy, and the third is the discovery of North Sea oil.

We can see the performance of the SNP in Table 1. From its foundation in 1928 until the beginning of the 1960s it was a very minor party. At various by-elections thereafter it did rather well, and in 1967 a nationalist candidate overturned one of the largest Labour majorities in the country at Hamilton.[1] From that time forward the fortunes of the party have gone up and down but the general trend has been upward. It is important to notice, however, that the growth began in the early sixties and the Hamilton victory

169

Table 1.   Scottish National Party votes and MPs, 1945-74

Year		Total SNP vote	SNP vote as share of Scottish electorate	SNP MPs
1945		30,595	1.2%	—
1950		9,708	0.4	—
1951		7,299	0.3	—
1955		12,112	0.5	—
1959		21,738	0.8	—
1964		64,044	2.4	—
1966		129,112	5.1	—
1970		306,796	11.4	1
1974	February	632,032	21.9	7
1974	October	839,628	30.4	11

Source: *The Times House of Commons* (London: Times Publishing House, 1945-74).

was no flash in the pan. Another point well worth mentioning is that at the last election the SNP was the second party in Scotland, leaving the Conservatives a very poor third. Thus its parliamentary representation underrepresents its strength in the electorate, for with few exceptions the SNP stands second in the districts where it does not actually represent the constituency.

This success story is hardly paralleled by any account of the Scottish economy. During the 1950s and 1960s Scotland lagged behind the United Kingdom as a whole: from 1951 to 1969 the gross domestic product of the United Kingdom nearly doubled in value while that of Scotland increased less than 70 percent.[2] If we consider any other indicator, such as unemployment, we find that there, too, Scotland was doing very badly, certainly less well than England. If the rise of the SNP can be dated from the early sixties, the decline of the Scottish economy began much earlier. Things began to go wrong in the 1870s, and after 1919 severe decline was evident everywhere. In several towns in the once prosperous Clyde Valley, half the menfolk were out of work. At the present moment the Scottish economy is still in a perilous state despite many government attempts to prop up the ailing shipbuilding industry, for example, and to induce such new industries as automobile manufacturing to come to the central belt. At the moment of writing, news has come through of the possible closure of the Chrysler plant at Linwood, with the consequent unemployment of 9000 and devastating effects on many more whose jobs depend on this large complex. If any large units such as Chrysler, Singer, or the BMC plant should close, the vast majority of the work force would have absolutely no immediate prospect of employment.

All this may seem strange to anyone who has read about the third well-known fact about Scotland: the discovery of oil in the North Sea. The find was first announced in 1971, and it quickly became known that very large quantities were involved. Has this discovery been of no benefit to Scotland? For a few years, certainly, unemployment in the northeast, from Montrose to Peterhead, has been low. Aberdeen has become crowded with American, Dutch, and other oil workers, and they have brought in a good deal of money. One should remember, however, that oil is not, in the long run, a labor-intensive industry. At the beginning many jobs are opened up in the construction of sites on shore, the laying of pipes, and so forth, but after this work is completed, all that is needed is a small core of maintenance workers. In Scotland no additional work was available in refining or in factories dealing with oil derivatives. The large refinery at Grangemouth that had been built several years before 1971 could handle North Sea oil and still work well below its capacity. There is a world surplus of refinery capacity, and no new refinery in Scotland could be contemplated. As MacKay and MacKay have pointed out,[3] the major returns from oil discoveries come in the form of either direct exploitation by the government or the taxes that oil companies pay to the government. In the British case the petroleum revenue tax and virtually every other impost goes to the central government. With the exception of the Shetland Islands Council, no authority in Scotland benefits directly in this way. Scotland benefits from oil revenues only in the sense in which every part of the United Kingdom benefits: increased income promotes better government services.

These three facts about Scotland—the Nationalist vote, the weakness of the economy, and the discovery of oil—have been linked in various ways. Many commentators have suggested that the causal link has been between the third and the first: the oil boom created the Nationalist upsurge. In view of what has already been said, it is clear that this cannot be, and I shall argue that Scottish nationalism has arisen in large part as a response to the

second factor: the collapse of the economy. It is clear from Table
1 that the increase of those voting Nationalist started about ten
years before the whole issue of oil came on the scene. It is possible
to argue that oil gave the SNP a boost and speeded up the turning
of voters to the Nationalists, but by 1971 the whole process was
well on its way.

The Cause of Scottish Nationalism

If the turning of large numbers of Scottish voters to the
SNP cannot be explained by greed for oil revenues, how can it be
explained? To answer this question we must put the movement in
a British, if not in a European, context.

Table 2 illustrates an important and little-recognized trend in
British politics. Whereas the traditional model of a two-party system could be accepted up to 1950, the situation changed quite
distinctively after that date until by October 1974 only a little over
half the electorate voted for one or the other of the major parties.

Table 3 throws light on another aspect of British voting behavior: the decline in turnout. In short, the increase of the SNP
vote has to be seen in the context of a general decline not only in
the popularity of the majority parties but, apparently, in people's
concern with politics itself. The 1960s was the decade of the Liberal revival, a time when voters sought an alternative that was not
corrupted by office or the dog-in-the-manger tricks of the "offi-

Table 2. Share of electorate obtained by Conservative and Labour parties, 1950–74

Year		Conservative	Labour	Conservative and Labour combined
1950		36.5%	38.7%	75.2%
1951		39.6	40.3	79.9
1955		38.2	35.6	73.8
1959		38.8	34.5	73.3
1964		33.5	34.0	67.5
1966		31.8	36.5	68.3
1970		33.4	31.4	64.8
1974	February	29.5	29.0	58.5
1974	October	26.1	28.5	54.6

Source: *The Times House of Commons* (London: Times Publishing House, 1950–74).

Table 3. Share of electorate that voted in general elections, United Kingdom, 1945–74

Year		United Kingdom	Scotland
1945		72.7%	68.9%
1950		83.9	80.9
1951		82.6	81.1
1955		76.8	75.1
1959		78.7	78.1
1964		77.1	77.6
1966		75.8	75.9
1970		72.0	73.9
1974	February	78.8	79.0
1974	October	72.8	74.8

Source: *The Times House of Commons* (London: Times Publishing House, 1950–74).

cial" opposition. But the late fifties and sixties were also the time of the "satire movement," the foundation of the magazine *Private Eye,* and a general feeling that British institutions were perhaps not the best in the world. Young people who were interested in politics tended to join the Campaign for Nuclear Disarmament or the New Left Club rather than work as Labour Party activists. In short, the pattern of British politics that had obtained since the end of the war became somewhat destabilized. It is possible that these conditions, which brought into question the monopoly of the traditional parties, were conducive to the rise of what was essentially a new party. It is also quite clear that this malaise or at least change was spread throughout Western Europe and was not confined to Britain.

Am I arguing, then, that Scots turned to the SNP not because they were seriously interested in independence for Scotland but because they were discontented generally? Of course Scottish independence has always had some support, but we must be clear about how the data are to be interpreted. Despite the fact that Nationalist votes have gone from less than 1 percent to about 30 percent of the Scottish electorate, polls from the 1940s to the present day show that a remarkably consistent 20 percent of Scottish adults support the idea of independence.[4] We cannot say, then, that the rise of the SNP is a result of an increase in the proportions of people who support this policy. It is even doubtful whether Nationalist support can be explained by an interest in

any constitutional arrangement. When Scottish voters are asked
to state the most important issues to which the government ought
to attend, the topics mentioned most frequently are economic
ones. In March 1978, for example, in a poll carried out for London Weekend Television, prices was the choice of most respondents (56 percent), with unemployment and wages close behind,
whereas only 17 percent mentioned devolution. But we must be-
ware. Support for a party may be nonetheless strong although its
electors do not support the main plank of its platform. Frequent
studies have shown that Labour voters are no more concerned
about Labour progress in nationalization or immigration, for
example, than are SNP supporters for Scottish independence.
This fact does not mean that they will not continue to vote for the
party.

I have argued that voting for the SNP is more likely to indicate
a general feeling that Scotland's interests should be supported
rather than a demand for devolution. This point of view seems to
be borne out by the data in Table 4, collected after the General
Election of October 1974.

It is notable that no party is supported by a large proportion of
its voters because of specific policies. Among the SNP voters,
however, almost half mention that the party would do more for
Scotland. They do not suggest that they support the party because
they believe in a particular scheme of devolution or independence
but generally that it would be better for their country. In a parallel answer the model group of Labour responses to this question
refers to the historic appeal of the Labour party: not that it will

Table 4. Reasons given by Scottish voters for supporting parties, 1974

Reasons for support	Conservative	Labour	SNP
Always voted for party	17	24	3
Dislike other parties	31	12	22
Put country on feet	14	6	2
Do more for Scotland	1	—	45
For working men	1	41	1
Deserve a chance	—	1	21
I agree with policy	17	10	4
Other	9	6	2

Source: British Election Study in Scotland, 1974, conducted by W. Miller.

nationalize the means of production or ensure a wage policy or any of the other specifically Labour policies but rather that it will be good for a particular social group.

The vote for the Labour Party has been based largely on the class consciousness of manual workers. Can it be that the vote for the SNP is based on a heightening of national consciousness among the Scots? I shall argue that this is indeed the case, and I believe that such evidence can be seen in Table 5. The data show various interesting points. It is clear that SNP votes have increased among both those who identify themselves as Scottish and those who identify themselves as British. This seems to argue that voting for a party may bear little relation to agreement with its fundamental positions. Undoubtedly some votes for the SNP were cast purely in protest, and it would be no surprise if many of those who cast them identified themselves as British. When we look at those who identify themselves as Scots, however, it seems very clear that the SNP votes are much more numerous. Perhaps even more important is the fact that the proportion of votes cast for the SNP has increased more rapidly among the Scottish identifiers than among the British identifiers. In 1970 the proportion was

Table 5. National identification of Scottish voters and support

	British	Scottish
1970		
Conservative	33.8%	27.6%
Labour	60.7	61.4
Liberal	1.0	0.9
SNP	4.5	10.1
	100.0%	100.0%
February 1974		
Conservative	31.5%	18.3%
Labour	53.9	53.7
Liberal	4.8	4.8
SNP	9.7	24.3
	99.9%	100.1%
October 1974		
Conservative	27.4%	23.1%
Labour	56.5	39.0
Liberal	3.5	2.3
SNP	12.6	35.5
	100.0%	99.9%

Source: *The Times House of Commons* (London: Times Publishing House, 1970–74).

only twice as large among Scottish identifiers but by October 1974
it had become almost three times as large. In October 1974 over a
third of all those who felt themselves to be Scottish rather than
British voted for the SNP. It seems, therefore, that being Scottish
is related to political action in the minds of a growing number of
Scots. I suggest that it is in this new development in what it means
to be Scottish that the important key to the rise of the SNP vote is
to be found. Let us look, then, at the nature of this identity.

The Scottish Identity

It is well known that, even though Scotland became part
of an incorporating union with England in 1707, it retained many
national institutions that are still prominent in the life of the society. The legal system, the church, the schools, and the system of
local government are distinctive and add a particular flavor to
Scottish life. But this is not all. Scottish society outside these elite
institutions has remained self-consciously Scottish, and many aspects of life, from football to music and drinking, are distinctive—
distinctive but often regarded as parochial and partly or wholly
rejected on that basis. One of the features of Scottish society that
distinguished the 1950s and 1960s was a new interest in social and
economic conditions, which may have formed the background to
political developments.

This new development arose in part as a response to the disas-
trous state of the economy. Newspapers contained regular articles
on unemployment, invariably pointing to the particularly high
levels of unemployment in Scotland. Added to the employment
problem was the fact that in Scotland, as in the rest of Britain, a
new spirit had developed after the war, which took the form of
various attempts to solve social and economic problems by creating jobs or by developing some aspect of Scottish life. In many
areas of life it is possible to see a renewed interest in the country
and a keenness to make it worth living in again. Thus the Scottish
Council (Development and Industry) brought together industrialists and trade unionists to plan for a revival of Scottish industry;
and the Edinburgh Festival, though it contained little that was
specifically Scottish, encouraged a confidence that Scotland could
be in the mainstream of European culture. At the other end of the

cultural spectrum, the establishment of a commercial TV channel, Scottish Television, meant that the London-centered monopoly of the media was broken and that henceforth Scottish news and concerns would have more attention.

Perhaps the development can be summed up in song. Up to about five years ago Scottish football and rugby crowds had dutifully sung "God Save the Queen" at international matches. About that time a member of a Scottish folk group (himself a nationalist) wrote "O Flower of Scotland," a song that is now sung virtually as the unofficial national anthem. Its sentiments are nationalist, and yet at the time of the 1976 England-Scotland International, both elite Scottish papers, the *Glasgow Herald* (a staunchly Conservative newspaper) and *The Scotsman* (certainly not a nationalist paper, though sympathetic to devolution), printed the full text so that the spectators would be prepared to sing out.

One last point should be made. It is that, depending on the poll chosen, between 70 and 80 percent of the Scottish electors think the SNP upsurge has been of benefit to Scotland whether they voted for the party's candidates or not.

What does all this tell us about the reasons for the increase in the SNP vote? Unfortunately, it is very difficult to be conclusive. Our survey evidence comes from a period when most of the changes had already occurred, and in any case, survey evidence does not provide wholly satisfactory answers to this sort of question. We must, then, make some rather speculative deductions.

I have already mentioned the separate institutions that survived the Union of 1707, which formed the basis for the further development of national sentiment. Though this outcome is in no way inevitable, the institutions formed what is called structural conduciveness. What triggered the change?

Of all the writers on nationalism, perhaps the most thought-provoking has been Ernest Gellner.[5] One of his major themes has been the effect of "differential modernization." A very similar argument has been put forward by Tom Nairn[6] and other Marxists and has been called "uneven development." Roughly, the argument suggests that nationalism grows out of a situation in which people are aware of modernization in other countries, usually in a country that dominates their own, and are also aware that their own land does not share the benefits of those new developments.

Scotland fits remarkably within this model. On the one hand Scotland was industrially an advanced country until the beginning of this century. In the twenties and thirties Britain shared in the world economic crisis, and there was little sign of nationalism. From the late fifties on, Scotland markedly slipped back in comparison with Great Britain as a whole. One can, of course, argue that the discrepancy between the economic performances of Scotland and England existed long before the rise of nationalism, but the relative positions of the countries are less important than the perception of a discrepancy. In the 1950s Scotland not only became worse off than England but experienced at least two new processes that drew the attention of Scots to this discrepancy. One was the very economic policy of the British government, which stressed the importance of regional policy to combat the problems of areas with special difficulties. Thus it became a commonplace that Scotland was a special case in the sense that its unemployment and industry generally were in a particularly bad situation. Second, the establishment of a specifically Scottish television service meant that, to a much greater extent than before, Scottish news and topics were discussed. Under these circumstances it would not be surprising if many electors got the idea that Scotland was not doing as well as England. It was perfectly clear that Scotland was not as prosperous as many parts of England, especially the southeast, which was the part that was usually presented as typifying English life. This still leaves open the question of why Scotland should have turned to nationalism at a stage when the country seemed less viable economically than in the past. Part of the answer almost certainly lies in a general feeling that the British institutions that once had been a source of pride were now seen as tarnished. The Scot could not comfort himself, as he drew his unemployment benefit, with the thought that he belonged to a nation on whose empire the sun never set.

The Impact on British Politics

What effect have these dramatic changes had on British politics? Before we review various institutions and procedures, a more general point should be made. The appearance of the SNP on the scene emphasizes the fact that the once dominant class dimension no longer is so important as it once was. The Liberal revival of the 1960s is part of the same movement. The political debate seems to be fought on grounds other than rich versus poor, the working class against the middle and upper classes. For the first time in many years, nonclass considerations are central in the debate. Nevertheless, the burden of my argument will be that not too many institutional changes have taken place except those in party stances, in Scottish government, and in questions of British administration.

Many of the most substantial changes have come about in the realm of party stances on Scottish government. It is the government that has been most directly in the line of fire of the Nationalist advance. Perhaps the first sign came in 1966, when the Liberals first tried to get a devolution measure into the parliamentary timetable. It was true, as Russell Johnson said, that home rule for Scotland had traditionally been a part of Liberal policy. It is difficult to find any traces of it in Liberal manifestos after 1939, and in any case, when the party was in power it did not do much to implement this policy. It may have been important for the 1966 action that Scottish Liberals were beginning to feel that the SNP were challenging them as the third party in Scotland.

The Conservatives present a complicated and peculiar story. They are traditionally the party of union, but it was at their Scottish conference in May 1969 that Edward Heath became the first leader of a major British party to recognize publicly the need for devolution. In March 1970 a committee chaired by Lord Home proposed a form of Scottish assembly. During their time in government from 1970 to 1974, the Conservatives showed no signs of implementing this policy, and several statements were made to the effect that it was not of top priority. After the election defeat the Conservatives eventually made it clear that they had abandoned any real devolutionist stance, and the new leader, Margaret Thatcher, declared that she and her colleagues were against any form of assembly for Scotland.

The Labour Party, which has often fought against the pressure of the Scottish section, has now, as the party in power, passed an act to establish a legislature in Scotland. This is a far cry from the situation in 1967, when the then prime minister, Harold Wilson, declared that his government had no plans for such a scheme.

One might sum up the situation by saying that the increase in the Nationalist vote in Scotland led all parties to think seriously about constitutional change where all had been satisfied with the status quo. The Labour Party so far reversed its position as to introduce measures of basic constitutional change.

Let us now turn to the administration of Scotland. Up to 1886 Scotland was administered under the departments of the crown in the same way as England and Wales. There were no special territorial arrangements. In the 1880s a strong home rule movement developed, emulating the movement in Ireland. It was supported by many of the social leaders of Scotland, including the civic heads of the major cities and leading figures in the educational system. Eventually the Liberal Party was persuaded to accept this policy in some form. Perhaps the most influential figure in this development was the young Marquis of Roseberry. It was under his influence that it was decided to appoint an undersecretary (later secretary of state) for Scotland. This decision was made in 1886 and was clearly reached under pressure from Scottish interests. Since 1886 the Scottish Office has assumed increased importance as a major bureaucracy. It is peculiar in that the administrative task was developed on a territorial and not a functional basis. Not until much later was a similar arrangement made for Wales.

It is significant that the Scottish Office enjoyed its greatest expansion in the 1960s and 1970s. In 1962 the Scottish Development Department, concerned with development in the economic and other spheres, was made one of the major components of the office. In 1973 the Scottish Economic Planning Department was established, making yet another expansion along lines now current in British government as a whole. This is the significant point. It cannot be said that these organizations came along exclusively because of Scottish pressure, but rather because they fitted in with the regional policies followed by the government. It is arguable that less attention would have been paid to Scotland had it not been for nationalism, but that is by no means clear. What is certainly true is that no part of the Scottish Office has the sort of wide economic powers that would make any real impact on the Scottish economy. Such powers are still very much in the hands of the Department of Industry, a U.K. department. It is true that one recently established Scottish government organization seems to have a special position. The Scottish Development Agency was launched with a flourish in 1975, with the suggestion that new funds were being made available to solve Scotland's problems. It was very soon pointed out that what appeared to be new funds were simply existing funds that had been previously distributed to other agencies. Hogwood has clearly shown that, although other British regions, such as the northeast of England, may resent the attention they believe is being lavished on Scotland, no evidence can be found that Scotland has become the recipient of any extra Treasury largess.[7]

Finally, have the events of Scottish politics had any long-term effects on other aspects of British politics? If it is true that they will lead to the breakup of Britain, then there might be some signs of a weakening in the general system. But up to this point, no such weakening can be detected. It is certainly true that many Labour back-benchers have voted against the government or have abstained during the course of the Scotland bill through Parliament. One cannot argue, however, that this breakdown of parliamentary discipline is the result of what has happened in Scotland. In the debate on Europe and whether Britain should stay within the EEC one saw a similar pattern. It is true that party discipline in Parliament is no longer so strict as it once was, but this is the result of other events and movements.

Conclusion

Politics in Scotland have changed fundamentally. This change is not of significance to Scotland alone. It affects the whole of Britain in that the Labour Party finds great difficulty in building a majority in Britain without Scottish seats. More generally, the moves toward devolution in Scotland could lead to the breakup of Britain.

Of the two major parties, Labour has responded to this threat by enacting legislation to establish a Scottish parliament. The Conservatives, after a brief flirtation, have returned to the Unionist orthodoxy. If we look at the Labour legislation, however, it is quite clear that it is a very minimal exercise. It transfers to the new assembly certain domestic powers, but the issues behind Scottish nationalism are economic, and in no sense could a future

Scottish government deal with economic problems under this legislation. Even in Labour's other policies, such as the setting up of the Scottish Development Agency, it is quite clear that no real change has been made.

It must be concluded that, despite the Scotland bill, the full implications of what has happened have not yet been grasped. There is no doubt that the SNP will have its ups and downs, but every downturn in the Scottish economy will turn Labour voters, and perhaps Conservatives too, into the arms of the SNP. In the long run, the policy of the Nationalists is to break up Britain as we know it. Nothing that has been done so far seems to stand in the way of their success.

Notes

1. The SNP victor was Winifred Ewing.
2. T. Johnston et al., *Structure and Growth of the Scottish Economy* (London: Collins, 1971).
3. Donald MacKay and A. MacKay, *The Political Economy of North Sea Oil* (London: Robertson, 1975).
4. This is the case from the early polls run by the Edinburg University Department of Psychology in 1948.
5. Especially in *Words and Things* (London: Gallery 1959).
6. See *The Breakup of Britain* (London: New Left Books, 1977).
7. See, for example, E. Page, "The Transformation of Decision into Activities: The SDA as a Case Study," M.Sc. thesis, University of Strathclyde, 1977, chap. 3.

12 | *Erosion of the Periphery*

MILTON J. ESMAN

I

The loss of Britain's worldwide empire in the two decades following World War II marked the greatest change in recent British history. Britain's rulers yielded reluctantly but gracefully to the inevitable. There were no Algerias, no Angolas, no Dien Bien Phus. In a generation Britain completed the transition. Despite gloomy forebodings, living standards have improved substantially, though at a much slower rate than in most industrial countries. A welfare state has been established which has increased the quality of life for the great majority. Though Britannia no longer rules the waves and its security depends very largely on the United States, its people seem to feel no less secure than they did during the period of imperial greatness. Yet there have been costs, material and psychic. Middle-class positions in the administrative and professional services of the colonies and dependencies and jobs in the military and police have disappeared, along with economic opportunities in the semiprotected colonial markets for the products of British industries, which were becoming increasingly uncompetitive in international commerce. The loss of empire has also shaken much of the old confidence in the superiority of British institutions and of the British people, and the pride of the common man in identifying with the country that counted most in the world's affairs.

Having lost its empire, Britain is now confronted with challenges from its own territorial periphery. In the center-periphery metaphor, which has provided a paradigm for considerable polit-

ical writing in recent years, London and the southeast have for
many centuries represented the center of the United Kingdom, as
the Paris region has represented the center of France.[1] Political
power, economic control, and cultural prestige tend to be lodged
in the center; peripheral areas are weaker and often dependent
along all these dimensions. Some peripheral areas of the United
Kingdom, including Ireland, Scotland, and Wales, happen to be
the homelands of ethnic minorities, though the north of England
is not. Thus London is to Wales as Paris is to Brittany, Madrid to
Catalonia, and Rome to South Tyrol. During the past half century
the growing participation of the state in economic activities and
the expansion of welfare services have further concentrated political power in their centralized bureaucracies. The expansion in
the scale of industrial enterprises has centralized power in financial institutions and corporations located usually in capital cities
and sometimes abroad. The growth of public-sector enterprises
has reinforced this trend. Peripheral areas have suffered from
both loss of control and economic deprivation, absolute in some
cases, relative in others. Meanwhile improved communications
have made living conditions in metropolitan regions the standard
for their own comparisons and expectations. Efforts by central
governments to compensate for these developments by such economic incentives and redistributive policies as DATAR and growth
poles in France and regional development policies in Britain have
been of only limited help. The result of this growing awareness of
relative economic deprivation, combined in many cases with reac-
tivated cultural grievances, has been the mobilization of ethnic
protest into nationalist political movements demanding increased
autonomy and sometimes national independence for peoples who
have long been attached to larger political systems.[2]

English chauvinism has played a role in the consolidation of the
United Kingdom, but Britain has never been a Jacobin state.
Though England has represented the dominant core, it has tolerated very considerable cultural diversity, so long as the political
and economic unity of the realm has not been impaired and its
international security has not been threatened. This toleration
extended, it is true, more to Protestant than to Catholic areas in
the peripheries. In many respects the United Kingdom has been a
multinational state containing several minority peoples whose cul-

tures and sense of separate identity survived in their ancient homelands.[3]

The politicization of ethnic differences may be located on a continuum between two poles, the cultural and the economic. The cultural pole is identified with the slogan of "self-determination of peoples," an expression of popular sovereignty, the inherent illegitimacy of foreign rule, and the right of every people to self-government. The economic pole is derived from perceptions of economic exploitation or regional economic deprivation politicized in ethnic or national terms. Most ethnic protest combines elements of both; together, as in Quebec, they can provide a powerful mobilizing drive. Before World War I, when the economic role of the state was limited, most of the ethno-national movements, including those in the Habsburg, Ottoman, and Romanoff empires and in Ireland, emphasized the inherent right of self-determination. Since World War II, however, economic grievances have been more common, as in contemporary Scotland. Indeed, as in the contemporary case of "Occitania," spokesmen for regions that have suffered economically may attempt to rediscover or to resurrect an ethnic identity in order to mobilize more effectively and to legitimize their demands externally.[4]

Contemporary writers who until recently glorified the United Kingdom as the prototype of the well-integrated polity have conveniently overlooked the Irish question.[5] The demands of the Irish Catholic majority for home rule dominated British politics from 1880 until the outbreak of World War I. Though formally annexed by an act of union in 1800, Ireland, like Algeria, had been a conquered province. Like most colonies, it was governed by people whom the local majority considered to be foreigners of a hostile religion and culture. Their lands and other major economic assets had been confiscated and awarded to members of the colonial elite and alien settlers; the Irish culture was demeaned, their religion was oppressed, and they themselves were impoverished and treated as both contemptible and subversive. The colonial status of Ireland was embodied in the concept of the "Protestant ascendency." The results were deep grievances and a profound and abiding hatred that was translated into militant action when nationalism became a respectable political doctrine after the French Revolution and the extention of democratic suffrage created rising expectations. The unwillingness of the British Parliament, particularly the House of Lords, to concede home rule—in effect to restore regional government and turn it over to its Catholic majority—made revolution and secession inevitable.[6] London's failure to manage the Irish crisis represents a notable exception to, or perhaps a refutation of, the well-cultivated legend that the British ruling class, unlike the Bourbons, knew how to make the timely concession to popular forces required to preserve the essence of their power and their domains.

When the Irish Free State was established in 1922, a major peripheral area was lost to the United Kingdom. A half century later, Ulster remains as its tragic legacy. Many, perhaps the majority in Britain, would be happy to forgo the high and apparently endless costs of maintaining Ulster in the United Kingdom and would be inclined to leave it to its own devices, but are trapped by fear of the bloody consequences of abandoning their residual responsibility to IRA terrorists and equally ruthless Protestant vigilantes. The Irish experience should serve as a reminder that the center of the imperial system sustained serious erosions at its periphery during the heyday of empire, more than a half century ago.

Space does not permit me to dwell on Wales, a second peripheral area that is the homeland of an ancient culture. A Protestant community, Wales has been administered as part of England; it has enjoyed no independent political status since the Tudor Acts of Union in 1526 and 1532. The core of modern Welsh nationalism is the Welsh language, which is now understood and used by a declining minority of about 20 percent, most of whom are bilingual and live in rural areas. Nevertheless, many Welsh maintain a pronounced sense of distinctive nationality. Though the Welsh nationalist movement formally demands independence, it is unlikely to mobilize politically significant demands in Wales on behalf of this goal. It appears that demands for official recognition of the Welsh language can be rather comfortably accommodated by the British government and that in the coming referendum the Welsh majority may not support even the limited regional administrative autonomy offered by Westminster in the recently enacted Wales bill. Welsh nationalism, it appears, does not represent an important threat to the territorial integrity of Great Britain.[7]

Scotland is a different story. Scotland was never a colony, nor was it ever dominated by an alien ruling class. The severe repressions of the Highland clans following the final defeat of the Stuarts at Culloden in 1745 and the brutal Highland clearances of the nineteenth century were carried out primarily by members of the Lowland Scots majority, not by the English. Under the terms of the Act of Union of 1707, which most Scots have regarded as a voluntary agreement on the part of their parliament, Scotland lost its parliament but retained and has managed to maintain its other major national institutions, including its distinctive legal code and procedures, its established church, its educational system, and its local government structures. Though much of Scottish life has been anglicized, Scotland has retained an indigenous popular culture and a distinctive style of speech, which have contributed to the maintenance of a sense of distinctive nationality with ancient roots. The British government conceded Scotland's distinctiveness by establishing the Scottish Office in 1885 and transferring much of the administration of internal matters to its headquarters in Edinburgh. All bills that concern Scotland are routinely reviewed by a Scottish Grand Committee before they are taken up in Parliament. Until well after World War I, Scots retained control of their own economy and of their major economic enterprises. Scots, as individuals, could and did move freely into all sectors of professional, business, and political life in England. Though there is a certain anti-English strain under the skin of many Scots, they have not been and never considered themselves to be an oppressed people.[8]

Scots had a major role in building and maintaining the British Empire. Enterprising Scots of all classes were prominent among the military and administrative agents of empire and in the plantations, financial and trading houses, schools and hospitals that were established under British protection. The Empire provided an outlet for Scottish enterprise and energies that were underemployed at home and a preferential market for Scotland's burgeoning industry. The profits of empire flowed back to Scotland, and during the latter part of the nineteenth century Glasgow was probably the richest city in the world. Scotland has been especially hurt by the end of empire, since the losses of employment opportunities and of protected markets have coincided with stagnation in its industrial base, especially in the Strathclyde area, and with the loss of control of many of its economic enterprises. By the late 1950s Scots were increasingly aware that their economy was depressed, that their living standards were substantially below the British average, that their unemployment was double the rate for southeast England and would have been even higher except for substantial out-migration. Scots felt an increasing malaise, a demoralization, a sense of dependency, and an apparent inability to do anything about it. Scotland was economically a depressed and declining economic region, and the measures undertaken by London through the redistributive expenditures of the welfare state and through regional investment incentives had cushioned the blow but were far from sufficient to reverse the trend.

During the late 1960s many Scots lost confidence in the ability of British institutions to respond to their economic plight. The failure of the Labour Party to improve employment and welfare conditions after its return to office in 1964 disillusioned many members of the working class and the intellectuals who identified with the Labour Party and with socialism. On the other hand, the threat of British socialism and the tendency of Labour governments to yield to militant unions and attacks on some of the remaining privileges of the middle class alarmed property owners, small entrepreneurs, rural nonunion workers, and members of the professional middle classes. The result was a series of stunning electoral successes for the previously insignificant Scottish National Party (SNP), which proclaimed that Scotland's redemption depended on the reestablishment of political sovereignty and separation from England. Virtually overnight the SNP became an important party of protest. Its prescription for independence, however, could not be taken seriously by most Scottish voters, because it seemed impossible for Scotland in its weak and dependent condition to go it alone economically. The SNP's proportion of the popular vote fell from 30 percent in the 1968 local elections to 11 percent in the general election in 1970.[9]

It was the discovery of oil in very large quantities beneath the broad continental shelf off Scotland's east coast that electrified

Scotland in the early 1970s and converted the SNP from a party
of protest to a serious force in Scottish politics. The SNP capitalized
on the theme "It's Scotland's oil"; only independence could ensure that the rich revenues from its patrimony would not be
appropriated by London and dissipated throughout a declining and overpopulated Britain, but would be used to rehabilitate
and modernize Scotland's decaying industrial structure and provide productive employment and amenities for its people. North
Sea oil provided renewed hope for Scotland's economic future
and, for many, confidence that Scotland could, if necessary, go it
alone economically. Branches of the SNP led by youthful en-
thusiasts multiplied throughout Scotland. The SNP vote grew
from 10 percent and one MP in 1970 to 21 percent and seven MPs
in February 1974 and 31 percent and eleven MPs in October
1974. The Labour vote fell from 45 percent in 1970 to 36 percent
in October 1974, the Tory from 38 percent to 25 percent.
Though polls indicated that only 20 percent of Scots desired full
independence, the SNP was able to capitalize on rising expectations resulting from North Sea oil and to persuade a majority of
Scottish voters that Scotland was in a position, for the first time, to
make important demands on London.

The Labour Party responded with alacrity by creating the Scottish Development Agency to sponsor and finance industrial
growth in Scotland, by promising to transfer several thousand
civil service jobs from London to Glasgow, by establishing the
headquarters of the new National Oil Corporation in Scotland,
and above all by pledging itself to a program of institutional
devolution—the establishment of an elected Scottish assembly and
a Scottish executive that would be responsible for a broad range
of public services in Scotland.[10] Scotland was being offered the
home rule it had failed to achieve before World War I, in effect a
quasi-federal status within the United Kingdom. To Labour's
strategists, devolution would go a long way toward pacifying Scottish discontents while keeping Scotland within the political and
economic framework of the United Kingdom, salvaging Labour's
Scottish seats in Westminster (without which it had little chance of
remaining or of ever again becoming the party of government),
and maintaining Britain's unrestricted access to and control of the
revenues from North Sea oil. The tactic worked in October 1974;

Labour retained its Scottish seats, which more than provided the margin of its slender parliamentary majority.

London's initial response to the challenge of Scottish nationalism was one of consternation and disbelief. Every major institution in British politics and society is intensely unionist, and large numbers of Scots are tied to such institutions as the trade unions, universities, professional societies, and economic organizations. From London's perspective, Scotland had few legitimate complaints, and those were shared by other economic regions of Britain. The political and economic unity of the kingdom is one of the nonnegotiable premises underlying the legitimacy of any political discourse. The revenues from North Sea oil and the oil itself are indispensable to the recovery and the future viability of Britain's weak and troubled economy, with its lagging productivity and its high rates of inflation and unemployment. Moreover, Britain borrowed heavily in anticipation of these revenues to finance its large balance-of-payments deficits on current account. Thus any measures that would appease the Scots would have to ensure the continued political and economic integration of the realm and London's control of oil revenues. It would be important from London's perspective, however, to make expedient concessions that would avert outbreaks of Ulster-style violence in Scotland.

The lengthy battles over Labour's devolution package which preoccupied Parliament during the 1976–77 and 1977–78 sessions resulted from the reluctance of the English majority, along with most Scottish Tories and several Scottish Labourites, to concede special treatment to Scotland, and their insistence that ultimate control must remain securely in London. That the proposed Scottish Assembly should enjoy any special access at all to oil revenues was not even considered in the debates. The Scotland bill that finally emerged in the summer of 1978, with numerous cuts and bruises, will be followed by a referendum in which a majority, including 40 percent of all eligible Scottish voters, must approve the devolution package if the new set of institutions is to be established. The bill was sufficient to redeem Labour's 1974 pledge on devolution, just in time for the 1979 general elections. The success of Labour, the disappointing performance of the SNP in two parliamentary by-elections in the Glasgow area in the spring of

1978, and subsequent surveys suggest that the Scots have been sufficiently mollified both by the priority that the Callaghan government has given to devolution legislation and modest improvements in the Scottish economy to reward the Labour Party with their vital support.

Will the SNP succeed in convincing a majority of Scots, once the devolution measures have been implemented, that Scotland should in its turn follow Ireland out of the United Kingdom? Probably not, according to available evidence. No more than 20 percent of Scottish respondents have ever expressed a desire for full independence, but a substantial majority have indicated their preference for some form of home rule along the lines of the recent devolution package. If the referendum carries, Scotland will regain an institutional political voice. But without the gingering effect created by the SNP, Scotland would not have its new set of political institutions, and most Scots acknowledge this. Any London government that takes a hard line against demands emanating from Scotland's new political institutions—demands that are likely to escalate—will probably benefit the SNP. The SNP will have many grievances to exploit, including (1) the size of the block financial grants that Whitehall will make annually or biennially to the Scottish Assembly, for the latter will have spending but not taxing powers, an arrangement that *The Economist* calls "representation without taxation," a prescription for political irresponsibility; and (2) the division of North Sea oil revenues, a subject that even the SNP had to suppress in order to see the Scotland Bill enacted.

During the past two and a half centuries, the average Scot has been able to reconcile his Scottish patriotism with loyalty to Britain and the English connection. Now, however, this dual allegiance cannot be taken for granted. The SNP has been successful, for the first time since 1745, in presenting Scotland, especially Scotland's youth, with a practical political alternative that puts Scotland's interest first and in restoring to the Scottish polity distinctive political structures in which Scottish grievances and conflicts of interest with the London government can find legitimate institutional expression. London has made important institutional concessions in the hope that Scots will be appeased by "home rule." It has not responded, however, to the economic grievances, which are far more salient and which Scottish voters believe can and should be alleviated by a fair share of oil revenues to be used by Scottish institutions for Scotland's benefit.[11] These institutional concessions by London may stabilize the English-Scottish relationship for a time, but not, in my opinion, unless a settlement can be worked out that gives the majority of Scots what they consider a fair deal on oil revenues, a subject on which many of them feel very deeply but which London has not yet been willing even to consider.

II

Unlike contemporary Basque, Breton, and Welsh nationalism, Scottish nationalism has not been fueled by major cultural grievances. Religion and language are not issues between England and Scotland, and because Scottish nationalism has lacked the emotional tensions generated by religion and language the SNP has remained a peaceful movement. The nationalist movement in Scotland has inspired virtually no political violence. Scotland's grievances have been primarily economic, based on a widespread sense of collective economic deprivation and a serious decline of confidence in the capacity of British political institutions to deal with Scotland's needs. Rising expectations resulting from North Sea oil and an effective organizational vehicle, the SNP, were sufficient to make Scottish nationalism a force to be reckoned with in Scotland and in all of Britain.

To what extent is Britain's experience with its Scottish minority unique, and how can it be explained in terms of developments common to all late industrial societies? Four important factors have conditioned or encouraged the recent emergence of nationalist movements among peoples occupying traditional homelands in Western Europe:

1. The Pax Americana. The American military deterrent has greatly increased the sense of security throughout Western Europe. For nearly three decades most Western Europeans have not felt threatened by the prospect of external invasion. They have been able safely to concentrate on other concerns.

2. Sustained affluence. A long and steady period of substantial economic growth, combined with the redistributive programs of

the welfare state, has lifted most Europeans comfortably above the subsistence level and reduced the salience both of material demands and of class orientations.

3. Increased levels of education. Greater educational opportunities have undermined traditional patterns of discipline and deference both of religion and of class, increased opportunities for mobility, stimulated intellectual independence and a willingness to make demands on the system, and enhanced tolerence for individual and group differences.

4. The end of European empire. Many small nations have succeeded in establishing their political independence and in gaining recognition of their new status as morally and politically legitimate.

Everywhere in the West, regardless of national boundaries, traditional values have been under strain.[12] New preferences have emerged, especially among young people and opinion leaders. Among the signs are the following:

1. Resistance to and rejection of the traditional institutional disciplines of sex, class, age, religion, and ethnic stratification—a process of desubordination along many important dimensions of interpersonal and intergroup relations, including the declining authority of industrial managers and trade union leaders.

2. Increased demands for individual and group freedom and for opportunities to influence and participate in decisions that affect the individual's working, community, and leisure environments.

3. Sharp reaction against centralization and large-scale units in both the political and the economic spheres. There is widespread rejection of allegedly impersonal, remote, bureaucratic, unresponsive, incompetent, overloaded, and overcentralized government and of similarly oversized, technocratic, dehumanizing economic enterprises, in both the private and the public sectors. This mood is accompanied by the declining appeal and salience of state-centered nationalism. The militant state patriotism that characterized all Western polities in the century before World War II now seems dated, irrelevant, devoid of emotional content, and even slightly hypocritical, especially to young people. Even the Keynesian faith in centralized economic management has lost its appeal: for all its large bureaucracies and its centralization of power, it has been incapable of dealing with persistently high

unemployment and simultaneous chronic inflation. This disenchantment is especially felt in the weaker economic regions, which have often been the unintended victims of macroeconomic management and have benefited little from redistributive policies. The substantial economic benefits and social security produced by large-scale industrial units and trade unions and by centralized planning and the welfare state now seem to be taken for granted. Young people and opinion leaders concentrate on their deficiencies and their costs while propounding new sets of aspirations and new life-styles.

4. A consequent search for new institutions and new objects of loyalty and respect, especially for institutions that can provide a more satisfactory sense of community both for governance and for socioeconomic activities—communities that can compensate for the alienation that many young people feel from the large but emotionally empty urban agglomerations in which they live and their dissatisfaction with the impersonal bureaucratic institutions of government and industry in which they work.

These changing values have generated politically significant protests against the status quo—demands that the governments of all late industrial societies, including the British, have felt it necessary to recognize and in many cases to respond to. Most of these demands place little emphasis on material living standards and less on economic efficiency, to the despair of neoclassical economists observing the stagnation in worker productivity and the relatively poor performance of the British economy, especially in international competition. Likewise, Marxists are distressed by the disinterest of these reform and protest movements in proletarian revolution and their tendency to deemphasize class conflict even when their rhetoric includes the leftist slogans of recent Third World liberation movements. The demands of these protest movements include the following:

1. Equal treatment of women, homosexuals' rights, and sexual freedom as expressed in liberalized provisions for divorce, contraception, and abortion.

2. Protection of the environment and enhancement of the quality of life, including the elimination of air and water pollution, protection of natural resources, restoration of historical sites, and increased public support and sponsorship of recreational and leisure facilities and the arts.

3. Workers' participation in the management of economic enterprises, as evidenced by the growing literature on self-management, the extension of *Mitbestimmung* in Germany, and the Bullock report in Britain, combined with efforts to humanize and democratize the work environment.

4. Increased attention to the devolution of political life to smaller units, both local and regional; for example, the Hunt-Peacock Memorandum of Dissent to the report of the Kilbrandon Commission on the Constitution in Britain[13] and the recent promises by President Giscard d'Estaing radically to decentralize public administration in the classically overcentralized French state.

5. The legitimization of ethnic interests, both cultural and economic, and the relaxation of the monopolistic claims of the centralized state on the individual. Concessions to ethnic-group pressures that would have been resisted during the two centuries following the French Revolution are now being granted: political devolution for Scotland, regional autonomy for Catalonia and the Basque country, official status for the Welsh and Breton languages, even bilingual education in the United States. Those who control the centers of Western states, while unwilling to countenance the dismemberment of their polities, have begun to accord reluctant legitimacy to ethnic pluralism and minority nationalism and to set aside their earlier insistence on cultural assimilation and a monopoly of power in the political center. They no longer insist on recognizing ethnic demands exclusively as regional economic problems amenable only to fiscal and economic concessions. Recent concessions to ethnic groups in regional homelands will stimulate less welcome demands from recent immigrant groups, including blacks, Asians, and Gypsies in Britain, Turkish and Yugoslav "guest workers" in Germany, and Spaniards and North Africans in France. Their demands are likely to include formal nondiscrimination, full civil and citizenship rights, and special services to permit the maintenance of minority cultures.[14]

While Scotland's grievances and demands are not typical of European ethnic minorities, in that they are overwhelmingly economic and have virtually no cultural content, the resurgence of political nationalism in Scotland must be assessed in the context of broader developments in late industrial societies.[15] The political emergence of ethnic groups and the legitimization of their demands are expressions of a general trend toward the redefinition of social priorities and increased tolerance of plural interests. Where cultural differences and national solidarities persist, grievances articulated and politicized in ethnic terms will be accorded at least a hearing. This applies especially to indigenous minorities that can claim traditional homelands. In some cases these demands can be rather easily accommodated by the center, as with the recent concessions to the Welsh language. Others, including demands from Scotland for a substantial share of North Sea oil revenues, will be resisted. Others may result in major institutional changes, such as the processes of institutional devolution now under way in Catalonia, Flanders, and Scotland. To forestall the erosion of their peripheries and to limit social violence, those who dominate the center in contemporary Western states are now prepared not only to accord legitimacy to ethnic solidarities but also to make timely concessions to their demands. It seems likely that ethnic-based demands will continue to be expressed and that concessions will continue to be made so long as ethnic spokesmen can demonstrate that they speak for substantial numbers of their constituents and so long as these demands fall short of the point that threatens the territorial integrity of these political systems. The sort of intransigence that contributed to the secession of Ireland is not likely, even under a unionist Tory government, to be repeated in the cases of Wales and Scotland.

The current strains on the British periphery are expressions of similar strains in most late industrial states, which have become more liberal and more tolerant of diversity than ever before. This does not mean, of course, that political leaders or public majorities necessarily support any of the proposed reforms or even that the causes are mutually supportive. Environmentalists do not necessarily support the goals of feminists, and neither may have any interest in worker participation in management or in ethnic minorities. Yet a certain synergism may be seen in these several forms of protest, especially in view of the favorable audience they continue to command among large numbers of young people and influential opinion makers. This situation has produced an environment favorable to the accommodation of moderate demands from such groups, rather than the neglect, ridicule, prompt rejection, or repression that they might have expected in earlier periods.

These accommodationist trends could be reversed if the Pax

Americana should fail and the security of these states should be threatened by the Soviets or by the breakup of Western defense alliances, or if prolonged economic adversity should result in conflicts that threatened a Gaullist-style right-wing reaction. Such developments might generate renewed demands for conformity on terms established by frightened and anxious conservative regimes. But this is sheer speculation. The current trend is accommodationist because changing conditions have evoked changing values, especially among young people, in the late industrial societies of the West. These changes have brought forth fresh demands and new life-styles. They have legitimized many expressions of protest and of pluralism, including the claims of such ancient national minorities as the Scots, who have begun to reassess their stake in the political structures under which they have lived for many generations.

On March 1, 1979, a year after this article was written, referenda were held in Wales and Scotland on the limited devolution schemes which Parliament had reluctantly authorized. As expected, the Welsh rejected devolution overwhelmingly, by 4 to 1. Although a decade of surveys had indicated that as many as 75 percent of Scots desired some form of home rule, the referendum carried in Scotland by only 51.6 percent, falling far short of the 40 percent of eligible voters required by Parliament. This margin was considered too slender to constitute a mandate for a major constitutional change. When Prime Minister Callaghan declined to put the matter to Parliament, the SNP withdrew its support, and the Labour government fell. In the ensuing general election, when the strongly unionist Conservative Party won a clear majority and formed a new government under Margaret Thatcher, the SNP lost 9 of its 11 seats in Parliament and its vote collapsed from 30.5 percent in October 1974 to 17.3 percent.

Why devolution fared so poorly in the referendum is still a matter of speculation. Many factors contributed to the outcome. The opposition was well organized and well financed, and campaigned effectively. They emphasized the economic risks to Scots preoccupied with unemployment; they attacked the increases in taxes and in bureaucracy that would result from an additional layer of government; and they played on fears that all of Scotland would be governed by a Glasgow majority. Though

the Labour Party sponsored the referendum, its support was uneven and tactical; enthusiasm came primarily from the SNP,
identifying devolution with eventual separatism, which the great
majority continues to reject.

The immediate future of home rule is not promising. The Tory
leadership is hostile in principle, does not depend on Scottish
support, and has other priorities. It is now impossible to hold that
the demand for home rule is so compelling as to require
institutional accommodation and to warrant the parliamentary
time and attention that another devolution battle would undoubtedly entail. At their moment of truth, the Scots responded
indecisively. The Scottish nation, Scottish nationalism, Scottish
interests, and Scottish issues will, of course, persist, but they are
unlikely to make waves in the British system for some time. The
SNP may recover from its recent setbacks, but in the absence of
opportunities to promote independence within the system, they
may resort to more militant tactics.

Notes

1. On the center-periphery paradigm see Edward Shils, "Center and
Periphery," in *The Logic of Personal Knowledge: Essays Presented to Michael
Polanyi* (London: Routledge & Kegan Paul, 1961), and Sidney Tarrow,
"From Center to Periphery: Alternative Models of National-Local Policy
Impact and an Application to France and Italy," Western Societies Occa-
sional Paper no. 14, Cornell University, Center for International Studies,
April 1976.

2. An analysis of this general trend and recent case studies are presented in Milton J. Esman, ed., *Ethnic Conflict in the Western World* (Ithaca:
Cornell University Press, 1977).

3. The royal warrants establishing the Royal Commission on the Constitution on April 15, 1969, directed its members to "examine the present
functions of the central legislature and government in relation to the
several countries, nations, and regions of the United Kingdom..." (italics
supplied) Cmnd. 5460 (London: Her Majesty's Stationery Office, October 1973).

4. James E. Jacob, "The Basques and Occitans in France: A Comparative Study of Ethnic Militancy," Ph.D. dissertation, Department of Government, Cornell University, August 1978.

5. Gabriel Almond and Bingham Powell, *Comparative Politics: A
Developmental Approach* (Boston: Little, Brown, 1966). For a standard history
of Ireland, see Edmund Curtis, *A History of Ireland*, 6th ed. (New York:
Barnes & Noble, 1950). A history from the perspective of the Anglo-Irish

is J. C. Beckett, *The Anglo-Irish Tradition* (Ithaca: Cornell University Press, 1976).

6. Of course the intransigent opposition of the Protestant majority in Ulster contributed to the outcome.

7. An analysis of contemporary Welsh nationalism may be found in John Osmond, *Creative Conflict: The Politics of Welsh Nationalism* (Cardiff, Gomar Press, and London: Routledge & Kegan Paul, 1977).

8. In his *Internal Colonialism: The Celtic Fringe in British National Development, 1536–1966* (Berkeley: University of California Press, 1975), Michael Hechter mistakenly treats Scotland as an internal colony. This argument is refuted by Tom Nairn in his chapter "Twilight of the British State," from his book *The Breakup of Britain: Crisis and Neo-Nationalism* (London: NLB Press, 1977).

9. The history of Scottish nationalism is discussed in H. T. Hanham, *Scottish Nationalism* (Cambridge: Harvard University Press, 1967). More recent events are discussed in Milton J. Esman, "Scottish Nationalism, North Sea Oil, and the British Response," in *Ethnic Conflict in the Western World,* ed. Esman, pp. 251–86. See also Christopher Harvie, *Scotland and Nationalism: Scottish Society and Politics, 1707–1977* (London: George Allen & Unwin, 1977).

10. *Democracy and Devolution, Proposal for Scotland and Wales,* Cmnd. 5736 (London: Her Majesty's Stationery Office, September 1974).

11. Repeated surveys have indicated that economic issues are far more important to most Scots than home rule or cultural concerns. See Esman, "Scottish Nationalism," p. 273.

12. There is a large literature on the attributes and dynamics of the emergent postindustrial societies of the West. The seminal volume is Daniel Bell, *The Coming Postindustrial Society* (New York: Basic Books, 1973).

13. Cmnd. 5460-1.

14. There is a large literature on migrant workers in Europe. See especially W. R. Böhning, *The Migration of Workers in the United Kingdom and the European Community* (London: Oxford University Press, 1972), and Ray C. Rist, *Guest Workers in Germany: The Prospects for Pluralism* (New York: Praeger, 1978).

15. One difference between most Scottish nationalists and many of the Continental ethnic minority organizations is the pronounced hostility of the Scots to the concept of a united Europe. The enthusiasm of many European intellectuals for a Europe of regions or of ethnic groups that would work in harmony with supranational European institutions and simultaneously weaken the power of the established centralized regimes has not been evident in Scottish nationalism. The SNP opposed British entry into the EEC and would be willing to consider joining it, once Scotland achieves independence, only on terms specially negotiated for Scotland. Tom Nairn's enthusiasm for the European option, expressed in his essay in this volume, is not shared by the majority of Scottish nationalists.

PART V : :

The International Problem

Whose Crisis?: Britain as an International Problem

LAWRENCE FREEDMAN

I

It is a very rare article or book on contemporary British foreign policy that does not find it necessary to quote at some point Dean Acheson's comment of December 1962: "Great Britain has lost an empire and has not yet found a role." The fact that this statement was uttered by such a senior international figure as Acheson, and one considered to be a friend of Britain, made it difficult to ignore. It pierced the cocoon of self-delusion, derived from past glories, that surrounded some sections of the British elite. Though it was then, and has been since, taken to be an important insight into the poignancy of Britain's position, as such it was unexceptionable. The winds of change had already been widely acknowledged. It is my suspicion that Acheson's jibe is so frequently recalled because it served as a challenge, for what he implied was that with a sufficiently thorough search a role was to be found. This role would be a substitute for empire, a position in international affairs of sufficient significance to satisfy the nation's self-esteem. In suggesting that such a role was to be found, Acheson did Britain a great disservice. Rather than shattering an illusion, he in fact perpetuated it.

There has been a continued search, increasingly desperate, for something unique and exceptional for Britain to contribute to the conduct of world affairs. The country has suffered from "top-tableitis," eager to be seen at the center of the stage, contributing solutions to the most important problems of our time. The performance has been one of the aging male lead, resisting bit and character parts when he can play the hero no more. The value of long traditions of diplomacy and familiarity with all regions of the globe has been asserted to justify participation in attempts to settle a variety of the world's troubles. International systems have been designed in which Britain is at the center, offering links with the English-speaking world, its old colonies, and Europe, helping mutual understanding because of its empathy with all. "We have country by country connections throughout the world," boasted James Callaghan as foreign secretary in 1975. "We have the experience . . . the *policy* which can enable Britain to make a contribution out of all proportion to our individual size and power to problems facing the world . . . we may well have found [our] role . . . We are the bridge-builders."[1]

For a country that no longer enjoys preeminence in international trade and finance or the ability to project military power far beyond its own locality, a collection of excellent contacts may be the best there is to offer. It is unfortunately difficult to elevate contacts and policy to a world role. Many channels of communication now exist through which nations can speak to each other, and Britain is necessary as an intermediary in very few of them. When West Germany and the United States were communicating imperfectly in 1977 and 1978, attempts by Britain to promote mutual understanding were not always appreciated. The Germans' problem could not be eased by Britain's use of its good access to explain the German position in Washington. The Germans' requirement was for comparable access of their own.

Another trouble with the bridge-building notion is that getting people to talk to and understand each other does not necessarily contribute to a reconciliation. Recalcitrant parties will need persuading and often pushing; international initiatives will need funding and personnel. A positive role in international affairs inevitably requires the expenditure of resources in some way. In the north-south dialogue, Britain could offer excellent schemes to ease relations between the developed and developing worlds, but they required amounts of money to make them work that Britain itself could not and would not offer.

In the bridge-building scheme, Britain is pictured standing outside the major conflicts of our time, without major interests at stake except for a general desire for peace and harmony in the world. The independent arbiter, the trusted mutual friend is a figure able to stand apart from the disputants. Yet Britain's interest in what is going on in the outside world is considerable, and its dependence on other nations is growing and not decreasing. Distant wars over territory may be of limited concern, but now the major issues pertain to the distribution of power and wealth in the world and the rules that govern international transactions. On these issues Britain has major interests that need protection and promotion.

II

In contrast to those who are still searching for some sort of unique role for Britain in the world are those who believe that Britain can have no role at all. Instead of acting on the world stage, Britain is in the audience watching the performance of others. This is a view I often encounter when explaining that I am engaged in a study of British foreign policy. The normal response is to ask whether such a thing actually exists. This popular view is based on a concept of foreign policy associated with policing functions or the cultivation of "spheres of influence." The recognition that Britain is no longer able to engage in this sort of international activity with its previous vigor and efficacy has encouraged many to believe that it is prevented now from enjoying such luxuries as a foreign policy at all.

This sort of approach can be detected in the recent Berrill Report on Overseas Representation. An introductory chapter treats with derision recent forays into international peacemaking:

> Its efforts . . . to help solve international problems by diplomatic or military means—Rhodesia, Cyprus, the Middle East, South Arabia, Vietnam, the problems of its own dependent territories—have not been conspicuously successful. . . .
> . . . If it maintains pretensions to a world role which it is palpably beyond its will or power to sustain, the UK is more likely to convince influential foreigners that we are still prey to delusions of post-imperial grandeur than to give them confidence that we are headed for an early recovery.[2]

In most accounts of Britain's postwar decline one can find variations on this theme. Some qualifications are in order. It is important not to exaggerate Britain's former strengths or the contemporary strength of other major powers. The fact is that the world has changed as much as Britain's capacity to operate within it. The withdrawal of British administrators and troops from Asia, the Middle East, and Africa has left vacuums that have been filled in a variety of ways. It is true that the superpowers, particularly the United States, moved in when the old imperial powers left, but their positions are not often so comfortable or secure as those of their predecessors and are rarely commanding. Power has shifted away from the industrialized world. The developing countries have achieved the attributes of sovereign states, which give them certain rights and leverage in international organizations. Some of their number have effective control over resources of vast importance to the industrial nations and have not hesitated to exploit them for economic and political benefit. New centers of power have emerged to complicate international life. The world is no longer so conducive to the interference of the major powers as it once was. While it is true that the superpowers can impose on others more than can countries of Britain's size and resources, even they are finding it difficult to order the world according to their preferences. Foreign policy, in the traditional sense, is becoming a much more unsatisfactory and tiresome activity.

It is important to emphasize this point; otherwise it might be thought that Britain's slide from great-power status was simply a reflection of its dismal economic performance. Even if Britain's average growth rate since the war had been over 5 percent rather than under 3 percent, the withdrawal from the colonies could not have been avoided. Britain might have spoken with greater confidence and authority in international gatherings but would still have found it difficult to maintain extensive overseas bases. To the extent that it was easier to do so, Britain's overextension might have lasted a little longer. But some contraction was inevitable; in order to have a military effort comparable to that of the mid-1950s, Britain's defense budget would have to be almost twice as much as it is today. We therefore have no reason to expect any basic change in Britain's international position resulting from an improvement in its economic performance.

Nor is there anything in Britain's recent foreign policy activity to suggest a great desire for a prominent role. Over the past few years the residue of Britain's empire has been occupying a disproportionate amount of the time and energies of the Foreign and Commonwealth Office. The attempt to complete the process of decolonization is frustrated by the reluctance of the colonies in question to substitute for the relative security of British rule the embrace of predatory neighbors. Beleiz fears Guatemala, the Falkland Islands fear Argentina, Gibraltar fears Spain, and Northern Ireland fears Eire. Most difficult of all has been the reluctance of white Rhodesians to accept the inevitability of rule by the black majority. In each of these cases, with the exception of Ireland, which is closer to home, the desire has been to extricate Britain from onerous responsibilities and international controversies without upsetting the subject populations unduly. The direction is clear, and it is confirmed by such recent episodes as the Cyprus crisis of 1974. Britain wishes to extricate itself from close involvement in the affairs of regions other than its own.

But this does not mean that Britain will no longer require a foreign policy. Disentanglement from the squabbles of others will never be complete, and as a permanent member of the UN Security Council Britain is required to have a view on the multifarious disputes that come before that body. Of greater significance is the fact that the major preoccupations of foreign policy have shifted from disputes about sovereignty and territory around the globe to the patterns of international trade and finance and the supply of oil and other raw materials. With a broader view of foreign policy as covering all attempts to structure external relations, it soon becomes apparent that foreign policy needs as much if not more attention than ever before, because Britain is more dependent on foreigners than ever before.

Once again we return to the fact of Britain's considerable stake in the affairs of the world. Britain is unusually dependent on foreign trade, poor in most raw materials, except recently (and temporarily) in oil and for somewhat longer in gas and coal; its capitalists own large portfolios of foreign investments, and many of its citizens still respond to the habits of empire or the pressures of tax laws and reside overseas. This is a country that can in no way be considered self-sufficient and for which autarky is therefore not an option. Consequently relations with other countries are of prime importance. Within these relations Britain does not have the leverage that was once available. In few areas are sufficient British troops on hand to compel compliance with the wishes of Her Majesty's Government. When the disruption of trading relations is considered, it is necessary to accept the fact that Britain often needs the foreign exchange more than the other country needs Britain's goods. These constraints do not mean that Britain can have no foreign policy, even in the areas of its greatest need, but that it needs a *good* foreign policy more than ever. Britain's relative weakness puts a premium on using available resources and points of leverage with care, skill, and ingenuity.

III

We have noted two views on Britain's position in the world: one sees Britain as eager to demonstrate some unique and valuable British contribution; the other, more cynical, points out that Britain has little to offer. I have suggested that attempts by Britain to play an honest broker within or to extricate itself from world affairs fail because it has definite interests to care for. Foreign policy is not an expensive luxury that Britain can afford no more but a vital element in any strategy to maintain Britain as a viable trading nation. As such it can be rather a selfish activity, not the selfless do-gooding on an international scale implied by the "role in the world" rhetoric.

Many would argue, in fact, that Britain has been insufficiently selfish in the conduct of its external relations. This view can be found among those who believe that Britain makes an excessive contribution to NATO by spending a greater portion of its GNP on defense than its European allies, signed the Treaty of Rome out of a mistaken internationalism, and accepted the collapse of key industries because of undue respect for rules governing free trade. As Britain's economic position has become increasingly parlous, the desire to put immediate interests to the fore has grown. For the rest of this chapter we shall be considering the implications of such a trend for British foreign policy.

The perception of Britain as a basket case is widespread.

"Never, surely, except under the impact of overwhelming military defeat . . . has a great country gone so rapidly from world power to extreme helplessness," writes George Kennan.[3] During the 1976 election campaign the British ambassador to Washington had to ask President Ford if he would please refrain from citing Britain as a negative example every time he wished to make a point about the evils of public spending. Britain has become viewed as an object of pity but not of respect. The spectacle of the 1974 miners' strike, the consequent demise of the Heath government, and the rampant inflation of the following years fed fears that Britain would either collapse internally or in attempting to survive would resort to siege economy measures. In either cases great strains would be put on Britain's relations with its major partners and on the whole Western system. The prospect of this former pillar of the international establishment turning into a deviant case was alarming. Others have viewed Britain as a negative influence before, as a colonialist power, for example. But that view was a consequence of Britain's strength, not of its weakness.

Britain has previously caused difficulties because its decline has left a vacuum in international affairs. Britain has stopped providing a stabilizing influence in the turbulent regions of the world. Thus Andrew Young's remarks about Britain's leaving America with the problems of South Africa as it did before with Palestine. But now Britain is viewed not merely as lacking in stabilizing influence but as being a destabilizing force. A change has been noted in Britain's international personality—from generosity and responsibility to an introverted parochialism. To its partners in the EEC Britain is always asking for concessions and special treatment without displaying great interest in offering anything in return. Its preoccupations are with short-term costs rather than long-term gains. The more Britain becomes dependent on others, the more it dwells on the trappings of national sovereignty. Beyond that there is a fear that Britain's economic disease may be terminal. The internal political consequences could be horrendous, with the ascent of totalitarianism of either the left or the right. The collapse of Britain as a trading nation or of the city of London as a financial center could have reverberations around the world. Britain, still a large and strategically placed country, could become a source of challenge to the basic tenets of Western liberal democracy or the institutional arrangements that have held the West together.

IV

This, then, is the international dimension to the British crisis. It is not the external eyeball-to-eyeball confrontation known to students of international relations but the external repercussions of an inner decline. To put all this into perspective, and to keep the alarmism in check, we need to look at the source of Britain's troubles—its economic performance.

The first thing to note is that the economic failure has been relative rather than absolute. Britain has a smaller share of an expanded world market. Its standard of living has risen, but less quickly than that of other industrial countries. Second, Britain's economic capacities have not suddenly deteriorated. Since the 1880s Britain has failed to achieve economic growth for any extended period at a rate above 3 percent. Other chapters discuss reasons for this failure—inherent laziness, obstructionist trade unions, incompetent management, obsolete industrial equipment, meek salesmanship, and so on. All I would note is the remarkable persistence of this minimal rate of growth.

Britain's economic defects were exposed with the withdrawal from empire and the associated loss of safe and protected overseas markets. The competition with more vigorous economies and the need to make way for them in the arrangements and institutions of international trade and finance has necessitated the series of adjustments, often somewhat traumatic—and made at the last minute—that have punctuated Britain's postwar history. In assessing the impact of Britain's economic performance on Britain's foreign policy, we need to take account of the consequence of these adjustments, with the associated appearance of impending calamity and panic in economic management, as well as the consequences of Britain's *relative* poverty among industrialized countries.

These adjustments, such as the 1967 devaluation, the 1974 miners' strike and following inflation, and the 1976 run on sterling, which led to the appeal for help from the IMF, did little for international confidence in Britain and were all indeed intensified by that lack of confidence. Countries with an uncertain future find their erstwhile friends, partners, and allies treating them gingerly. A main reason for the anxiety about Britain in the mid-1970s was less the objective indicators of Britain's economic health than the appearance of sheer incompetence and recklessness in domestic, economic, and industrial management. Thus in the fall of 1977, a year after the dark days of the collapse of sterling in 1976, Britain was being praised at the IMF for getting its inflation and money supply under control. Its foreign currency reserves were bulging and the value of sterling was rising. Yet during this period what is now described as the "real economy" had progressed not at all. The indicators of industrial production remained stagnant while the atmosphere of crisis subsided.

More was at stake, however, than an appearance of competence. During the 1976 sterling crisis the British experienced the basic foreign policy consequences of economic weakness: the growing interference of foreigners in domestic economic management. The crisis was in part precipitated by the desire of leading American Treasury and banking figures to force Britain into cutting back on public expenditure by refusing extensive support to the pound on the exchange markets and thus forcing Britain to the IMF, where any loan would carry stringent deflationary conditions. There then followed a battle in which the British government tried to convince its creditors that a too severe deflationary package would be so traumatic that it would have grave effects on the country's economic and political stability, while at the same time indicating a willingness to do enough to bring down public spending and thus reduce the borrowing requirement.

A recent account in the *Sunday Times* of the events of late 1976 quotes Brent Snowcroft of the U.S. National Security Council as saying: "It was considered by us to be the greatest single threat to the Western world." William Rogers, former U.S. secretary of state, said, "As I saw it, it was a choice between Britain remaining in the liberal financial system of the West as opposed to a radical change of course. . . . [If Britain turned its back on the IMF] the whole system would have begun to come apart. God knows what

Italy might have done; then France might have taken a radical change in the same direction ... We tended to see it in cosmic terms."[4]

The British government did not discourage this view, anxious that the political consequences of strict monetarist rectitude not be forgotten. Drastic public spending cuts could well necessitate a severe reduction in the British Army of the Rhine (BAOR) while the siege atmosphere engendered by the pressure from the IMF might lead to import controls.

In this situation Britain's bargaining strength lay in its weakness. It was like a large company on the brink of bankruptcy. Propping it up could be justified not in terms of any positive attributes of efficiency or productivity but only in terms of the negative consequences of a collapse. The threat of collapse, however, cannot be resorted to too often. One day the bluff may be called. It is also worth asking how serious the options of withdrawal of troops from Germany or the adoption of protectionism really were.

The extreme expense of BAOR in foreign exchange—an estimated £574 million in the 1978–79 period—provides the incentive for a cutback here rather than in other elements of the defense budget. Such a cut, however, would involve little saving on public expenditure. If the withdrawn troops were to be based at home, new accommodations would have to be built; if total manpower were to be reduced, redundancy payments would be needed. Savings would accrue only gradually, so there would be little relief for a short-term economic crisis.[5] A move to protectionism is often portrayed as an advantageous strategy that is eschewed only out of a regard for some international code of conduct. There is no reason to believe, however, that Britain, as a country that needs to export to survive, would prosper in a protectionist world. The retaliation of others would hurt Britain considerably.

The major difficulty with both these options is that they presume a freedom of maneuver that Britain just does not have. Over the past decade Britain has not been able to avoid going into debt and thus could not dispense with regard for the opinions of major creditors. The account of the 1976 sterling crisis cited above quotes an exchange in a key cabinet meeting. Tony Benn, adopting the "siege economy" metaphor, argued that power lay in the citadel. The only question was who was inside—Labour or the international financiers. Denis Healy replied: "He wants us to withdraw into the citadel, but only so long as we can slip out occasionally to borrow the money to buy the bows and arrows we'll need to shoot at the besieging armies." In the end the government could get the IMF's deflationary package modified and launch an international initiative to tackle the problem of the sterling balances, but the creditors could not be ignored.

The need to borrow just adds to Britain's dependence on the outside world. A truly radical option involving economic conflicts with trading partners, creditors, and sources of raw materials is best avoided. In the melodramatic sense, prevalent in the mid-1970s, of a country diverging markedly from close cooperation with the rest of the West and from the norms of international behavior it had helped to create, Britain is unlikely to be a major international problem.

Yet one cannot ignore the fact that if Britain's economic performance fails to improve, more problems will emerge. With the next sterling crisis the conditions imposed by Britain's creditors may be too much to swallow and could result in a convulsive reaction. More likely, a persistent lack of economic growth will increase the pressure on the defense budget and prompt reductions in some aspect of the contribution to NATO. Persistent unemployment will encourage protectionist pressures in specific industrial sectors. Continued decline in the sources of national wealth will result in a distrust of cooperative ventures, with alarm over what others are taking rather than gratitude over what they are giving. National resources, be they North Sea fish or North Sea oil, will be watched over with increasing chauvinism.

The most depressing thought is that in this situation Britain may not be unique. The big "if" concerns international economic recovery. If it arrives and is sustained, Britain and its partners will be less tense in their mutual dealings. Failure and a low growth decade for all OECD members will have major repercussions throughout the Western world. Britain's crisis has its own peculiar aspects and has caused the international community some anxious moments. But many of the problems resulting from Britain's low growth may well be generalized through the 1980s. In the long term, Britain's viability as an industrial nation is in its own hands. In the short term, Britain's ability to avoid a new crisis is in many ways out of its hands, because the international circumstances favorable to economic recovery and the reform of its manufacturing industry depend on the actions of others—America, Japan, Germany, and the OPEC countries. Without this support Britain will once again face grave problems and difficult decisions. Its only consolation may be that as it suffers, everybody else is suffering too.

Notes

1. James Callaghan, *Challenges and Opportunities for British Foreign Policy* (London: Fabian Tract 439, December 1975), p. 10. I am indebted to Chris Hill of the London School of Economics for drawing my attention to the importance of the concept of role in British foreign policy. His own thoughts on this matter should be published shortly.

2. Central Policy Review Staff, *Review of Overseas Representation* (London: Her Majesty's Stationery Office, 1977), p. 10. Nor, of course, have the efforts of other powers, including the United States, to solve the problems mentioned been "conspicuously successful."

3. George F. Kennan, *The Cloud of Danger* (London: Hutchinson, 1978), pp. 135–36.

4. The story of the 1976 crisis was told in a series of detailed articles in the *Sunday Times* by Stephen Fay and Hugo Young on May 14, 21, and 28, 1977. They are to be published as a pamphlet: *The Day the Pound Nearly Died.*

5. The BAOR question is explored in detail in Lawrence Freedman, "Britain's Contribution to NATO," *International Affairs,* January 1978.

14 | *The Pax Britannica and British Foreign Policy*

RICHARD ROSECRANCE

Foreign policy depends on power. It thus becomes important to discuss the British concept of power in international relations and the way it was expressed over the past two centuries. I shall seek to do so only in the most general terms, for it is impossible to do justice to the subject in a short paper. My concern will be largely with Britain's changing economic position in the world and its implications for foreign policy. Britain's power in the world stemmed directly from its economic preeminence, from the Pax Britannica.

Broadly speaking, one may say that an international economic imperium may be operated in either of two ways. The imperial center may acquire its dominance through a strong surplus of merchandise trade which enables it to lend the proceeds to the rest of the world and thus to serve as an international clearinghouse for world finance; or the dominant nation may obtain its financial surplus through "invisibles": shipping, insurance, brokerage commissions, and financial services. In this case the imperial center may maintain a continuing deficit in merchandise trade without encroaching upon its creditor status. In either case, the imperial nation confronts the problem of providing the means by which others are to be enabled to pay their debts. And in each

I am indebted to Thomas Ilgen, Ronald W. Jones, Judith Reppy, and Barbara Rosecrance for advice and criticism. None of them is thereby implicated in the conclusions that follow.

case some combination of foreign investment, foreign loans, and debtor exports offers an answer.

Many believe that changing patterns of comparative cost cause international capitalism ultimately to equalize the fruits of early industrial development and initial trading advantage. "Early developers" gain leverage that is gradually lost as others industrialize.[1] Creditors use their surpluses to finance the development and export trade of the initial debtor nations. The concentration of resources and capital in one particular industry or region of the world bids up wages and prices and tends to make other industries and other regions more competitive. There has never been any doubt that this theory operates among industrial states, and nineteenth-century and twentieth-century economic development bear testimony to the growing competitive position of late developers,[2] to the change from Pax Britannica to Pax Americana, thence possibly to a Pax Europa. What has been questioned is whether the development process is necessarily worldwide and whether it can be financed from agricultural and raw-material production.[3] Ricardo and the Hecksher-Ohlin theorems tend to support an affirmative answer, but at the very least historical experience has lagged behind their predictions.[4]

If this theory is correct, no economic imperium can be expected to endure. "Secular stagnation"[5] slows growth, and the incentives to invest may decline. At this point new and more profitable outlets will be sought, and other nations or regions of the globe will begin to grow more rapidly. There will naturally be impediments to this process: wars, trade disruptions, and economic nationalism. Nonetheless, the intrinsic tendency will be for latecomers to catch up and for the returns on investment gradually to equalize.

This is not to say that all imperiums are alike or that they have equal and similar consequences. The second pattern, involving a surplus earned from invisibles, is actually more beneficial to the other members of the system, at least in the short run, for it permits the debtor countries to achieve quick and dependable surpluses in merchandise trade, providing a healthy stimulus to their export industries. The rise in the export sector may then be used to stimulate industrial development overall.[6] The first pattern is less benign initially in that it deprives the debtor countries of an export strategy and forces them to rely on loans or foreign investment for the solution to their balance-of-payments problems. It may thereby postpone the day of balance-of-payments independence.[7]

In other terms, however, the first strategy may be preferable. For the imperial country, at least, the export surplus sustains and further stimulates industrial growth at home. The success of the export strategy may delay a competitive challenge in one's home markets. In the center country's economy it strengthens economic and industrial factors and diminishes financial ones. The second strategy has corresponding disadvantages. Since the surplus is not to be obtained by exports, its continuance is seen to depend on financial primacy: on attractiveness and solidity of lending agencies, on interest rates, on financial expertise and information. It thereby slights industrial and export competitiveness and weakens the export stimulus to home development.

These two strategies may have other implications. When the sun has set on the erstwhile economic imperium and the surplus has vanished—when the lending agencies no longer can serve as banker to the world or purvey the world's "top currency"—there will be a domestic reckoning. It is well known that top-currency countries gain (at least temporarily) great benefits in world trade.[8] Because their national currency is also the world's reserve currency, they may invest abroad in grand amounts. They may import on a prodigious scale, paying for deficits with their own national issue. When imperium has ceased to bestride the financial world, however (and when its currency is no longer the major medium of international exchange), the imperial center must begin to export to live. Its ability to achieve merchandise trading surpluses will be a partial function of historic wont. If export industries have been neglected in the past—if industrial investment has lagged—the necessary exports will not easily be forthcoming. Thus the nature of the choice between imperial strategies may be of continuing economic significance long after the imperium is over.

The Pax Britannica operated more nearly on the second theory than on the first. While Germany and later the United States sought to gain economic power in the world system through exports, in the nineteenth century the United Kingdom did not have an export surplus after 1822.[9] This was, of course, not simply a matter of necessity for Great Britain.[10] During the eighteenth century Britain had maintained a steady surplus in its trade with continental Europe. Its industrial development was reaching its relative peak in the 1830s and 1840s. Its industrial exports might have won it surpluses in any market, even the most protected, because other nations did not have competitive substitutes for British manufactured goods, particularly textiles.[11] Nor was Britain's failure to earn surpluses the result of the free-trade policy that opened its markets to a flood of foreign imports. Until the end of the 1840s the Corn Laws and the Navigation Acts protected the British market; yet even in the early nineteenth century Britain did not achieve surpluses in merchandise trade. Britain's concept of economic (and derivatively of national) power was not forced on it; it was freely chosen.[12]

What was the choice? After the Napoleonic War, Britain in effect decided to concentrate its international energies on services, on invisibles—shipping, insurance, and returns from the financial services performed by the British capital market. Until 1889 the surplus on invisibles more than offset the deficit on visible or merchandise trade.[13] After 1890 and up to 1910, however, invisible earnings no longer counterbalanced the deficit on merchandise trade. England's total favorable balance on current account came to depend upon earnings from foreign investments. It was not until the 1930s that Britain's overall balance fell into deficit. The failure of investment earnings and invisibles to counteract the heavy merchandise deficit led to an outflow of gold and foreign currencies. This pattern was repeated after World War II.

As we have seen, Britain's choice was a salutary one from the standpoint of its European partners and the United States. Because Britain accumulated deficits in visible trade, they were enabled to run surpluses. As long as the City dominated international finance, there was no disadvantage on either side, because Britain always made up its deficit. But the approach itself contained a crucial weakness: if Britain conceded export surpluses to others, sooner or later they would build up capital markets that would challenge the ascendancy of London. At this point the strategy provided no answer. The first theory, in contrast, left much more initiative in the hands of the center country. Since its own exports would be the basis of financial dominance, and since the deficits of its creditors could be made up only through capital flows, the imperial country was in a position virtually to administer the international financial system. The initiative would remain with the capital markets of the center nation.[14] The Pax Britannica, on the other hand, lost initiative to the peripheries. It conceded merchandise trade surpluses to others and sought to compensate for the deficit by attracting funds to London. The allure of the London money market might be virtually irresistible, but it was left to others to decide whether or not to resist it.

Indeed, after World War I, the inner logic revealed itself, and Paris and later New York began to compete with London, both offering and drawing investment funds. They began to invest heavily overseas. At the end of the twenties and the beginning of the thirties Britain decided to reemphasize its financial as opposed to its strict trading interests, to strengthen London, and to reestablish temporarily the prewar value of the pound sterling. But despite valiant efforts, London never regained its old dominion, and British exports languished. The French, who devalued the franc several times, made gains against an overvalued pound, and the Americans administered a punishing blow with their own large devaluation of 1933. Britain was trying to resurrect the Pax Britannica and the nineteenth-century financial system at a time when neither its exports nor the pound sterling could stand the strain.[15]

Britain's choices in the 1920s and 1930s were reflections of a fundamental imperial strategy adopted one hundred years earlier. But that strategy was not axiomatic. Other countries chose to emphasize an export-oriented thrust toward economic power.[16] Export surpluses were believed to display industrial competence. They would force cultural attention to one's goods. The surplus derived might be used to build military power. One observes these tenets in German and American practice. Though Germany and afterward the United States were latecomers in the process of industrialization, both were quick to develop surpluses in the markets of the European continent. With the exception of Spain and Portugal, traditional British preserves, Germany had equaled or surpassed British exports to all major Continental countries by 1910 and had surpluses with every country but Russia.[17] Its greatest noncontinental surplus was with Britain, and its only deficit with an industrial country was with the United States. The American record was even more striking. Aside from a pair of two- to three-year lapses, the United States had a surplus on merchandise trade from 1874 to 1970, nearly a century.[18] Further, the United States earned surpluses in industrial markets, first for its agricultural products but later for its manufactured goods. Germany and the United States benefited initially from protective tariffs. But both continued to win surpluses even when the apparatus of tariff protection had been largely dismantled.

Britain's forte, in contrast, was in judging the credit-worthiness of others, their fitness to receive loans from the British market. In the words of Walter Bagehot, Britain lived by and maintained its overall surplus by financial acumen:

> ... a very great many of the strongest heads in England spend their minds on little else than on thinking whether other people will pay their debts.... Each banker ... is a kind of "solvency-meter," and lives by estimating rightly the "responsibility of parties" as he would call it.... The moment any set of traders want capital, those whose promises are known to be good, get it in a minute, because it is lying ready in the hands of those who know, and who live by knowing, that they are fit to have it.[19]

That the British capital market dominated others can hardly be denied. In the early 1870s it was not only three times greater than its largest competitor (New York) but twice as large as its rivals taken together.[20] But while the money market was homogeneous in a larger sense, the specialized firms that handled foreign loans and issues dominated the market, and the share allotted to foreign entrepreneurs and governments greatly exceeded that available to British domestic manufacturers.[21] Neither British industrialists nor the domestic banks that served them were represented in the inner councils of the Bank of England.[22] This did not present a problem so long as London was able to draw in funds from all over the world, more than counterbalancing its merchandise deficit. But when capital centers burgeoned in Paris and New York, the deficiency in British exports meant that London might begin to be starved of funds.

But this problem did not become evident immediately. Because of its financial surplus, England did not initially have to capture

Continental markets where competition and protection would present obstacles. Thus after the mid-nineteenth century the British began increasingly to export to "soft" markets, where British goods did not confront a major competitive challenge or where they had a special entrée.[23] They sent their goods overseas to the New World, Africa, Australia, and New Zealand. As late as 1872 Western Europe took 43.8 percent of British exports, but by 1910 the share had dwindled to 25.1 percent.[24] On the other hand, while Canada, Australia, India, New Zealand, and South Africa took only 17.9 percent of British exports in 1872, their share rose to 30.8 percent in 1910.[25] The Empire became the refuge for British exports even though free trade technically allowed competitors an equal access. Insofar as Britain was able to make up its merchandise deficit, the Empire was responsible. In 1910 London had a large deficit in visible trade with continental Europe, and also a growing deficit with the United States. Some of the older dominions, such as Canada, had ceased to be earners of gold and foreign exchange, and South America no longer provided substantial rewards. Thus in the years before the war India became the jewel in the imperial crown. Britain had favorable balances with Australia, Japan, China, and certain African countries. But India alone financed two-fifths of Britain's deficit with the rest of the world.[26] The triangular trade in these years was roughly as follows: European and American surpluses in trade with England were partly made up in imports from Empire countries and territories, and the British surpluses with the Empire helped greatly to reduce the overall deficit.[27]

The Empire was relevant to British power in more than one way. British emigration provided a safety valve for domestic discontent, and it operated very effectively during the nineteenth century. As early as 1820 the British government had recognized emigration as a means to alleviate social distress and as a remedy for unemployment. Beginning in 1834 it set up the first of a series of assisted emigration schemes to Australia. Many disillusioned Chartists of the late 1840s shared in this movement of population. The Scottish crofters, whose land had been taken out of cultivation to provide pasturage for sheep, migrated initially to Canada. In Ireland, the repeal of the Corn Laws and the Irish potato famine of 1846–47 helped depopulate the country, and over a ten-year span the Irish population actually decreased by 1.7 million.[28] The gold rush at mid-century, first to California and then to Australia, drew many laborers who had become redundant with the onset of the machine and factory system.[29]

Initially the great preponderance of these migrants went to the United States and other independent countries, but by the end of the century the Empire had become their dominant destination. Emigration, of course, fluctuated with economic conditions at home and abroad—the former providing push and the latter pull. The 1840s and 1850s saw three-quarters of 1 percent of the British population leave home. The rate declined to one-half of 1 percent until the Great Depression of 1873–96, when it increased by 30 percent.[30] The boom conditions overseas after the turn of the century also facilitated emigration from Britain: many more embarked for new lives in Canada and Australia. In 1913 a full 1 percent of the British population left to live elsewhere, and the Empire provided the preferred location.

The Empire remained as haven for the surplus population in Great Britain until the 1930s. Then the net movement turned inward, and during the depression of 1933–37 Britain absorbed a foreign population of nearly one-half million.[31] The pattern repeated itself after World War II, and by 1961 the inflow and outflow of population attained approximate balance. Without immigration restrictions, however, the influx would have greatly exceeded the number wishing to leave. Thus the United Kingdom could no longer count on an exodus of population as a means to relieve economic distress at home.

The Empire was important in another way: it provided occupations for the middle class. According to one British scholar, the Empire

> employed directly about 20,000 men as colonial administrators, 146,000 as soldiers permanently garrisoning the colonies (8,000 officers and 138,000 men), and many more as clerks, agricultural advisers, forestry officers, education officers, engineers, surveyors, policemen, doctors, and the like besides countless others engaged in directing and supplying them at home. The empire, therefore, was a source of employment and a means of satisfying ambition. Nearly all the men it employed except the non-commissioned soldiers were from the upper and middle classes. Many of them were good at what

they did, but good for little else, which made their dependence on the empire even greater. This was how they had been educated; for the public schools, too, were geared to the empire's needs. Many of the ideals they aimed at, the qualities they worked to instill in their wards—notions of service, feelings of superiority, habits of authority—were derived from, and consequently dependent upon, the existence of an empire: of colonial subjects to serve, feel superior to, and exert authority over.[32]

But even more important, the Empire drew Britain further into the web of financial as opposed to economic and industrial strategies.[33] If the Empire could yield a financial return on investment and trade, England had less need to export to its industrial competitors. Indeed, it had less need to export at all. The returns on foreign investment and lending could more than make up for deficits in foreign trade.

In certain respects the control of the Empire is a key to the British notion of power: it was administrative as much as political. It was financial more than economic. Britain's power in the Empire resided in its intelligence—its ability to gain information and to evaluate indigenous rulers and their subjects. It was the same skill the City of London used in evaluating the credit-worthiness of a prospective borrower. The British acceptance and discount houses were at the heart of the Pax Britannica. Any bill that was "accepted" by a British house would be easily purchased by others. And the British knew just how much discount to charge their customers. They had unparalleled sources of information and great financial discernment. It was this key intelligence that made London a great financial center and drew funds from the remotest corners of the earth.

Of course the strength of the pound sterling was critical in this process, since sterling was equivalent to gold and a less bulky means of settling accounts. But the pound was strong not because of an export surplus but because of the surplus in invisibles.[34] Thus the pound was strong because British financial institutions were awesome, and here British expertise and knowledge were the essential commodities.

The same was true of the British armed forces. Except for Chinese Gordon's artificially contrived last stand at Khartoum against the Mahdi,[35] the British never lost a campaign during the nineteenth century. Yet at its maximum their empire was much more exposed than America's extreme recent version of the Pax Americana. Britain's forces were stretched over an arc that extended from the Mediterranean to the Middle East and Africa, thence to India, Burma, Southeast Asia, and the Pacific. They were ready to protect Canada, Australia, South Africa, and the Fiji Islanders. That these commitments could be carried so long with such a small complement of land forces was a tribute, again, to British intelligence and expertise. Britain knew how to intervene and was master of the unflurried exit. It was expert at the disciplined use of force, and much better than the United States it knew when to compromise and reach agreement. Even as late as the early 1950s Britain defeated foreign adversaries before reducing its global commitments. In this respect Britain's military prowess can be usefully compared with the U.S. record. In the American Civil War, the presumed superiority of industrial output, the sheer weight of productive effort, was established. It was reinforced in two world wars. The deductions drawn were similar to those in America's export strategy: that productive weight and increasingly sophisticated industrial technology would tip the military as well as economic scales in one's favor. It was precisely this view, *ceteris paribus,* that led to the U.S. blunder in Vietnam: that power massively applied would always win, regardless of the cultural values and tenacity of the other side. But Britain did not make this mistake. In Malaya, Kenya, Cyprus, the critical requisite was intelligence, and the British largely attained their goals because they knew more than their adversaries. They knew how to co-opt local leadership and how to persuade. Thus Britain fought a few battles but not many sustained campaigns. When battles extended into vast theaters of war, Britain was less successful—in the Crimea, against the Boers, and along the Marne. Even World War II, the "finest hour" of the British nation, did not display British superiority in mass terms. It offered in the RAF, in the Royal Navy, and in the British intelligence services another example of superiority in intelligence. The ULTRA secret was typical of British achievements, and it helped turn the tide of the war.

In sum, British power was based on an incomparable ability to take the measure of opponents, clients, allies, competitors, and dependents. The ruling of an empire helped to hone many skills, and acumen was certainly one of the sharpest. Thus, in a way that overstates the case, one may say that British power was more financial than economic. It was based less on crude industrial output than on an ability to assess people. Once this habit of mind was acquired, it was difficult to shake. As late as the 1950s and 1960s one finds British economic policy returning to its financial roots.[36] The British once again placed sterling uppermost and the British economy and industrial growth second. This priority represented yet another attempt to acquire the financial surplus that had been the key to the Pax Britannica in the nineteenth century.

It is fruitless to speculate on what might have happened if Britain had chosen another path in the 1830s and 1840s. If Britain had chosen to base its imperium on exports, several results might have followed. Because of the pressure of foreign competition both at home and abroad, Britain would have modernized its plant more quickly and effectively, and probably a smaller proportion of British investment funds would have gone overseas. This would have been a great disadvantage to the Empire and to the United States, but it might in the long run have been beneficial to Britain.[37] Britain would have placed less emphasis on the Empire, except as a source of raw materials, and the dominions would probably have developed an outward-looking orientation at an earlier date. Whatever its disadvantages, however, a different strategy for the Pax Britannica might better have prepared Britain to cope with the challenges of Continental exports, the European Community, and the United States in the late 1970s.

Thus one approaches the problems of British foreign policy of the last twenty years or so. The basic trouble was that Britain's material position had been outpaced by that of others no later than the 1930s. Britain entered the 1950s as a tightrope walker, relying heavily on the balance provided by past success. This balance made possible a number of significant victories. In the Third World, in continental Europe, and in the Far East, Britain's position often determined American policy. In 1955 it was Anthony Eden who came to the rescue when John Foster Dulles botched his relations with the French and Europe. While the French had lost Indo-China and were suffering in Algeria, the British were on the way to success in Malaya. And they defended their position with great valor and success in Southeast Asia as late as 1964.

But the Pax Britannica predisposed Britain to make two crucial mistakes. The first was to seek a position midway between the United States and Europe. The second was to strive to carry out overseas a policy that ultimately could not be based on the slender margin of Britain's resources. The first error led others to devalue Britain's role. Britain could influence Europe only as the greatest and most committed of Europeans, but its hesitancy in 1957 and for more than a decade afterward reduced its prestige and influence on the Continent. Britain could have influenced the United States only as the chief European spokesman, a role it had abjured. Britain was European enough for neither Europe nor the United States. Its policy had no fulcrum of power on which to rest.

Overseas the greatest reversal was Suez. When British weakness was suddenly revealed, no ready-made solution was available. If Britain's forte had been intelligence and administrative skill, what should one do when acumen was lacking or when British financial superiority was no longer accepted? Suez was the great turning point in British foreign policy, not only because of the concrete failure that it represented but because things had been going so well immediately before.

The Anglo-French invasion represented two mistakes. First, it showed a misunderstanding of what military force might accomplish in a contemporary colonial context, and it entirely misjudged the reaction of the United States. Second, it displayed a lack of financial power to carry on a wrongheaded policy. Britain was simply not strong enough to do what America did in Vietnam for ten years: to defy the opinion of the rest of the Western world. The American objection was critical and in an immediate financial sense. Thus when British power collapsed at Suez, it was like a crust crumbling under the fork. There was no secondary or reserve layer of strength to resist further penetration. The failure of British foreign policy after Suez was a failure that required, in essence, a new modus operandi. Since the British did not have a reservoir of industrial strength to return to, the deficiency in intelligence was decisive.

In this respect the British foreign policy record has in recent years been more difficult than that of the Germans and Japanese. Perhaps Britain's disadvantage, as some have said, was that it never lost a war, and therefore never had to start afresh. But one must still start from somewhere. After World War II the Japanese and Germans (great beneficiaries, it is true, of American foreign assistance) had less to do than the British in the 1980s. They had only to return to previous modes of economic behavior: seeking to develop surpluses in merchandise trade and to win a place for their goods in competitive markets. After 1950 or so their course of action was relatively clear, and the Korean war boom gave them a chance.

The weakening of the Pax Americana taught the same lessons. If the United States could no longer act as an economic royalist, sending great quantities of its currency overseas in payment for debts incurred through too much foreign investment (part of it military) and too many imports, an answer still remained: a return to export strategies of the recent past.

Britain's problem in the late 1950s and then in the 1960s, when government after government put off the devaluation of sterling, was to do something entirely new: to begin to earn surpluses in Continental and developed-country markets—to return to habits not of the nineteenth century but of the eighteenth. The European Community was to be the great stimulus to British exports; it was to provide the needed challenge and opportunity. And it might have turned out that way if new investments and new capacity had been laid down to sustain the impetus. But while the record is still being written on these points, an external observer wonders whether the British are still not treading outworn paths. Britain is still probably making more profitable investments overseas than at home. And the hoped-for solution to the export problem seems not to be a well-sustained development of industrial goods: motorcars, electronics, consumer durables, chemicals, machine tools. Rather, it seems that North Sea oil is to provide the solution. The enormous sums that Britain acquired from foreign sources were lent on the prospects of the North Sea gusher. But that oil will not be the answer to British problems in world politics after 1990, and one wonders what the strategy will be then.

This is not to say that there is, for any of us, *a* solution to the foreign policy problem. The United States confronts great difficulties as well in regaining its export balance. The Germans and the Japanese are having to learn to make foreign investments and not to rely wholly on domestic production for sales overseas. But one can afford to make large foreign investments only if trade is not greatly out of equilibrium. Outward capital flows are a luxury to be sustained from a trade surplus; they are not a remedy for a deficit in merchandise trade. If British power is to regain some of its past potency, London will have to devise a new way of influencing others. Exports and productivity provide such a way. It is not too late to switch concepts of international power.

Notes

1. W. A. Cole and Phyllis Deane, "The Growth of National Incomes," in *The Cambridge Economic History of Europe*, vol. 6, *The Industrial Revolutions and After*, ed. M. M. Postan and H. J. Habakkuk (Cambridge: Cambridge University Press, 1965), p. 19.

2. See, among others, Alexander Gerschenkron, "Economic Backwardness in Historical Perspective," in *The Progress of Underdeveloped Areas*, ed. Berthold Hoselitz (Chicago: University of Chicago Press, 1952).

3. See Johan Galtung, "The Structural Theory of Imperialism," *Journal of Peace Research* 2 (1971): 81–117.

4. An interesting critique of the "factor proportions" approach is given in Staffan Burenstam Linder, "Causes of Trade in Primary Products versus Manufactures," in *International Trade and Finance*, ed. Robert E. Baldwin and J. David Richardson (Boston: Little, Brown, 1974).

5. Alvin Hansen, *America's Role in the World Economy* (New York: W. W. Norton, 1945), p. 24.

6. See Joan Robinson, "Understanding the Economic Crisis," *New York Review of Books* 25, no. 20 (1978): 33.

7. The British strategy, which was to permit debtors to win export surpluses in the British market for most of the nineteenth century, was in this way even more favorable to others than the American strategy of the twentieth century. This difference may help to explain why developing countries have moved more slowly to challenge the trading and financial ascendancy of Western Europe and the United States than their counterparts did to challenge British industrial exports in the last half of the nineteenth century.

8. See Susan Strange, "The Politics of International Currencies," *World Politics* 23, no. 2 (January 1971): 227.

9. Brian R. Mitchell and Phyllis Deane, *Abstract of British Historical Statistics* (Cambridge: Cambridge University Press, 1971), pp. 333–34.

10. Eric Hobsbawm observes: ". . . we also find—and this is rather odd—that at *no* time in the nineteenth century did Britain have an export surplus in goods, in spite of her industrial monopoly, her marked export-orientation, and her modest domestic consumer market. Before 1846 Free Traders argued that this was because the Corn Laws prevented our potential customers from earning enough through their ex-

ports to pay for ours, but this is doubtful" (*Industry and Empire* [New York: Pantheon Books, 1968], 2: 119). (Italics in the original.)

11. David Landes notes that French textile mills were not competitive: "In general the French cotton industry continued to lag far behind that of Britain. Plants were smaller; machines were older, less efficient; even allowing for differences in equipment, labour was less productive. It was a high-cost industry..." ("Technological Change and Industrial Development in Western Europe, 1750-1914," in *Industrial Revolutions and After*, ed. Postan and Habakkuk, pp. 392-93.

12. It is of course questionable whether such a "choice" was a matter of national policy. It was rather the result of hundreds of individual choices by financiers, Treasury officials, magnates, and industrialists. Nonetheless, the result constituted a national strategy in the economic sector.

13. Mitchell and Deane, *Abstract of British Historical Statistics*, p. 334.

14. The criticism of U.S. economic "imperialism" rests partly on this foundation. Since developing countries could not export in quantity to Western markets, their position depended on foreign loans or investment to make up the deficits.

15. See the account in Leland B. Yeager, *International Monetary Relations: Theory, History, and Policy* (New York: Harper & Row, 1966), p. 274.

16. See, among others, Michael Kreile, "West Germany: The Dynamics of Expansion," in *Between Power and Plenty: Foreign Policies of Advanced Industrial States*, ed. Peter J. Katzenstein (Madison: University of Wisconsin Press, 1978).

17. Ross J. S. Hoffman, *Great Britain and the German Trade Rivalry* (Philadelphia: University of Pennsylvania Press, 1933), pp. 115-19.

18. Arthur S. Banks, *Cross-Policy Time-Series Data* (Cambridge: MIT Press, 1971), pp. 203-4.

19. Quoted in John B. Condliffe, *The Commerce of Nations* (London: George Allen & Unwin, 1951), p. 338.

20. Ibid., p. 342.

21. Alexander K. Cairncross notes "that in the *long* run foreign investment was largely at the expense of home investment or vice versa" (*Home and Foreign Investment, 1870-1913* [Cambridge: Cambridge University Press, 1953], p. 187). (Italics in the original.)

22. Condliffe, *Commerce of Nations*, p. 347.

23. Hobsbawm, *Industry and Empire*, 2: 121.

24. Alfred E. Kahn, *Great Britain in the World Economy* (New York: Columbia University Press, 1946), pp. 209-10. See also François Crouzet, "Trade and Empire: The British Experience from the Establishment of Free Trade until the First World War," in *Great Britain and Her World, 1750-1914: Essays in Honour of W. O. Henderson*, ed. Barrie M. Ratcliffe (Manchester: Manchester University Press, 1975), p. 221.

25. Kahn, *Great Britain in the World Economy*, pp. 209-10.

26. Crouzet, "Trade and Empire," p. 227.

27. S. B. Saul, *Studies in British Overseas Trade, 1870-1914* (Liverpool: Liverpool University Press, 1960), p. 45.

28. D. A. E. Harkness, "Irish Emigration," in *International Migrations*,

vol. 2: *Interpretations,* ed. Walter F. Wilcox (New York: National Bureau of Economic Research, 1931), p. 274.

29. The long-run impacts of the introduction of labor-saving machinery are discussed in John R. Hicks, *A Theory of Economic History* (Oxford: Clarendon Press, 1969), pp. 148–54.

30. Mitchell and Phyllis Deane, *Abstract of British Historical Statistics,* pp. 8–10.

31. William Douglas Forsyth, *The Myth of Open Spaces* (Melbourne: Melbourne University Press, 1942), p. 177.

32. Brian Porter, *The Lion's Share: A Short History of British Imperialism, 1850–1970* (London: Longman Group, 1975), p. 200.

33. Hobsbawm notes: "The British economy as a whole tended to retreat from industry into trade and finance, where our services reinforced our actual and future competitors, but made very satisfactory profits. Britain's annual investments abroad began actually to *exceed* her net capital formation at home around 1870. What is more, increasingly the two became alternatives, until in the Edwardian era we see domestic investment falling almost without interruption as foreign investment rises. In the great boom (1911–13) which preceded the First World War, twice as much, or even more, was invested abroad than at home; and it has been argued—and indeed is not unlikely—that the amount of domestic capital formation in the twenty-five years before 1914, so far from being adequate for the modernization of the British productive apparatus, was not even quite sufficient to prevent it from slightly running down" (*Industry and Empire*, 2: 161). (Italics in the original.)

34. In the last quarter of the nineteenth century Britain faced a great "overhang" of overseas sterling balances compared to its relatively small gold stock. But, unlike the situation in the late 1960s, this did not disturb the repose of the international financial community. Condliffe observes: "The ultimate source of cash was the Bank of England. Therefore the gold reserve of the Bank became in effect the reserve of the whole trading world. It was for this purpose minute. Bagehot, writing in 1873, reported that for some years it had averaged about £10 million but had formerly been much less" (*Commerce of Nations,* p. 348).

35. See Lytton Strachey's ironic account in *Eminent Victorians* (London: Chatto & Windus, 1948), chap. 4.

36. See Stephen Blank, "Britain: The Politics of Foreign Economic Policy, the Domestic Economy, and the Problem of Pluralistic Stagnation," in *Between Power and Plenty,* ed. P. Katzenstein (Madison: University of Wisconsin Press, 1978).

37. This is the essential conclusion of Hicks, *Theory of Economic History,* p. 154.

PART VI : :

The Future

I

In Great Britain, "crisis" has long been a permanent state of affairs that inexplicably never seems to change anything. The word has associations with the sickroom or even the deathbed—an aura certainly responsible for its evergreen appeal. But here we are dealing with an invalid who constantly resurfaces from his ordeals, orders a large breakfast, and with exasperating complacency tells those who have gathered to mourn that there was never really anything to worry about. It will all be different from now on, he adds. This cheerful prediction is as regularly mistaken as the doom-laden prophecies in which he indulges when the thermometer shoots up and he feels "it" overcoming him once more.

One is tempted to dismiss him as a hypochondriac, of course. The United Kingdom then appears to have a foreseeable future of such minor crises, more imaginary than real, with small effect on the patient's underlying rude health. The great collapse feared for so long will never happen, or is so far away there is no point in dwelling on it now.

An alternative diagnosis, to which I subscribe, is that there are two levels of crisis built into Britain's recent history (by which I mean the history of the last century), the enduring or chronic disorders of imperial decline and the temporary eruptions or fevers to which that disorder has made Britain susceptible. British society recovers from the latter, true enough: one need only think

233

back to the winter of 1977 or the election of February 1974. Such
episodes might have led more vulnerable polities straight to the
morgue, yet were quickly forgotten in Britain. Such recovery,
however, does not mean there is really nothing wrong. All it
means is that a continuously worsening disease is still accompanied by great though diminishing reserves of political strength.

This politico-cultural fortitude reasserts itself against the bouts
of obvious sickness, and so disappoints the facile prophets of an
English apocalypse. But it does nothing whatever to cure the underlying ailment because it is itself organically linked to the
pathological conditions. The same imperial history and the same
conservative state have bred both the illness and certain characteristic homemade remedies, or rather palliatives, which come
automatically into action if a collapse is threatened. Thus actual
dissolution is averted. The cohesion of the body is resoundingly
reaffirmed, to the delight of functionalists and other votaries of
tradition; the snag is that it can be resurrected only in the old,
flawed form. And this structure is charged with the germs of the
next overt crisis.

Where are we now in this century-old history? And what will
happen when the patient finally discovers that this time he lacks
even the strength to stage his recovery act? These are the questions I want to consider.

I shall not attempt a historical overview of the notion of the
Great British Crisis, "from Matthew Arnold to Tony Benn," as it
were, through the well-known and depressingly numerous stages:
Great Depression, New Imperialism, the National Efficiency
campaigns, Lloyd George, the effects of World War I, the noncrisis of 1926, Second Great Depression, "national governments,"
effects of World War II, the nonrevolution of 1945, 1947, the new
cycle of sterling crises, stop-go, Harold Wilson's nonrevolution
from above, Edward Heath's noncounterrevolution from above,
1974, Third Great Depression, the IMF saga, and the current
anxious speculations about whether or not another general election can be held before the next visit to the sick bay.

The topic is monumental, and ghoulish. Since 1910 at least it
has all been crisis, save for those few years in the 1950s when
Britain had it so good (a slogan invented, characteristically, just
when it had become plain that the postwar U.K. boom was over

and Britain would soon be back to crisis as usual). These perennial difficulties have created a vast, insanely repetitious literature of self-censure and prophecy. There never was a time, either, when U.K. governments were not inundated with stern reproofs, sermons on foreign virtue, warnings of calamity, thunderous reports about scientific education, and urgent advice—much of it sound—about the need to change our ways. As regularly, these tracts have settled into the instant oblivion of archive and library shelf. Apart from a few suitably patrician and timely reformers such as Keynes, Beveridge, and Lord Kilbrandon, has any society ever produced so much dramatic good counsel, or esteemed it so little?

Rather than plod through this jungle, I think it better—and certainly more entertaining—to prospect the future. What can be said about Britain's propensity to crisis from the angle of political futurism? This is what one always wants to know, talking about crises. Why not address the problem directly? It goes without saying that in doing so one must employ reference points from what is known of the long past history of the malady.

II

Political futurology is difficult, of course. As George Lichtheim wrote, "Neither Comte, nor Marx, nor J. S. Mill, nor any other major political thinker of the nineteenth century ever supposed that the political process as such lent itself to scientific description or analysis. It would be truer to say they regarded politics as a madhouse, or at most a stage on which the actors declaimed lines of their own composition."[1] Hence there can be no point in trying to foresee the actions of lunatics or extempore thespians.

Scientific prediction belongs elsewhere. It is in the area of economics, demography, and technology that we find law-governed behavior. These disciplines have furnished both Marxists and twentieth-century futurologists with supposedly discernible trends of continuity, and with "innovation" in an apparently graspable form. If politics is more than sound and fury, then it merely manifests such underlying forces.

I shall have something to say about the Marxist model later. But first we should look at the futurological one first outlined by

William F. Ogburn fifty years ago. He saw "invention, accumulation, diffusion, and adjustment" as the four propellants of social
change, which together furnish "a general explanation of any one
culture, such as that of China or India or Greece." Invention and
accumulation are basic; the adjustment of social relationships and
social philosophy follows on. "Thus," he continues, "the invention
of the factory with machinery driven by steam produced a change
in the family, by taking occupations out of the home, especially
those of women." In this way "significant inventions" (including
"social inventions") disturb the equilibrium of placid societies and
drive them forward, compelling them to re-form their customs
and ideas. Evolution is adjustment to novelty.[2]

Ogburn's model—and, I believe, those of most futurologists—
reflect the circumstances of past American society. They certainly
do not mirror British conditions of the last century. One need
advance but a small way into the thickets of the long imperial crisis
to feel this. Wave after wave of exasperated critics have, in effect,
cursed their homeland for being hopelessly unlike Ogburn's
ideal. Not enough innovation, too little adaptation to change,
clinging to outworn social patterns, unwillingness to face challenges—this is the invariable burden of their accusations. Unable to credit the fact that a bourgeois society may simply want to
be that way, these tribunes must believe it is asleep, and will be
roused by the forthcoming book or royal commission report. This
raging indictment will accomplish what two world wars failed to
do and bring round the Prometheus who inexplicably dozed off
sometime last century.

One can deduce the real model of British change from their
railings as well as from the direct study of social history. British
culture is governed by what I am tempted to call the anti-Ogburn
cycle. Its mainspring is not open adaptation to the accumulation
of innovations but the alert containment of novelty. The aim is to
preserve an older social equilibrium undisturbed, not at any cost
(which would entail a strategy of mere reaction) but at as low a
social cost as possible. Invention does not compel shifts in social
relationships and finally alter even the prevailing social philosophy. Britain's social philosophy, embodied in an authoritative
politico-cultural hegemony, sustains social relationships in a way

that defuses invention. On the level of pure science and Nobel Prizes the British have done well enough. But lower down their record with significant inventions is systematically poor, except in time of war. Technological and economic innovation has often been crippled or forced abroad. Social and political invention has been somehow cramped and devitalized. So, while there have been many changes, and above all much talk about change, the essence of the older equilibrium has always come through. Beneath a smoke screen of earnest rhetoric about new starts and vanishing class barriers, unavoidable episodes of change are permitted and quickly integrated into this status quo. The feat is then described as "the social revolution this country has undergone since . . ." 1832, 1900, 1945, and so on.

All this has given futurologists a hard time in Britain.[3] I shall try to explain why later. For the moment we should note only that these would-be scientific forecasters have shared a mistaken assumption with a very large number of British politicians and pundits: the idea that Britain is a fairly standard member of the troupe of advanced capitalist nation-states and is therefore capable of self-propulsion on Ogburnian lines. Marxists tend to suffer from the delusion like everyone else. It is not only the existence of the large industrial sector of British capitalism that persuades them of this notion. History plays its part by reminding people of that puissant piece of mythology, the "workshop of the world." Having created the original "economic miracle," Great Britain must forever be deemed capable of another.[4]

It is also worth noting that creative writers have never been much taken with such official optimism. "Futurologists," wrote Daniel Bell, "usually have no awareness of the nature of social systems: their boundaries, the interplay of values, motivation, and resources, the levels of social organisation, and the constraints of custom and privilege on change. . ."[5] But Britain is the modern Holy Land of such constraints. Since World War II its literature has undergone a thorough reaction in precisely this sense. A generation of self-consciously "realistic" and traditional novelists has gloated over all those constraining social nuances and delectable impediments to mobility and progress. Literature can be too easily dismissed as a witness of the social condition; in modern Britain it has actually been quite important in justifying the old ways of the state to man.[6]

The literary evidence is still more striking if one looks at visions of the future. From Aldous Huxley's *Brave New World* through George Orwell's *1984* and up to the current television series "Survivors" and "1990," Britain's contribution has been seminal. I suspect this potent seam of cultural pessimism has had far more popular influence than all the exhortations to turn over a new leaf. What is the normal theme of such literary nightmares? It is that an England deprived of its rich, decaying humus of constraints and class barriers must collapse into gruesome and rather foreign ways.

Technology is invariably associated with the disaster. It always gets out of control and into the wrong hands. Englishmen are reduced to the condition of Morlocks or proles. Only a few members of the liberal intelligentsia have somehow survived the deluge, shorn of their books and country cottages. They embark upon a lonely struggle to put the cultural clock back. Their lack of success underlines the fable's arcadian moral, which runs something like this: things are not *too* bad as they are, and will get a lot worse if any fool tries *too* hard to improve them. As with the traditionalist mainstream of letters, there is a fairly transparent celebration of social immobilism.

This strain of gloomy dystopia is not confined to novels or the media, either. It is a simple matter of observation that intellectual conversation in present-day Britain frequently makes the same plunge. The only imaginable future seems to be a black one. A soporific "middle ground" still dominates all big party conferences and general elections in Britain. Yet an uninformed visitor could be pardoned for believing that the National Front had already almost taken the country over. It is as if the eternal present of the old regime prevents any effective view of the future. So when a future crisis is mentioned, nobody seems able to stop this side of total disaster: fascism, race war, or worse.

These imaginings are themselves mostly symptomatic. But symptomatic of what? There will be future episodes of crisis, after all, quite likely worse than others we have known and quite capable of bringing big political changes. Is it really so impossible to foresee at least some aspects of this development more realistically?

III

Let me now return to the anti-Ogburn model and try to explain it better. Obviously it contradicts what most political commentators have said about the century-old crisis. Their stance has always been that Great Britain has an economic problem, which can be cured if certain economic policies are adopted. With only rare exceptions, they assume that the British state is sound and quite capable of taking up such policies. It may require a few minor changes, of course, scientists in the civil service and that sort of thing, but will otherwise remain intact. In this familiar perspective each successive failure to solve the problem is dismissed as some sort of accident: "We didn't get it quite right that time," "Our policies did not have time to work," and so forth. But next time it *could* be different, the long-heralded economic miracle could actually come about.

Any more realistic predictive model is bound to detect something fishy here. An endlessly repeated accident cannot be accidental. It must simply be part of the patient's behavior. We are not dealing with a mere problem but with part of the political ideology of being British in recent times. Italo Svevo's novel *La coscienza di Zeno* has as its hero an incurably heavy smoker who writes in his diary each day, "U.S.," "ultima sigaretta." He always sincerely intends to stop smoking. But he never does, and actually cannot. It is just that the idea of stopping and turning over a new leaf has long ago become an integral part of the smoking ritual. The thought of reform is an occasional opiate that eases his downhill progress; one doubts whether he would decline so happily without it.

No, it is not the case that Britain has an economic problem that gives rise to persistent episodes of crisis but will one day be cured by a supremely crafty government. The country has plenty of economic difficulties, of course, and each panic has particular causes of this kind. But *the* crisis, in the sense that interests us here—the long-drawn-out spiral of decline—arises from the state's inability to resolve the problem. That incapacity is neither accidental nor curable by any of the stratagems that so tediously recur through the modern history of British politics. So it would be more accurate to say that the nature of the state is the proximate cause of the British crisis. It is Britain's constitution, its political and administrative system, and an associated penumbra of civil hegemony, powerful yet hard to define, that maintain society on its hopeless course.

What is this nature? The subject is so well known that I need spend little time on it here: the unwritten constitution reposing sovereignty in the crown-in-parliament rather than the people; a two-party political order placing stability before democracy; an elite-controlled bureaucracy no one has ever been able to reconstruct; and a civil structure exhibiting low individual mobility, high group deference, and such prominent forms of ideological control as the monarchy and the famous British media. The term "system" has had a bad press recently because of the ultraleft usage denoting a baleful and omnipotent monster who has thought of everything. Although far from omnipotent, a "system" does exist in the sense that these elements do support one another unusually strongly and have been remarkably slow to disintegrate.

The resultant overall mixture is one of anachronism and strength. As I hinted earlier, the two things are inseparable. The ever recurrent economic crisis is, by near-universal consent, caused by failure to "modernize" the industrial sector. This conventional view identifies weakness with backwardness. It deplores (in the language of the Hudson Institute) such culpable failure to "re-orient British society to fit it for the high industrialism of the twentieth century." But actually this blatant social archaism has its own strength, too. Furthermore, radical modernization would probably destroy that strength. It would dramatically augment mobility, undermine traditional class consciousness, make the old hierarchies unworkable, menace the comfortable sloth of everyday existence, alter the political party system, upset the City and the Treasury dreadfully, and so on.

Of course, such conservative strength actually conserves. The great majority of actors in U.K. politics depend upon this fact. They *all* want Great Britain to catch up and (in the words of Sir Alan Cottrell, master of Jesus College, Cambridge, a former chief scientific adviser to the government) "have a second go at what it has failed so dismally to achieve during the past century: true regeneration of British industry, based on commercial policies, investment, technology, understanding leadership."[7] Well, naturally, who has ever been able to carp at this objective? But wait a minute: not *at any cost*—not, for example, if it means letting a lot of French-type technocrats run the economy instead of the Treasury, not if it means compelling the City to direct investment into domestic industries, "comprehensivizing" the public schools, turning Oxbridge into a polytechnic, sacking most of Whitehall, thoroughly annoying the United States, and ceasing to be the "good boy" of the Western alliance.

The trouble is that any actual program of crash modernization is bound to mean such things. It implies giving up a lot of the good, comfortable habits everyone depends on, as well as the notorious bad habits holding us back. These comfortable habits include the way we are ruled. In short, modernization is not, and perhaps never has been, a merely economic strategy under U.K. conditions. It could be enacted, as distinct from endlessly prospected, only through what would really be a revolution; that is, a relatively radical upheaval in the state and the governing ethos. In the past it was only under the special and transient circumstances of wartime, particularly between 1940 and 1945, that anything like this was ever seriously attempted.[8]

A revolution *or* a counterrevolution; a movement of the left *or* of the right. One need not prejudge this issue when predicting that at some point a political break must occur and a new regime must actually try to realize the content of all those modernization programs. By "break" I mean that the change of route must be forced by some novel combination of circumstances. It is inconceivable that it will be chosen through any agency of the existing system. Going back to the first of the two questions I posed, "Where are we now in this century-long history?" I believe that the conditions of such a break are now relatively imaginable. And I *will* prejudge the issue by suggesting that it is most likely to be of the right rather than the left. Also I believe (this is the second question I asked) that its form is more foreseeable than is usually thought.

IV

Some further development of our predictive model is needed first, however. I have suggested that we are discussing a society in which, contrary to many received opinions, the political culture is all-important and economics, at least in the sense of industry, is secondary. The true purpose of that culture, manifested in what its leaders do as distinct from what they write down in their diaries, is self-preservation. Behind all the new resolutions is a kind of Venetian consensus, built around a number of familiar taboos and constraints. And this consensus has been erected *against* modernization in precisely that sense trumpeted by a century of economic pundits and other apparent scourges of the status quo.

But, it is bound to be objected, this argument awards a somewhat mysterious character to the state. Marxists especially will be prompt to see the hand of idealism at work. How can a system of hegemony be said to enjoy this degree of autonomy, if not outright independence, *against* the body of economic and social relations on which it stands?

In approaching this problem, let me draw your attention to one outstanding recent analysis of the economic crisis. Stephen Blank has argued that in any overview of these persistent failures and false starts, one remarkable fact stands out plainly: the domestic economy was consistently sacrificed to a variety of *external* factors. The repeated body blows of stop-go deflation were administered to U.K. industry in order to maintain "Britain's position" vis-à-vis the outside world. What was that position? "The function of international economic policy was to restore and enhance Britain's role as a world power and, in particular, to contribute to the maintenance of the Commonwealth and Sterling systems (as well as the special relationship with the USA)," comments Blank, and the core of that role was "the re-establishment of sterling as a general international currency and of London as an open financial market-place."[9]

This aim was the consistent obsession of the state. It was upheld by the Treasury, with approval from the City, and with scarcely any critical opposition. This was the general strategy worked out by J. M. Keynes toward the end of the war and implemented at Bretton Woods. Afterward, finance capital did not have to fight to impose its view upon the state; its assumptions and world view were, by and large, taken for granted inside the general tableau of the British great-power mentality. Britain had to stay great; this meant putting sterling first; that in turn implied balance-of-payments constraints and manhandling the industrial sector to fit. The tale has been told so often, and to the accompaniment of so much gnashing of teeth and futile rage, that one hesitates even to mention it again. "Every single measure taken by British governments in the postwar period, whether Labour or Conservative, to spur exports . . . led to a curtailment of exports," writes one typical commentator. "Every single one penalised the efficient and technologically advanced industries on which growth and exports depend. Sometimes these measures hurt the domestic economy more than they did at other times. But none of them produced permanent improvement in British international accounts even though this was the sole aim of the policy."[10] Still, we can see now what the goal of the vicious circle has been: preserving the United Kingdom's place in the capitalist world, both politically and economically.

This dominant aim bears an ancient and unfashionable title: imperialism. The "external" strategy meant putting the Empire first, and it clearly made almost no difference to this attitude that there was less and less empire to defend. What was left, at any given stage, was somehow always more important than the long-suffering industrial sector. Efforts to redress the balance, such as Sir Stafford Cripps's Economic Ministry after 1947 and George Brown's Department of Economic Affairs after 1964, were weak and short-lived. After only a year or so, Treasury mandarins could be heard scrunching their bones with discreet relish.

Imperialism, therefore, in the sense of maintaining this special, outward-leaning equilibrium of the U.K. economy, has been the counterpart of that internal, conservative cohesion I referred to before. Not only do the various elements of our state support each other in that comfortable stagnation the critics have so deplored; they are all in their turn supported by this particular inclination of the economy. This is the material reality.

It is for this reason that I believe a generally Marxist model of Britain's condition is sufficient.[11] But it has to be a historical and specific model, one that takes in the *longue durée* of British capitalist development—the longest in existence—and, above all, locates that development in wider context. One may then perceive that it is no Hegelian *Geist* that maintains the remarkable entrenched authority of the British state. It is a set of equally remarkable entrenched interests that, because they have been in the saddle for generations, have assembled around themselves an unusually extensive and varied battery of political and civil hegemony.

Some other recent work helps us gain insight into the way this status was achieved. In a brilliant article titled "Wealth, Elites, and the Class Structure of Modern Britain," W. D. Rubinstein argues that it is a fundamental mistake to overlook the internal contradictions of the capitalist class in modern U.K. development. One can get nowhere with a one-dimensional model of capitalism, above all in this case. "It is a logical fallacy," he points out, "to infer from the central importance of industrial capitalism in the dialectical process the central importance of industrial capitalism for the bourgeoisie. The notion of the preeminent importance of industrialism and the Industrial Revolution has, moreover, affected our view of nineteenth-century British history totally, and in so insidious a way as to be accepted virtually without thought."[12] In reality, one may more accurately read the history of late-nineteenth-century Britain as first the containment of industrialism, then its defeat by an older, more powerful, and more political bourgeoisie. This bourgeoisie was of course the southern, London-based elite, first mercantile and then financial in its interests, which during this epoch built up about itself what Rubinstein calls "its London-based associates of great influence in twentieth-century society, like the Civil Service and the professions—the familiar Establishment of fact and fiction." This strong hegemonic bloc then colonized and took over the growing state power of the Edwardian decade and afterward.

Consequently, the sinister mystery of "deindustrialization" has fairly ancient but quite understandable roots.[13] They lie in the ever more dominant interests of what has become the most successful and politically crucial sector of British capitalism: the City of London. By 1914 the northern-based industrialists had been reduced to a subordinate role. It is in this quite secondary position that one may trace the origins of the extraordinarily feeble struggle they have put up against the policies imposed upon them.[14]

The imperial interest made industrialism its tributary. In this manner the only social class likely to fight effectively for modernization has been neutered over most of the period of Britain's modern crisis mythology. At approximately the same time—say between 1900 and 1918—both wings of the bourgeoisie enjoyed combined victory over the emerging political forces of the working class. This wider class struggle was institutionalized in the form of the new Labour Party. Through an able strategy of "social imperialism" its leaders were persuaded of the soundness of Constitution and Parliament, from their point of view; once inside the state, and exposed to its prodigious range of ideological influences, they found it impossible to get out.[15]

But space is not available here to expand too much on this theme. Suffice it to say there is a quite nonmystical explanation of the anti-Ogburn cycle, Great Britain's peculiar resistance to change, or what Peter Jay used to call "Englanditis." I doubt, for example, that British intellectuals are more irrecuperably Tory by instinct than those of any other society. A vociferous minority among them has always been outraged by the system; and in any case antitechnological humanism and precapitalist fantasy appear to be endemic in all capitalist states. It is certainly true, however, that in Britain objective conditions have favored a rather insouciant, romantic traditionalism on their part. As I suggested before in discussing literature, the same conditions have awarded real weight to such attitudes by locking them into a larger, more pervasive ideology that binds together the educational system, politics, and the state. It is in this way that the distinctive climate of modern British society was formed. While this can be called a capitalist ideology in an almost uselessly vague way, it is much more important to recognize its specific nature: it is a mercantile, old-bourgeois *Weltanschauung* and not a neocapitalist one. Many of its impulses are frankly hostile to "capitalist" ideas in this narrower, more modern sense; and of course this is one important reason that the working class, which has its own motives for hatred of such factory-capitalist virtues, finds traditionalism palatable.

I have no space, either, to say much about the history of British archaism. In a longer perspective it can be traced to the characteristics of the postrevolutionary mercantile state. In the more limited context of interest to us here, its founding moment was undoubtedly the containment and curbing of the industrial revolution: at that point the state chose a strategy of predominantly external development—the kind of imperialist consolidation most congenial to its inherited (and already quite ancient) structure. Considering it in comparative context, one may say it elected *not* to separate itself more authoritatively from civil society and to become the interventionist guiding structure for which the great majority of radical critics from Matthew Arnold onward have pleaded in vain.

The cost of this strategy was a peculiarly decentered development and hence a peculiar dependence upon the wider framework of the capitalist world. Priority was given to overseas investment and to the great complex of banking and other capital institutions that so effectively serviced world capitalism for so long. These institutions had little concern for the lagging industrial economy but an overwhelming interest in the state of worldwide trade and investment. So, therefore, did the British state. Since World War II especially, all its governments have subscribed to a uniform foreign-policy consensus that (as Stephen Blank says) effectively determined all the internal economic vicissitudes there was so much fuss about. Disputes occasionally arose between the parties over Europe, true; but they were fairly easily resolved, and nobody challenged the primary policy of adhesion to America's definition of the new free-trade world.

Depictions of the coming Great Crisis have normally contained an image of the hard, cutthroat world of advanced industrialism—those conditions to which the British had to adapt by modernization if they were not to suffer some even worse fate, such as revolution. As a matter of fact, the U.K. *ancien régime* did not find world conditions all that distressing until very recently. Notoriously, it benefited from victory in 1945, then from the postwar boom of the 1950s—when most of the competitors were in no state to cut anyone's throat—and afterward established a tolerable place within the sustained growth of the 1960s. This was an ever more dependent place, certainly. Yet as long as a general expansion was proceeding, dependency was classified as sin only by the modernizing, industrial-minded pundits. They could complain that the British overseas-oriented economy was being confirmed in its parasitism by these conditions, and sinking back into the ruts of anachronism. But the spokesmen of the Establishment could reply, also quite correctly, that the really successful sector of

British capitalism was flourishing anew and keeping the entire system afloat.[16]

These were, surely, the general conditions referred to initially, the crisis that has been ever with us yet never truly critical. The industrial base fell farther and farther behind, its periodic troubles provoking ever wilder schemes for Great Leaps Forward, and ever increasing cynicism when, inexorably, these leaps faltered into a few nervous sideways steps. But it was kept in forward motion none the less by the massive advance of the whole world economy. And as long as this was the case, the booming City sector could afford to ignore the problem. Once the specter of white-hot technological revolution had been exorcised, the state, too, evolved normally. Social imperialism was pursued into the last age of a shrunken empire as state expenditure and employment continued to mount. Right-wing critics found this growing top-heaviness of the state insupportable and identified it as the newest cause of "Britain's economic problem."[17] Outbursts of impotent rage such as those once associated with the present U.K. ambassador to the United States were the common result.

V

As far as the external force field is concerned, things have begun to change since 1973. The global economy has sunk into stagnation. With its peculiar degree of dependence, Britain has begun to suffer much more severely than at any time since the 1930s. From Bretton Woods up to the IMF rescue operation of 1976–77, Britain enjoyed a relatively complaisant international framework. But if the recession continues for years—the most widely held view at present—this amiability will disappear. The circumstances of Britain's negotiated decay are on the way out. Should there actually be a relapse, even partial, into protectionist strategies among the main trading nations, then one may visualize conditions in which the British state is *compelled* to undertake the salutary steps so many prophets have urged.

This is crucial, of course. That type of *redressement* will be contemplated by *this* type of polity only when it becomes not just inevitable—one might say it was always inevitable—but bitingly urgent. I argued previously that it entails a political revolution, or counterrevolution. What signs are there of internal changes in this direction, to match the ominous external trends?

The "sweet fog" has lifted a bit, though not because of the reforms Bernard Crick hoped for. It has been dissipated by straightforward disenchantment. This creeping delegitimization was expressed in moderate yet decided terms by Roy Jenkins when he left Westminster to become president of the EEC Commission: "When all possible qualifications have been made, there can be no doubt that the British political system has failed adequately to promote the long-term interests of the British people—not merely over the last twenty years, but over a much longer period. In my view there can also be no doubt that that failure has been due, not merely to obdurate circumstances, but to some features of our system of government and politics and to the conventions and assumptions which underpin it."[18] I know one must be cautious in taking such prescriptions at face value. There is a long history of useless thunder about Parliament, as there is about the economy. But it is the quiet certitude of Jenkins's indictment that impresses, plus the fact of its coming from a party that produced so many resonant justifications of constitutionalism in the recent past.

In his more academic survey of the system, Dennis Kavanagh writes that every single one of the old textbook chestnuts about British politics is now exposed to question, if not to outright contradiction. "In contrast to much of the what's wrong with Britain literature of the 1960s, which focused on the economy and society," he says, "there is now more criticism of the political institutions, particularly the workings of the two-party system and the sovereignty of parliament. . . . For the present, given the change from stability to instability, one should suspend assumptions about politics as usual."[19]

There is, in short, far more realization now than at any time in the past that the nature of the state has something to do with the crisis. The 1960s and the early 1970s saw both old parties wrestling with the decline, and both failing. Thus the party system went into the long recession after a prolonged period of attrition and demoralization. Since 1974, as Kavanagh notes, nearly all its supposed rules and virtues have ceased to function. Sustained only by an uncertain parliamentary coalition, government has been al-

most wholly devoted to two defensive operations; that is, to com-
bating the effects of the economic downturn, mainly by classical
deflationary policies, and to saving the political system itself by
conceding a degree of self-government to Scotland and Wales—
the argument here being that if political separatism took stronger
root in these countries, the old two-party machine would be permanently crippled.

In his analysis of the crisis, Eric Hobsbawm maintained that the
Scottish middle class's loss of faith in the British state was the most
serious single symptom of the new phase.[20] A growing part of a
social class that played a most prominent part in the imperial
history of that state has come to define its new attitude in one
four-letter word: exit. Devolution is in one sense a liberal, ac-
commodating measure. Yet what has been most striking, in the
perspective of political decay, is that the great majority—
including the majority who have trooped in and out of House of
Commons lobbies voting for it—do not believe in this liberalism.
Few think that it is really likely to stop nationalism. Among the
wider English public there is yawning incomprehension and
boredom with the subject. They merely see a parliament obsessed
with the irrelevant, in the midst of deepening recession.

At the same time as the Constitution itself is under mounting
assault, a new wave of resentment against the civil service has
arisen. That older "what's wrong" critique to which Kavanagh
refers saw the bureaucracy as corrupted by the Establishment's
general civil elitism. Partly in consequence, reform was started ten
years ago. The purpose was to end for good what the Fulton
Report (June 1968) called "the obsolete cult of the amateur" in
administration, and so strengthen at least some of the sinews of an
effective interventionist state. Had this been done it would have
been a significant fruit of the 1960s, even in the context of the
all-round failure of Labour's program. But what actually happened? In the last year we have been treated to a series of investigations on the subject, and their conclusions have been doleful
and unanimous. It is not merely that nothing has been done: the
process of reform has been systematically sabotaged by a successful rear-guard action of the mandarins. And finally, almost
twenty years after Lord Balogh's famous battle cry against the
ancien régime, *The Apotheosis of the Dilettante*, a miserable white paper

put out by the present government has stated that, after all the
fuss, there is really nothing to worry about.[21]

No change at the top, for the sempiternal reasons. As Peter
Kellner concludes, the snag is that as the enraged critics "advance
down this line of reasoning, it is not long before they start challenging some fairly substantial assumptions about class, education
and culture in British society."[22]

On the other hand, there has been a good deal of change lower
down in the structure. This is perhaps no less ominous than the
rigidity of the mandarins. Petty corruption has become a fairly
widespread and recognized phenomenon in certain areas of the
civil service and police during the same era—widespread enough,
at any rate, to be worth its own royal commission. The commission
produced its due, balanced underestimate of the problem in July
1976, and has been duly censured for skating over the surface.[23]
Whatever the real dimensions are, public expectations have certainly altered very noticeably. It would not be an exaggeration to
say that in particular regions such as the northeast of England,
southern Wales, and western Scotland they have fallen to zero.
Some years ago I wrote an account of the workings of the Labour
Party, trying to explain how it had turned into a principal pillar of
the old state, and I recently had occasion to reread it with a view to
another edition. What now struck me as most surprising about it is
that it said absolutely nothing about Labour involvement in local
government scandals, of the sort that has been weekly reading for
years in Cardiff and Glasgow. That kind of thing simply failed to
impinge upon our Hegelian reasoning in 1965. And (I sadly concluded) the task of writing about *this* mode of "integration" had
become too big for me.[24]

One must be cautious in calculating the decay of such stalwart
forces, I know. After all, the threatened collapse of winter 1974
was followed by a vigorous tripartite restoration of consensus and
by Labour's remarkable success in rallying the workers to an almost wholly conservative economic program. Deepening cynicism
about aspects of the state seemed to be counterbalanced by the
mighty hysteria worked up around the Jubilee in 1977. Still, I
think it can be said that political decline has become more evident
in the present round of crisis: paralysis, loss of sovereignty, the
threat of territorial disintegration, failure to reform, and corrup-

tion are all distinctly more prominent than they were a decade ago. And there seems no more chance of curing this malady than of finally solving the economic problem.

If so, then what is likely to come forth from the encounter of darkening recession and a wasting polity? Although no one can predict political gyrations exactly, I would have thought there could be little doubt as to the general form they will assume. Here the ground is so well prepared, both by precedent and by constantly reiterated ideology, that a modest amount of straightforward prediction is in order.

When compelled to, political systems change according to their own nature—or at least try to. Obviously, the U.K. polity must attempt restorative, essentially conservative change: however "radical" its short-term expedients, the firm underlying aim can be only a return to the status quo. This might be said of any country coping with crisis, I know. But the particular dimension here relates to the antichange syndrome in Britain. A society so intensively conservationist in outlook must need correspondingly strong defenses, or techniques of return. After all, the very things mentioned above—empire and external dependency—were bound to expose Britain to the storms of this century, such as the world wars and the Great Depression. A state open to such external buffeting should therefore have evolved emergency techniques of preserving its internal hierarchy and stability.

In fact it does possess such resources: the gray side of its twentieth-century political story. Not the black side, because there has never been any risk of military dictatorship or fascism. Yet a muddy, disreputable zone lies between these extremes and the overcelebrated virtues of two-partyism. The United Kingdom state is thoroughly at home there. It is even possible to argue that this is its real home, because—and this is merely a matter of record—the system has retreated into it each time it has been under really major threat. More than that: from this "crisis" experience it clearly drew new energy and authority and was thus enabled to survive the relatively minor upsets of the calmer eras that intervened.

This emergency formula is usually called "national government," the title worn by the 1930s version. The idea itself, however, originated with Lloyd George in 1910, as a response to the imminent revolutionary crisis of that period. His conception was simply an all-party coalition based on agreed objectives, which would enable the system to surmount an immediate menace; afterward there could be a swift return to normal. Although not realized before 1914, it was fairly quickly implemented once the war had begun—that is, when it was grasped that the war would last a long time and was posing crucial social and economic problems to the whole old order.

The resultant Lloyd George coalition lasted from 1915 until 1922. It had evolved from a strictly wartime deal into a project for postwar reconstruction in the national interest. So the model had established a peacetime validity. After the Great Crash and the failure of MacDonald's Labour government, it was employed again, and this time it lasted for thirteen years, from 1932 until the end of World War II. During the ten years following 1935 there was no general election at all, although there was a major shift of government when Churchill assumed control.

These governments were in office for a total of twenty-one years and one month. The total for straightforward Conservative rule is twenty-seven years and seven months. Labour lags a long way behind, with only eighteen years and six months (to March 1978). The winning Tory total, however, is due to the Conservatives' long tenure of office during the post–World War II boom: the thirteen years of relative noncrisis, having it so good, and so on. In terms of *qualitative* significance or fatefulness, national government has been the dominant mode. These periods when the normal functioning of the system was placed in abeyance "for the duration," when the underlying consensus manifested itself as a sort of qualified one-party rule in the national interest—these have been the decisive, founding experiences. They are still constantly harked back to, in both popular psychology and the rhetoric of politics.

This is true above all of the war coalitions. Wartime furnished the ideal conditions for a form of externally directed mobilization. Especially during World War II, the energies usually screwed down by Britain's social conservatism were released in a huge, spasmodic discharge. This release was revitalizing and yet safe. It increased the circulation and healed the festering wounds of the depression era, yet was directed outward and designed to validate the old ethos and class structure. This was the surrogate revolution Labour inherited in 1945—as many critics have noted, the war provided British socialism with its only real opportunity of dramatic forward movement. But this overspill from the emergency period also circumscribed its motion and ordained Labour's failure. For there was never any chance that "national unity" would be channeled into socialist construction.

It is virtually certain that this formula will be attempted again. It is repeatedly appealed for by a wide chorus of Establishment voices each time clouds pile up or the pound falls. A kind of magic attaches to it. It is the only available way of saving the system which looks both radical and yet romantic-conservative. It recalls wartime modes and legitimates a nationalism more overt and sentimental than ordinary British conditions allow.

VI

Edward Thompson has written, "My sense of history suggests that any rightist take-over in Britain will come, not through the agency of fascists, but by steady, vegetable pressures from within the State itself.... This ... will be presented in full colour to the British public, perhaps as the formation of a National Government in the public's own interest."[25]

My own sense of history, as past controversies have shown, is not very close to Thompson's. Yet on this issue I find we are in close agreement. England's foremost radical historian has amplified his view of the likely movement of contemporary history in another place, too, the forthright introduction to the State Research Collective's 1978 *Review of Security and the State*.[26] Here he describes how such recent events as the ludicrous "secrets trial" of the summer and fall of 1978 show once again that

> the ruling group within the State in Britain has a kind of arrogance about it which may be historically unique. It has a settled habit of power, a composure of power, inherited from generations of rule, renewed by imperial authority, and refreshed perennially from the springs of the best Public Schools. It is a group which does not bother, or need to bother, to get itself elected. It knows what "British interests" are, and defends these through every change of political weather ... It rules, unobtrusively, from within.

In a great number of ways the operation of the British state is quiet and genteel. But the implacable corollary of such gentlemanly patterns—agreeable enough in their way, by contrast with heavier bureaucracies—is this: the survival of a Venetian patriciate, secure, secretive, aloof, immovably committed to its own "responsible" power.

A "national government" is the apotheosis of such patrician responsibility. Men of all parties swallow their differences in the national interest. But this interest is defined, inevitably, by these more permanent guardians of the state tradition. The "adversarial style" of British parliamentarism (as it has come to be called by academic commentators) evaporates in the name of consensus; the plastic swords are put away for the time being, and for the sake of salvation. The experts explain what steps must be taken to avert disaster. But both the experts and the executors can come only from this same charmed circle of intellect and authority. There are historical examples of democracies that have abdicated power to an alternative force during crises of this kind—the most recent and relevant being that of the French Fourth Republic in 1958. In the conditions of U.K. political life, however, there *is* no alternative; or rather, the alternative is merely the abiding, inward reality of British state history, advanced from the wings to the forefront of the stage.

There was a good deal of puzzled discussion about the reknowned "intelligence" of the British ruling class during the first day of the Cornell conference. It revolved around the obvious question: How can such an intelligent, flexible, alert ruling group have presided so serenely over several generations of disaster? The perplexity arises from failure to see the special character of that intelligence. Intelligent it certainly was, and remains—but this intelligence has always been the calculating, conserving awareness of a patriciate and not the innovating, constructive outlook of a rising class, a new movement rebuilding its world. It undoubtedly has sensitive antennae for disturbances to its basis, and a ready will to accommodate and compromise with forces it has learned are here to stay. Long before Marcuse worried out the notion, it had perfected strategies of a containing tolerance, spiritual disarmament, and absorption.

The limitations of this old imperial consciousness, however, are its virtues. And this is why the puzzlement was mistaken. The profile of these limitations coincides with that of the long post-imperial fall from grace—the point being that, in the successive stages of the fall, Britain's rulers have encountered dilemmas ever more resistant to intelligent compromise, reasonable accommodation, decent pragmatism, and so on. The *real* dilemma of "modernization" or "marrying one's century" (to use General de Gaulle's famous phrase) demanded a different sort of intelligence and will altogether. And—as I indicated earlier—it is simply an additional (and of course characteristic) trait of the United Kingdom's ruling *Weltanschauung* that the leaders developed early on the technique of *talking about* new starts and amazing mutations of the national essence in order to stave off the need to undertake them.

It is in this perspective that one may estimate the likely fate of any emergency coalition to come. It is bound to fail. The formula succeeded in wartime and managed to keep the system going in the 1920s and 1930s, when imperial reserves still remained to be mobilized. Under both those conditions, the profound conservatism at its heart was compatible with a degree of forward movement and adaptation. Those conditions, however, have disappeared. There will never be another imperial war, and the IMF and EEC will not indefinitely cushion Britain's fall. National-government regimes promise to be both radical and restorative; but the whole point of the crisis conditions that have slowly accumulated over the past twenty years is that restoration is impossible. The actual undertaking of renovation has become inevitable.

One may extend this contradiction over an even broader range. Almost all of modern Britain's character—territorial, urban, administrative, cultural—derives from one key fact: it has been ruled, in astonishing continuity, by a homogeneous civil elite of a certain type. What the "crisis"—at that deeper level I referred to at the beginning—really does is demarcate and undermine in stages the distinctive limitations of this class. With all its amazing capacities of adaptive finesse, all its resilience and cultural power, it cannot change its historical skin. That is, it cannot replace its own state form with another. Yet this is, unquestionably, what the break demands: a different *sort* of state. Intelligence cannot provide it. And it is very difficult to see what can.

We may appreciate the crux of the problem by turning to an outstanding recent analysis of the Constitution. No study in modern times has given us a more incisive portrait of its state than Nevil Johnson's *In Search of the Constitution* (1977). I would recommend this book with particular warmth to those who believe that Marxists enjoy a monopoly of gloom and foreboding in the field of British studies. Though written from a political standpoint quite contrary to E. P. Thompson's and my own, it exposes the senile dementia of the old order more effectively than any of us have done.

"My contention is," Johnson begins grimly, "that the root of the trouble is now political, not economic and social: we have an old and tired political order under which it has proved increasingly difficult to solve serious economic and social problems."[27] Then in one chapter after another the patient's shaking limbs and faltering faculties are laid out for inspection. "Pursuit of illusions" is all he is good for nowadays. Keynesian-based "socialism" led to the formation of a "static State" where distributive equality took priority over growth; the patrician administration of this stagnant polity bred a quietism of decay, beneath all the "febrile and pointless" half measures of successive governments; Parliament itself "has become a shadow" of the nineteenth-century original, "teetering dangerously on the brink of discovering the truth about itself" and dragging the House of Lords and an unreformed electoral system into the age of the European Parliament; yet without such self-discovery, the author admits, there is small chance of constitutional reform, let alone the creation of a German-style *Rechtstaat* of the kind he admires. Both the customs of the elite and "the sentiments of the people towards government" (the title of his Chapter 10) act against it.

None the less, when it comes down to recommending what ought to happen, even this most acerbic of critics relents. "The repair and re-shaping of an indispensable political framework is not, however, quite out of reach," he insists, trying very hard not to be funereal. How could they be undertaken? Well, the best thing would be if "at some stage a government might be ready to entrust the review of a range of fundamental constitutional questions to . . . an inquiry body" with unrestricted terms of reference. It would be manned by such people as Mr. Johnson or his colleagues from Nuffield College, Oxford, naturally. Such a super-royal commission would carry out the vital task of political reeducation and nudge or entice Westminster bit by bit toward "a step-by-step yet coherent reform." Thus, by a supreme act of self-transforming intelligence, the old carriage would endow itself with a new motor and wheels.

No historical-materialist grid is needed to identify this plan for reform as an illusion—as, indeed, one of those illusions for which Mr. Johnson so shrewdly indicts the British establishment in his own book. And the point is, surely, that beyond the inevitable palliative phase of a national government it will be not intelligence but stupidity that calls the tune. Our *ancien régime* has negotiated its own decline ably enough; no regime negotiates its own foundering or transformation. These are things it backs into, when the traditional antennae and modes of control fail completely. And because it has given an impression of perennial omnicompetence for so long, the old state's failure is likely to be all the more total, and totally unintelligent.

In this sense, then, what one ought to be looking out for in the contemporary U.K. scene is not the subtle new formulae secreted at Oxbridge but the idiocies on offer far lower down. It is down among the hacks, vulgarians, brash careerists, and loud renegades that the new *idea forza* is probably gestating. Here, in the strata traditionally marginalized and condescended to by the patricians, one is more likely to discern a few clues to the future. After all, they have played a prominent part in the modern politics of many other countries. In certain conditions they could come into their own even in England. Let me add at once (to answer a possible accusation of double standards) that in my own country, Scotland, they have already made palpable progress toward some sort of power; and this has been invigorating as well as risky.

I do not want here to embark on a survey of the prospective *bestiarium* of English politics in the 1980s. Suitable varieties of daftness exist on both left and right. But—as one would expect— those on the right are currently more vociferous, influential, and jubilant. Benefiting from the broader international climate of philosophical reaction and anticollectivist humbug, they have ac-quired a fair purchase on the media and public opinion as exemplified by newspaper editorials and publishing lists. Given the inert strength of the old order (and especially of the Labour Party), they have not yet penetrated far into practical politics. Official Toryism has shifted in their direction, true, under the inspiration of Margaret Thatcher. But repeated past history has shown what a gap may still remain between ideological rhetoric of this kind and its translation into power.

Still, they are a lot closer to access to the *possibility* of power than their enemies on the far left. And if it remains difficult to imagine just how, in English conditions, they could do the trick, the explanation lies in another significant absence. Two things have been precluded from the normal course of peacetime politics by the very style of Establishment politics: populist nationalism and (normally linked to it) a populist, antisystem style of political leadership. Again, these are quite familiar animals in many other lands (notably in the United States). And all one is really trying to imagine is a postcrisis Britain, or England, where they have become abruptly naturalized, with a correspondingly great sense of novelty.

In this connection, it is salutary to recall the Powell adventure. No one was more evidently (and self-consciously) marked out to swing politics onto a new course than Enoch Powell. There has been no more relentless critic of both main parties, no fiercer adversary of Establishment liberalism and self-deception. No would-be tribune has enjoyed half so much popularity or employed half his skill in the exploitation of racism and other festering resentments. And yet, without dismissing someone who is still a force, one is forced to register the failure of his essential mission so far. Why has it failed?

It was already clear some years ago that there were serious obstacles in the messiah's path. I made an effort to work out just what they were at that time, and later elaborated the argument in *The Break-up of Britain*.[28] There are objective constraints on that sort of mobilization in English political culture, associated with both the imperialist inheritance and the patrician stranglehold. And (I also held) Powell has remained too addicted to pure laissez-faire capitalism and the semisacred taboos of Westminster parliamentarism. These judgments still appear right to me, and indeed they are repeated in his own way by Douglas Schoen in the most serious study of Powellism yet published, *Enoch Powell and the Powellites* (1977). For instance, Schoen declares that "another significant reason why Powell has not been more of a force . . . is that the population by and large does not share his concern over parliamentary sovereignty and the more general issue of U.K. nationalism. Except when they have been directly threatened (as in war), the English public has never been susceptible to mobilization over questions of sovereignty and nationhood in the way the Americans have."[29]

Schoen added something, however, which I had not perceived at all. Powell has always thought that some sort of mass upsurge of public opinion would "catapult him into leadership" (in Schoen's phrase), most probably through the Conservative Party's conversion to his ideas. And he has also believed that personal charisma alone would solicit such energies—as expressed in speeches, electoral pronouncements, and his lone crusader's drama of renunciation and prophecy. As a result, he has never undertaken real political organization or allowed it to be done for him (although many offers have been made). Afraid that a Powellite party would be crushed and eliminated by the system (like past new parties), he has stuck to a strategy of takeover from within.

This failure (I can now see) is as important and revealing as any other. It is by no means obvious that a Powellite movement would have shared the fate of other new departures in British organized politics. Yet Powell chose to join the Ulster Unionists. Although vociferously pro-British, this party belongs to the alien logic of Irish political life and (given dominant U.K. popular attitudes on Ireland) represents a hopeless *practical* platform for his message. He seems to regard presence in the House of Commons as vital to that message. In fact, he may be the one figure in recent British politics who could have dispensed with the sacred imprimatur and conducted an effective antisystem mobilization from without.

Reflection on this crucial failure may help us estimate just where the crisis is, politically speaking. It should cause us to be distinctly less complacent about those "objective" barriers to a new, Gaullist-style English nationalism. They are there, all right. But we do not really know how high they are, for the simple reason that as yet nobody has seriously tried to build a a political vehicle capable of crashing them. The National Front, an extreme right-wing racist movement active in and around immigrant ghettos, is almost certainly *not* open to that kind of evolution. My own guess (but it can be no more than a guess, even with Schoen's careful analysis in mind) is that if Powell had taken such a path, he would have found the going very difficult but far from impossible. And the very existence of the new movement would have seriously hastened all those trends toward disintegration listed above.

Hence, one may very well imagine that Powell is only a precursor of some more emphatic national-populist leader of the 1980s—of another messiah less closely tied to the old regime, less "principled" and more unscrupulous, more politically innovative and adventurous. A transitional national government might open the door to him, both by its general incompetence and its destructive effect on the cohesion of the old parties. That effect would be much worse than the exercises of the 1930s (which none the less gravely damaged the Labour Party for most of the decade). And the resulting movement would be far more massive than Oswald Mosley's attempt to invent a British variety of fascism. It would "normalize" U.K. politics with a vengeance (whether one takes the United States or continental Europe as the reference point). And this would be *the* crisis, at last!

VII

During the debate in the House of Lords on the formation of the International Monetary Fund in 1944, John Maynard Keynes spoke these words:

Sterling must itself, in due course, become once again convertible. For, without this, London must necessarily lose its international position, and the arrangements ... of the Sterling Area would fall to pieces. To suppose that a system of bilateral and barter agreements, with no one who owns sterling knowing just what he can do with it—to suppose that this is the best way of encouraging the Dominions to centre their financial systems on London, seems to me pretty near frenzy. As a technique of Little Englandism, adopted as a last resort when all else has failed us, with this small country driven to autarchy, keeping itself to itself in a harsh and unfriendly world, it might make more sense. But those who talk this way ... can have very little idea of how this Empire has grown up or by what means it can be sustained. ...

So said the acme of the old ruling-class intelligence thirty-five years ago. There is not much in the fate of his nation since that did not lie implicit in those words: the primacy of the "international position" and its sterling accompaniment (which meant the secondary place of domestic industry and ultimate deindustrialization), City dominance over the rest of U.K. capitalism (which entailed Treasury control of economic policy), a foreign policy based on being the "good boy" of the new Atlantic world (a prerequisite of the "special relationship" and special protection under the American wing), and so on.

If the magician of Bretton Woods could be wafted back to us today on some suitably well-padded cloud, what would he think of the crisis? Other contributors to this volume have explained the disappearance of his economic world, with an abundance of illustration and commentary. Most of the external conditions of his imperial-survival strategy have gone. So has the Empire itself. In spite of a tenacious rear-guard action, the City has been edged farther and farther away from that nodal position he thought essential. We are in the decade of the sliding dollar and on the edge of a European monetary union that cannot fail to challenge its hegemony in the next decade, regardless of what London and sterling do.

I think he would be astonished that "frenzy" had not struck us long before now. Nearly all else *has* failed us. His insurance policies have served the old state well, admittedly; but there is small chance that the world will be less "harsh and unfriendly" in the coming decade. So why have the English been so long in resorting to the techniques of Little Englandism? Since Keynes was a genuine *political* economist in the old tradition, he would presumably look for the political explanation. And here quite a few shocks would await him.

The first, immediate one is very simple. He would be unable to buy a copy of the *Times*. The ineffable house paper of his elite has vanished, in a final flurry of editorial trumpetings about the Crisis and its Rational Solution. Keynes was as susceptible to its tedium and pomposity as any other reader. Although he was too clever to fall for journalistic frothings on "England is not England without the *Times*," nobody would comprehend more accurately than he that patrician, Established England is indeed no more itself without this organ. There is (at the time of writing) real uncertainty about whether, or when, its Canadian proprietor will authorize its resurrection. Only one other fact might inflict a more chilling sensation on the shade: he would not be able to relax with his favorite weekly on Friday, either. The *Literary Supplement* has gone down with the rest of the ship.

Hovering in the ghastly foyers of the new *Times* building in Grays Inn Road, he would take only a few seconds to grasp the dilemma. A management of unbending incompetence, fumbling with "modernization" techniques in a last desperate effort to break even; floors full of unusable high technology imported from California; a mutinous working class steeped in imperialist corruption and malpractice, prepared to struggle "to the end" for the old customs. So here the crisis is not merely prospected. It is happening. And the best newspaper in Great Britain, the *Sunday Times,* has been washed down the drain alongside the Thunderer's Court Circular, Bernard Levin, and the letter page, where appeals for a national government are habitually launched.

When he picked up the *Guardian* and the *Telegraph* for background on the political situation, a second frightful blow would fall. For they, along with the rest of the press and media, are devoting every available column inch to scandalous revelations about the former leader of the Liberal Party. Little in the sexual detail of these escapades would surprise Keynes. Norman Scotts and gentlemanly deviations were familiar in his circle. The fact that they now stand exposed to mass ridicule, however, would deeply dismay him. What a deterioration in civilized standards! The allegations that a leader of his old party had to resort to hiring murderers to keep the whole thing quiet would—it goes without saying—more than dismay him.

Liberalism must be in bad odor and bad shape, he might conclude. But it would take him some time with such old friends as the *Spectator* and the *Observer* to grasp just how bad. Jeremy Thorpe's vicissitudes alone give no hint of the wave of asphyxiative reaction drenching the country. Reaction against what? An ectoplasmic ghoul called "collectivism" or "socialism" is usually pilloried in these fulminations; however—since there were few signs of triumphant bolshevism in Grays Inn Road—one would have to conclude that the British interventionist state is what they are talking about. I doubt that Keynes would have liked many aspects of the Labourite mixed economy that arose after his death. But he was one of its principal architects, and would certainly have preferred it to his recollection of the twenties and thirties. So we must picture him more than mildly depressed at this feverish onslaught, especially at the pitying tone it so often adopts. Poor Keynes, he meant well; what a shame that sort of thing never works.

The notions returning to fashion would remind him in numbing detail of the old fetishes of the 1920s. The truculent skeleton of laissez faire has sprung out of the tomb and parades across the front pages of the financial press. Such old enemies as Friedrich von Hayek have become celebrities, crowing over the end of the Keynesian era and the return to sanity. Keynes and Sir William Beveridge thought that a responsible social extension of liberalism was the cure for the ills of laissez faire; now a stiff dose of pure capitalism is seen as the cure for social democracy. The abstract lunacies of monetarism have turned into comfortable clichés, soothingly advanced as the "sensible" antidote to crisis, low productivity, inflation, and everything else.

More awful yet has been the party-political destiny of liberalism. Though it ceased to dominate Parliament directly after World War I, the liberal tradition remained vital. It changed parties but gained new authority. Through his influence and under the brand name of socialism it furnished the Labour Party with a reforming credo. In this grand enterprise the intelligent elements of the patrician elite discovered a new life. Capitalism was saved and improved from above, even if a lot of the pressure had come from below.

Now, with a return to world slump and the end of the welfare-state compromise signaled in every editorial, should not the great tradition once more rise to the challenge? Could not liberalism and the Liberal Party, which has survived in spite of everything, formulate some fresh radical approach? A second *General Theory* is hard to imagine, perhaps. But even without that, could not the system be saved and built up again by a new questioning of orthodoxies and a further generation of practical, piecemeal reforms? People said in the thirties that the old tree was exhausted, and were wrong. Might not the new chorus of reactionaries be equally mistaken?

With the best will in the world, I believe that Keynes would see nothing but darkness here. He has returned to an England governed by a Labour administration of the most overwhelming, unmitigated conservatism. Mrs. Castle has been honest enough to admit that it has pursued policies indistinguishable from those of a national government led by genuine Tories. No effort is required to conceive what Keynes would think of Sir Harold Wilson's later antics, or of an unemployment rate rising toward 1930s levels, or of the conjunction of the two. But he would be more dispirited still at the news that for over a year the Liberal Party shed all semblance of an alternative approach and propped the regime up "in the national interest." Thus it died politically even before Mr. Thorpe's culpable secrets tumbled out of the closet. Grimond and Thorpe had stood out, at least, for reform of the Constitution and Parliament; the Steel party stands only for "responsible moderation," with an alms bowl perpetually extended for whatever crusts of reform the national interest may allow.

Hence, liberalism has decayed into a formula for creeping national government. The lugubrious little coalition of 1977–78 was like an unavowed rehearsal of the next round; so (we must hope) were its failure and the recent collapse in Liberal support. The center has no hope of holding—let alone of reconstructing the drifting hulk. Up at the great shade's old university, the Cambridge Group has consecrated itself to frenzy and Little Englandism: the vision of an embattled socialist economy destroying all that is left of the old international position, quite unaware this may also mean doing away with the old state (including its Labour Party). On the right, he sees an army of remorseless logicians who (as he once wrote of Hayek) have started with a mistake and ended up in Bedlam. They intend taking us all there in 1979.

By now Keynes would have seen enough. I doubt very much that he would want to stay around and witness the next round of the British Crisis.

Notes

1. George Lichtheim, "Ideas of the Future," *Partisan Review* 33, no. 2 (Summer 1966).
2. William F. Ogburn, "Social Evolution Re-considered," in *On Culture and Social Change,* ed. O. D. Duncan (1964).

3. The most interesting episode here was the tour of the Hudson Institute forecasters, which resulted in *The United Kingdom in 1980* (New York: Wiley, 1974). Greeted with howls of rage by almost the whole U.K. press, this inquiry started off conventionally enough with a treatment of the "economic problem." But it recognized that the economic problem could not be isolated. "A kind of archaism of the society and the national psychology . . . a repeated and characteristic flight into pre-industrial, indeed pre-capitalist, fantasies" rendered piecemeal advice on the economic front alone useless. Unable quite to prescribe revolution, the Hudson reporters collapsed into rather tame suggestions of a "change of style" from above, which might eventually "re-orient British society to fit it for the high industrialisation of the later twentieth century." It should not be thought, incidentally, that this kind of cosmetic counsel has come only from futurologists. One of the shrewdest observers of British parliamentary politics, the late John P. Mackintosh, arrived at the same point of despair in his *Britain's Malaise: Political or Economic?* (1977).

4. In a recent and penetrating piece of demythology, Raphael Samuel has shown just how limited and backward-looking were the actual foundations of the fabled epoch: "The industrial revolution rested on a broad handicraft basis, which was at once a condition of its development and a restraint on its farther growth." There never was a *machine* "workshop of the world" capable of the feats so often ascribed to it, in other words. See "The Workshop of the World: Steam Power and Hand Technology in Mid-Victorian Britain," *History Workshop*, no. 3 (Spring 1977).

5. Introduction to the Hudson Institute's *The Year 2000,* ed. Herman Kahn and A. J. Wiener (New York: Macmillan, 1974).

6. A useful survey of the politics (and nonpolitics) of U.K. authorship over the last generation is Peter Firchow's *The Writer's Place: Interviews on the Literary Situation in Contemporary Britain* (Minneapolis: University of Minnesota Press, 1974). A malicious "review" of this work appeared in the literary magazine *Bananas,* no. 3 (London, 1975), underlining its social content. In the anthology *Bananas,* edited by Emma Tennant (London, 1977), I attempted a more serious treatment of the role of the literary intelligentsia in relation to the state.

7. Sir Alan Cottrell, "After the White Heat Cooled," in the *Times* Special Royal Jubilee Supplement, January 5, 1977.

8. A fine example of the neurosis on display is provided by the *Times*'s dramatic and quickly forgotten proposal of December 19, 1973: "Should We Invest £20,000 Million to Modernize British Industry?" After some prefatory hemming and hawing on the otherwise admirable quality of British life, the argument was that "the problem of Britain is industrial" and it is "consistent failure on this front" that has engendered the suspicion that Britain is doomed to be "the wallflower of the world." Not so: all we need is £20,000 million to do the trick. This sum could be got together by a wartime-style bond issue. The great leap forward would then be consummated "in a spirit not of Napoleonic dream but of realism and flexibility." Ah! But what does "realism and flexibility" actually mean? These are of course code words for the very *Times*ish consensus, "quality

of life" and all, which condemns all such notions to dreamland. Realism and flexibility defeated both the Wilsonian and the Heathite formulas for radical modernization, staged a grand ceremonial return to office in 1974, and have reigned uninterruptedly ever since.

9. Stephen Blank, "Britain: The Problem of Pluralistic Stagnation," in *International Organization* 31, no. 4 (Fall 1977): 686–87.

10. Peter Drucker, *The Age of Discontinuity* (New York: Harper & Row, 1969).

11. As long as overabstraction is avoided. The main abstraction that has dogged analysis here is the idea that the functioning of British society and state can be explained mainly (or even wholly) in terms of the internal industrial economy and its "relations of production" (the class struggle). There is a theoretical error at work here: all state forms are the products of some specific historical balance between these internal factors and the external relations imposed by the world system of capitalism. But there is an extra, practical dimension of error in failing to see the United Kingdom's *exceptional* dependence on such external relations.

12. W. D. Rubinstein, "Wealth, Elites, and the Class Structure of Modern Britain," *Past and Present*, no. 76 (August 1977), p. 126.

13. For the last cheerful word on deindustrialization, see Ajit Singh, "U.K. Industry and the World Economy: A Case of Deindustrialization?," in *Cambridge Journal of Economics* 1, no. 2 (June 1977): 134: "All that one can say in general is that the structural disequilibrium may be so deep-seated, and the economic and political environment may be such, that in spite of the benefits of North Sea oil, it may not be possible to bring about the required modifications in the production system without fundamental institutional changes."

14. Here see Stephen Blank's *Industry and Government in Britain: The Federation of British Industries in Politics, 1945–65* (Farnborough: Saxon House, 1973), above all the section "The Political Culture of British Industry," pp. 201–9; also Graham Thompson, "The Relationship between the Financial and Industrial Sectors in the United Kingdom Economy," *Economy and Society* 6, no. 3 (August 1977).

15. An important recent study of the origins of Labour's integration into the state, taking up the seminal work of Bernard Semmel, is Robert J. Scally, *The Origins of the Lloyd George Coalition: The Politics of Social Imperialism, 1900–1918* (Princeton: Princeton University Press, 1975).

16. Efforts have been made to justify the City's dominance directly and simply to throw overboard the "economic problem" of industry. The most recent and entertaining such work is Bernard D. Nossiter, *Britain: A Future That Works* (Boston: Houghton Mifflin, 1978). The London correspondent of the *Washington Post* is so fond of the Arcadian aspects of British decline that he sees the future of the West in them. Hence he advocates a positive strategy of deindustrialization as an example to others rather than a grim warning: the transfer of resources from manufacturing "to those areas where Britain has the greatest comparative advantage," such as banking, insurance, English-language instruction, the staging of

uniformed parades, crossword puzzles, and so on. But I doubt if Nossiter entirely believes his own attractive vision. Half of his concluding chapter ("A Model of Sorts") is devoted to a witty excoriation of British state secrecy, the legal system, and the supineness of press and parliament—those well-known inseparables of the English Arcady.

17. The book summing up this view of The Problem is Walter Eltis and R. Bacon, *Britain's Economic Problem: Too Few Producers*, 2d ed. (London: Macmillan, 1978), "Our view of Britain's crisis is to a startling extent similar to Quesnay's account of the crisis of the Ancien Régime in France," note the authors in their preface. Quesnay's celebrated *Tableau Economique* of 1758 demonstrated the vicious economic circle of the old French state, which could lead only to eventual breakdown. Eltis and Bacon substitute industry for agriculture in their version. Pushed to the limit, this analogy would situate the British dénouement in an uncomfortably far-off 2007.

18. Roy Jenkins, "What's Wrong, and What Could be Set Right: Reflections after 29 Years in Parliament," *Encounter*, February 1978.

19. Dennis Kavanagh, "New Bottles for Old Wines: Changing Assumptions about British Politics," *Parliamentary Affairs* 31, no. 1 (Winter 1978).

20. See E. J. Hobsbawm, *The Crisis and the Outlook* (London, 1975).

21. See Peter Kellner, "A Failure to Reform?," *Sunday Times*, March 19, 1978. In 1977 Bruce Page and Isabel Hilton produced a stimulating longer study of the same failure in the *Daily Express* (April 5-6), while at the same time the *Guardian* ran a series, "The Whitehall Ascendancy," reaching the same conclusion. Not long after that a subcommittee of the House of Commons Public Expenditure Committee (the English Committee) resoundingly confirmed all these verdicts. The recent White Paper is *The Civil Service: Government Observations, etc.* (H. of C. 535, March 1978).

22. Kellner, "A Failure to Reform?"

23. See M. Pinto-Duschinsky, "Corruption in Britain," a review of the Royal Commission Report *Standards of Conduct in Public Life* (Cmnd. 6524, July 1976), in *Political Studies* 25, no. 2 (June 1977). "The Commission considerably underestimated the problem and was mistaken in rejecting the proposed independent inspectorate," wrote Pinto-Duschinsky. Royal commissions for this sort of thing are a waste of time, he concludes (in more revolutionary vein), since such a culture of insiders will never tolerate any mechanism of external review: they always believe that they can best repair leaks and malfunctions.

24. The essay referred to is "Anatomy of the Labour Party," recently reprinted with only minor changes in *Revolution and Class Struggle: Readings in Marxist Politics*, ed. Robin Blackburn (1977).

25. E. P. Thompson, "The Secret State within the State," *New Statesman* 11, no. 10 (1978).

26. Julian Friedmann Books, London, 1978 (a collection of the collective's bulletins for 1977 and 1978).

27. Nevil Johnson, *In Search of the Constitution: Reflections on State and Society in Britain* (Oxford: Oxford University Press, 1977), p. 1.

28. "Enoch Powell and the New Right," *New Left Review*, 1970, reprinted in *The Break-up of Britain,* ed. Tom Nairn (London: New Left Books, 1977).

29. Douglas E. Schoen, *Enoch Powell and the Powellites* (New York: St. Martin's Press, 1977), p. 278.

16 | *Toward 1984: George Orwell and Today's Britain*

PETER STANSKY

I would like to attempt, no doubt idiosyncratically, to put the British crisis in perspective, using the life and work of George Orwell, with whom I've been preoccupied in recent years, as a way of gaining some insight into the nature of the crisis and perhaps to indicate the direction it is likely to take. Orwell, of course, has been dead for many years—he died in January 1950—and I admit at the outset that this sort of extrapolation is a risky business. We know what Orwell thought about the world he knew, but how can we be certain what he would think of things now? In a word, I must speculate.

It seems the roots of the crisis go back a long way. But I would argue that the very origins of Britain's great power in the Industrial Revolution already contained the seed of its later troubles. (The country that brought you the Industrial Revolution brings you the postindustrial world.) Certainly a lot of the attitudes that have become troublesome, particularly class attitudes and attitudes toward business, have deep roots in Britain's past. Undoubtedly many of the problems we have been considering have their early development in the period from 1870 on (and quite a few references have been made to this), when Britain began to experience economic difficulties, and these problems reached a climax at the time of the First World War. That war ended, technically at least, in a victory, but it was a victory won at a great price. Now, with the advantage of hindsight, one can see Britain's problems clearly prefigured, as the United Kingdom would develop in the years between the wars and after. One can understand that the Empire was plainly in decline long before Churchill and his successors presided over its terminal phase. One recognizes now that the need to be associated with Europe in a new way was unavoidable. But however clear the theoretical analysis, it is hard to believe that Britain has quite found a way to work things out as advantageously to itself as might have been hoped. Can Orwell provide any assistance in understanding why?

One is struck by his early recognition of the crisis in values in British society, and his forceful statement of the case in a rather unexpected source, his bitter look back to his prep school days—that essay, ironically entitled "Such, Such Were the Joys," which was published in the United States shortly after his death but remains unpublished in England until 1968 for fear of libel. In that essay he wrote specifically about his school and symbolically about the England in which he grew up.

"The essential conflict," he points out,

> was between the tradition of nineteenth-century asceticism and the actually existing luxury and snobbery of the pre-1914 age. On the one side were low-church Bible Christianity, sex puritanism, insistance on hard work, respect for academic distinction, disapproval of self-indulgence; on the other, contempt for "braininess" and worship of games, contempt for foreigners and the working class, an almost neurotic dread of poverty, and above all, the assumption not only that money and privilege are the things that matter, but that it is better to inherit them than to work for them. Broadly, you were bidden to be at once a Christian and a social success, which is impossible.[1]

Orwell had an almost prophetic sense of Britain's coming dilemmas—the need to find a new role for itself, without the Empire, without its commanding financial power, without its industrial might. He arrived at this accurate enough judgment during the later years of the Second World War. Earlier in the war he had been quite wrong in his predictions, spelled out in a series of letters from London to the *Partisan Review,* which itself had rather ambivalent feelings about the war. There Orwell argued that Britain must become a socialist society in order to survive. This argument was based on his experience in Spain, where he had seen an emerging socialist society thwarted for the sake of winning the civil war—and despite this change of course, victory was never achieved and the revolutionary dream was permanently obliterated. So far as England is concerned, he turned out to be wrong in his short-run prediction (as he later admitted), but his sense of what might happen casts an interesting light on where England finds itself today, and the sort of change—easy to call for, hard to make mean anything—that might be necessary if the situation is going to improve.

What is particularly striking about Orwell was his profound belief in England—his patriotism, beaten into him at the time of the First World War and wonderfully suggested in the title of the essay he wrote at the beginning of the Second, "My Country Right or Left." When he returned from Spain, he was already concerned and doubtful as to how England would respond to a worsening, potentially catastrophic world situation. His anxieties dominate the concluding paragraph of *Homage to Catalonia*:

> And then England, southern England, probably the sleekest landscape in the world. It is difficult when you pass that way ... to believe that anything is really happening anywhere. Earthquakes in Japan, famines in China, revolutions in Mexico? Don't worry, the milk will be on the doorstep to-morrow morning, the *New Statesman* will come out on Friday. The industrial towns were far away, a smudge of smoke and misery hidden by the curve of the earth's surface. Down here it was still the England I had known in my childhood: the railway-cuttings smothered in wild flowers, the deep meadows where the great shining horses browse and meditate, the slow-moving streams bordered by willows, the green bosoms of the elms, the larkspurs in the cottage gardens; and then the huge peaceful wilderness of outer London, the barges on the miry river, the familiar streets, the posters telling of cricket matches and Royal weddings, the men in bowler hats, the pigeons in Trafalgar Square, the red buses, the blue policemen—all sleeping the deep, deep sleep of England, from which I sometimes fear that we shall never wake till we are jerked out of it by the roar of bombs.[2]

Spain had been a traumatic experience for Orwell. He had seen what he took to be the socialist future and also what he saw as its betrayal, and he ended his Spanish experience mounting guard on top of a movie theater in Barcelona on behalf of a splinter Marxist group, the POUM, supporting the anarchists against the socialists and the communists. He had glimpsed the ennobling possibilities of socialism, had been stirred by a William Morris–like conviction—no matter that he happened to disapprove of Morris and the whole arts-and-crafts tradition—that fellowship is life and the absence of fellowship is death. Orwell's period after Spain, when he was writing *Homage to Catalonia* and *Coming Up for Air,* was rather confused: the time in the chrysalis before the new Orwell emerged, ready to come to terms with England. His attitude toward authority would always be ambivalent, perhaps more negative than positive, a mix of respect and disdain. Allowing for the biographical peculiarities in Orwell's case and emphasizing in particular the revulsion he felt after serving in the Burma police, I think that this ambivalence toward authority is an ingrained English attitude and may explain something about the strengths and weaknesses of British society at this moment. Many English tend to have a deep sense of responsibility, indeed almost a reverence for established authority, combined, rather paradoxically, with a profound sense of individualism and a belief in the rights of the freeborn Englishman. It may be in this area—where the ideas of Burke and Mill (both of them utilitarians, after all) can be said to meet and the ideas of Coleridge and Bentham to intersect—it may be in this area that the two great traditions of British political philosophy have their continuing conversation with one another and have an evident effect on the makeup of British society.

Orwell was so upset by his Spanish experience, his conflicting thoughts about authority and individualism and socialism (he had been caught in Barcelona at the time of the May uprising because he was there to arrange his transfer to the International Brigades; he had found the POUM far too undisciplined), that in the year before the outbreak of war he ricocheted among various positions, for a while believing in pacifism, which he would turn against violently and attack in the first years of the war. He despaired of the situation. He saw the threat of fascism but he had no faith that traditional government would be able to cope in either an effective or a morally attractive way. But once war broke out, he was desperate to help, and attempted to join the army. His health, rather than his "premature antifascism," kept him out. But he became an active member of the Home Guard, and he did his bit in his literary work. Convinced of the need to preserve literacy and literary standards even during the war, Orwell acted as literary editor of the *Tribune* and wrote his splendid weekly column, "As I Please." Before that he had worked for the BBC, that model he drew upon for the Ministry of Truth in *1984*, as a talks producer, broadcasting to India—an ironic continuation, in some sense, of his earlier experience as a police officer in Burma. With T. R. Fyvel he also edited a series of Searchlight books, designed to give expression to what Britain was fighting for. One of the books, *The Lion and the Unicorn,* was written by Orwell himself. The title, drawn from Britain's coat of arms, can be taken to stand for patriotism and socialism, a perhaps unexpected fusion of ideals that would be central to his politics through the later years of the war, and indeed to the very end of his life.

The development of his political attitudes can be followed in the letters to the *Partisan Review*. There, as I've said, he predicted, or prescribed, for Britain a social revolution if the war was to be won. But the manifesto-like note in the early letters was gradually muted as it became evident that the dreamed-of full-scale social revolution would not be accomplished. One hears a new note, a kind of grudging admiration, as he acknowledged that the powers that be in England were able to preserve their traditional society to an amazing degree and still win the war. (Which raises an abiding question about British society: Is it a sign of strength or of weakness that so many of the old values still persist? If they had been even more eroded than they are, would Britain be in better shape today, or worse?)

But with the survival of England assured and a Labour government that he supported committed to some measure of socialism, Orwell turned in his last major publication to the world of the future. I stoutly maintain, accepting Orwell's own statement of his intention, that *1984* is meant as a warning of what might happen if socialism were deflected from its true course and ideal and became, with the consent or ignorance of the governed, yet another totalitarianism. But a warning is not to be mistaken for a conviction, and I think it is a distortion of Orwell's purpose to read his novel as no more than a prophecy of inevitable doom-to-come in a socialist state. Admittedly the book has more prophetic aspects than we might have thought possible in the brief period of British prosperity of the early 1960s, before the incursions of inflation and unemployment, when the Keynesian solutions seemed to be working and one had an impression that Britain was entering a more joyful, generous, and rewarding period than the years of austerity that followed upon the war. Surely that period of the early 1960s, justifiably or not, was more optimistic in spirit, and we were not so conscious then as we are today of the brutalities in the world, which are a vivid memory from Vietnam, which are called to our attention now from all over the globe by Amnesty International, and which are not notably ameliorated by pious political talk of "human rights." (How Orwell would have detested that new form of newspeak, unless we have in mind the human right to torture other humans.) Immediately after the war, when Orwell was writing, one felt more hopeful that we had left behind the world of torture and the concentration camp, the world represented in *1984* by the Ministry of Love, but we seem closer to those horrors now—more horrible, we know from the documented evidence, than anything Orwell was able to imagine.

Happily, torture has not become an accepted part of the way of life in England, nor has Ingsoc, nor the extreme division between the mindless proles and the privileged functionaries of Big Brother. Granting the sci-fi accuracy of much of Orwell's detail— in an age of bugging, the telescreen surely must be waiting its turn to spy upon us—*1984*, though it seems an obvious first choice among Orwell's work, doesn't have all that much relevance to the present crisis of Britain. I would argue we have less to learn from his nightmares than from his ironic, sympathetic, and still valid analyses of the English character. For those analyses we can do no better than to turn to the pages of *The Lion and the Unicorn,* and I will take the liberty of citing two extended passages that seem to me of special relevance to the subjects under discussion here.

England is not the jewelled isle of Shakespeare's much-quoted passage, nor is it the inferno depicted by Dr. Goebbels. More than either it resembles a family, a rather stuffy Victorian family, with not many black sheep in it but with all its cupboards bursting with skeletons. It has rich relations who have to be kow-towed to and poor relations who are horribly sat upon, and there is a deep conspiracy of silence about the source of the family income. It is a family in which the young are generally thwarted and most of the power is in the hands of irresponsible uncles and bedridden aunts. Still, it is family. It has its private language and its common memories, and at the approach of an enemy it closes its ranks. A family with the wrong members in control—that, perhaps, is as near as one can come to describing England in a phrase.[3]

The second passage reads:

In whatever shape England emerges from the war, it will be deeply tinged with the characteristics that I have spoken of earlier. The intellectuals who hope to see it Russianized or Germanized will be disappointed. The gentleness, the hypocrisy. the thoughtlessness, the reverence for law and the hatred of uniforms will remain, along with the suet puddings and the misty skies. It needs some very great disaster, such as prolonged subjugation by a foreign enemy, to destroy a national culture. The Stock Exchange will be pulled down, the horse plough will give way to the tractor, the country houses will be turned into children's holiday camps, the Eton and Harrow match will be forgotten, but England will still be England, an everlasting animal stretching into the future and the past, and, like all living things, having the power to change out of recognition and yet remain the same.[4]

These remarkable passages not only represent Orwell's attitudes toward his country but also serve to remind us of the source of England's continuing strengths and weaknesses: the English themselves. It would seem that when it comes down to the essentials, or the essences, of English life, not much has changed, after all. Dare one say: For English problems there will have to be English solutions? I would like to think: Yes.

My hope is that England may soon be leading the way, demonstrating how it is possible to live *humanely* in a postindustrial, postmodern age, and that "economic growth" is not the one indispensable key to the good life. It is hard, however, to see how the good life can be paid for without economic growth, and at the moment England seems, rather crankily, to be caught in a conundrum.

Notes

1. George Orwell, "Such, Such Were the Joys," in *The Orwell Reader,* ed. Richard H. Rovere (New York: Harcourt Brace Jovanovich, 1956), p. 443.

2. George Orwell, *Homage to Catalonia* (London: Secker & Warburg, 1938), p. 314.

3. George Orwell, *The Lion and the Unicorn* (London: Secker & Warburg, 1941), pp. 34–35.

4. Ibid., p. 55.

Contributors

STEPHEN BLANK is senior research associate, The Conference Board, New York. He directs The Conference Board's Multinational Corporate Conduct Program. His major publications include *Industry and Government in Britain: The Federation of British Industries in Politics, 1945–65* (1973), *Multinational Corporations and National Elites: A Study in Tensions* (with Joseph La Palombara) (1976), *Multinational Corporations in Comparative Perspective* (with Joseph La Palombara) (1977), and *Multinationals in Contention* (with Robert Black and Elizabeth Hanson) (1978).

JACK BRAND is currently director of the Strathclyde Area Survey at the University of Strathclyde. He was educated at Aberdeen University and at the London School of Economics. He has held a number of academic appointments in England and Scotland and was a Ford fellow at the Survey Research Center, University of Michigan, 1971–72. His major interest is comparative nationalism.

BARBARA CASTLE has been a Labour member of Parliament for Blackburn since 1945. She was minister of transport from 1965 to 1968, secretary of state for employment and productivity from 1968 to 1970, and secretary of state for social services from 1974 to 1976. In this last position she was responsible for carrying through Parliament the Equal Pay Act, which extended equal pay to women.

GERALD A. DORFMAN is associate professor of political science at Iowa State University in Ames. He is interested in the problem of producer-group politics, with special emphasis on union-government relations in Britain. He is author of *Wage Politics in Britain* and the forthcoming *Government versus Trade Unionism in Britain since 1968*.

MILTON J. ESMAN is the John S. Knight professor of international studies and director of the Center for International Studies at Cornell University. He has recently edited *Ethnic Conflict in the Western World* (Cornell University Press, 1977), which includes his essays "Scottish Nationalism, North Sea Oil, and the British Response" and "Perspectives on Ethnic Conflict in Industrialized Societies."

LAWRENCE FREEDMAN is a research fellow at the Royal Institute of International Affairs, responsible for a project on the future of British foreign policy. He has previously held research positions at Nuffield College, Oxford, and the International Institute for Strategic Studies. In 1978 he published his first book, *U.S. Intelligence and the Soviet Strategic Threat.* He has also published a number of articles on defense issues in European and American journals.

EDWARD HEATH has been Conservative member of Parliament from Boxley since 1950. He has been government chief whip and minister of labor. He served as leader of the Conservative Party from 1965 to 1975. In this capacity he was leader of the opposition from 1965 to 1970 and again from 1974 to 1975, and prime minister from 1970 to 1974.

IRA KATZNELSON is associate professor of political science at the University of Chicago. He is the author of *Black Men, White Cities* (1973), co-author of *The Politics of Power* (1975), and author of *City Trenches: Urban Politics and the Patterning of Class in the United States* (forthcoming).

ISAAC KRAMNICK is professor of government at Cornell University. He is the author of *The Politics of Nostalgia* (1968) and *The Rage of Edmund Burke* (1977), and co-author of *The Age of Ideology* (1978).

ROBIN MARRIS studied at King's College, Cambridge. He taught for many years at Cambridge University and is now chairman of the economics department of the University of Maryland. He is the author of many books, including *The Machinery of Economic Policy* (1954), *Economic Arithmetic* (1958), *The Corporate Economy* (1971), and *The Theory and Future of Corporate Economy and Society* (1978).

RALPH MILIBAND taught at the London School of Economics for many years and was professor of politics at the University of Leeds from 1972 until 1978. He is currently visiting professor of sociology at Brandeis University. His publications include *The State in Capitalist Society* and *Marxism and Politics.*

TOM NAIRN is a native of Fife, Scotland. He joined the editorial collective of the *New Left Review* in 1963 and has contributed numerous articles to it. He now works with the International Institute in Edinburgh. His books include *The Beginning of the End* (with Angelo Quattrocchi) (1968), *The Left against Europe?* (1973), and *The Break-up of Britain* (1977). A forthcoming volume edited by him is devoted to the theory of nationalism: *Marxism and Nationality: The New Debate.*

JORGEN RASMUSSEN is professor of political science at Iowa State University. He is also executive secretary of the British Politics Group. He is the author of *Retrenchment and Revival: A Study of the Contemporary British Liberal Party* (1964) and *The Process of Politics: A Comparative Approach* (1969), and the co-author (with Alex N. Dragnich) of *Major European Governments.*

RICHARD ROSECRANCE is the Walter S. Carpenter, Jr., professor of international and comparative politics at Cornell University. He is the author of *Action and Reaction in World Politics* (1963) and *Defense of the Realm: British Strategy in the Nuclear Epoch* (1968), and editor of *America as an Ordinary Country: U.S. Foreign Policy and the Future* (Cornell University Press, 1976).

PETER STANSKY is the Frances and Charles Field professor of history at Stanford University. He has written extensively on modern England, most notably *Ambitions and Strategies: The Struggle for the Leadership of the Liberal Party in the 1890s; England since 1867;* and *Gladstone: A Progress in Politics.* With William Abrahams, he is the co-author of *Journey to the Frontier: Two Roads to the Spanish Civil War* and *The Unknown Orwell,* a study of the early life of George Orwell. He is currently working on a study of Orwell's life in the 1930s.

Index

Is Britain Dying?

Designed by Richard E. Rosenbaum.
Composed by The Composing Room of Michigan, Inc.
in 10 point VIP Baskerville, 2 points leaded,
with display lines in VIP Baskerville.
Printed and bound by Fairfield Graphics.

Library of Congress Cataloging in Publication Data

Main entry under title:

Is Britain dying?

    Essays originally presented at a conference held at Cornell University, Apr.
13–15, 1978, and sponsored by the Western Societies Program of the Center for
International Studies.
    Includes index.
    1. Great Britain—Politics and government—1964-   —Addresses, essays,
lectures. 2. Great Britain—Economic policy—1945-   —Addresses, essays,
lectures. I. Kramnick, Isaac. II. Cornell University. Western Societies
Program.
DA592.I8   320.9′41′0857   79-12895
ISBN 0-8014-1234-X